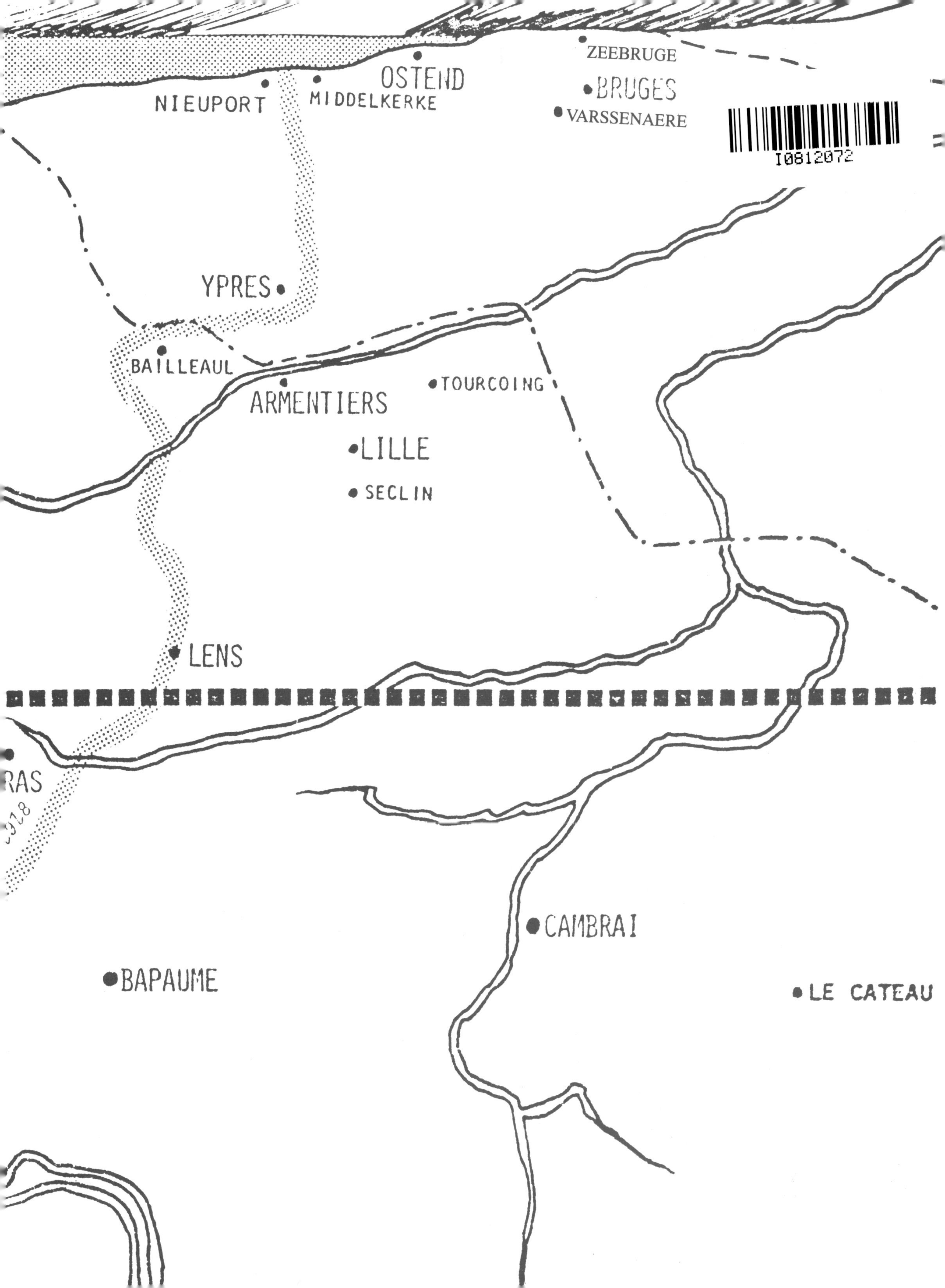
ZEEBRUGE
OSTEND
BRUGES
NIEUPORT
MIDDELKERKE
VARSSENAERE
YPRES
BAILLEAUL
ARMENTIERS
TOURCOING
LILLE
SECLIN
LENS
RAS
CAMBRAI
BAPAUME
LE CATEAU

The Camel Drivers

The Camel Drivers

The 17th Aero Squadron in World War I

Otis Lowell Reed and George Roland

Schiffer Military/Aviation History
Atglen, PA

For all the brave young men who once waged aerial warfare without parachutes.

Book Design by Ian Robertson.

Library of Congress Catalog Number: 96-67286

Printed in China.
ISBN: 0-7643-0071-7

We are interested in hearing from authors with book ideas on related topics.

Published by Schiffer Publishing Ltd.
77 Lower Valley Road
Atglen, PA 19310
Phone: (610) 593-1777
FAX: (610) 593-2002
Please write for a free catalog.
This book may be purchased from the publisher.
Please include $2.95 postage.
Try your bookstore first.

CONTENTS

Acknowledgements

Early in the effort to produce this book (more than twenty-five years ago), the authors engaged Mr. John J. Curtin of the Philadelphia area to help with the writing of a manuscript that just wasn't getting done. He wrote, and we wrote, and we rewrote him, and he rewrote us (and on and on) until finally it was somewhat finished—if a bit frayed from having so many fingers plying at the task. Since being retired we have rewritten all to give it one voice, bring it up to date, and resolve the many problems that developed in the early manuscript. Nevertheless we want to acknowledge the presence of Mr. Curtin's fine hand in the original work.

In order that we might hire Mr. Curtin and get on with it, Mr. Lorenz K. Ayers provided an interest-free loan in the early 1970s. While the debt was retired very shortly, it was a handsome thing for Mr. Ayers to do and we salute him for it.

Not enough can be said about the work of Mr. Michael Dickinson, of London, on behalf of this project. During the 1960s and 1970s he dug into a mountain of obscure material probably not often visited by anyone following the end of World War I. As if that did not present enough problems, a post office strike then came upon him and made it nearly impossible for him to discover if his work was reaching us or not. Despite these difficulties, he uncovered many things not previously known by most and managed to put them into our hands. The British view of this story would not have been possible without Michael Dickinson.

In chapter 9, the passages relating to the escape of Theose Tillinghast and others from captivity is drawn from *My Capture and Escape* by John O. W. Donaldson; copyright © 1919 by Harper's Magazine. All rights reserved. Reproduced from the July issue by special permission.

We wish to thank Mr. John Bell who encouraged the authors through thirty years of madness. In addition to urging the work unstintingly, he built a museum-grade model of Burdick's Camel for the 50th reunion at Dayton, attended the 55th reunion in Otis Reed's stead, and, finally, read our book in manuscript and advised us wisely. More than this cannot be expected of a friend.

Additionally, we must thank Mr. Jeffrey T. Hartley of the National Archives at College Park, Maryland, who located some obscure material and came up with a difficult title almost at the last minute.

Regrettably, many of the people who helped us in this effort have long since gone to their rewards. Nevertheless, in addition to those mentioned above, here are some others: Mr. James Ackerman; Mr. John P. Armstrong; Mr. Charles Biddle; Mr. Claud L. Booth; Ms. Karen Brown; Mr. Clinton Burdick; Mr. George Campbell; Dr. Milnor W. Case; Mrs. Irene Castle; Dr. Frederick Mortimer Clapp; Mrs. Anne Springs Close; Mr. Raymond Collishaw; Mr. Loran J. Cooper; Mrs. Irving P. Corse; Des Moines Iowa Museum; Mr. Douglas Desson; Mr. Frank Dixon; Mrs. John B. Dixon; Mr. John Donoho; Mr. Samuel Baltz Eckert; Mr. James Ellison; Mrs. Karen H. Enderle; Mr. Albert Everett; Miss Agnes Fowler; Mr. Charles France; Mr. Martin G. Giesecke; Mr. William N. Goff; Mr. Edward B. Goodnow; Mr. E. H. Graves; Mr. Alfred V. Haig; Mr. George R. Hamilton; Mr. William D. Hamilton; Mrs. Maxine Henderson; Mr. Eldon Hively; Mr. Roy Hively; Mrs. Gordon Kellogg; Mr. William H. Kellum; Mr. Howard Knotts, Jr.; Mrs. Molly Flagg Knudtsen; Mr. Bradley Lawton; Mr. Ernest S. Mason; Mrs. Marjorie Roberts McBride; Mrs. Frank J. Maxian; Mrs. Dorothy Myers; Mr. James F. Myers; Ms. Grace Myrick; Mrs. Louise T. Muller; Herr Heinz J. Nowarra; Mrs. Esther S. Phares; Mrs. Frank Pogue; Ms. Brenda L. Reed; Mrs. Ann B. Ridgeway; Mr. Eric Roberts; Mr. Charles Ross; Mr. Harry E. Ross; Miss Stephanie Saeler; BG Martin F. Scanlon; Mr. Charles A. Schadt; Ms. Ida Schuder; Miss Callie M. Shearman; Mr. Thomas B. Shearman; Mrs. Lois Meier Shoemaker; Mr. Robert J. Smith; Mr. De Villo Sloan; Mr. Ralph W. Snoke; Mr. Lewis C. Spidell; Mr. Theo. H. Spidle; Mrs. Dorothy Steiniger: Mr. Steven St. Martin; Mr. Theose E. Tillinghast; Mr. John M. Tipton; Mrs. Dorothy Todd; Mr. Miles Todd; Mr. Harry D. Traxler; Mr. Arthur Treacher; Dr. Cuthbert Tunstall; Mrs. Louise Umstead; U. S. Records Center; U. S. Air Force Museum; BG George A. Vaughn; Col. David T. Wells, Jr.; Mr. Edgar G. White; Mr. Roger M. Wicks; Mr. Rodney Williams; Mr. Scott Wilson; Mrs. Helen Woodward; Mr. Harold E. Young; and Mr. Frank J. Zoubeck.

Finally, we must acknowledge our long suffering families: Betty, Brenda, and Linda Reed; and Vera, Susanna, and Emily Roland. All must have gotten heartily sick of this long, long, ago.

Preface

(Otis Reed) When I was a boy in West Virginia fifty years ago, my neighborhood buddy, Bob Everett, and I used to climb up to the tiny attic of his home and examine his father's World War I uniform hanging there in the gloom. The blouse was especially curious, in that it sported lapels instead of the regulation stand-up collar typical of American uniforms of that earlier war. I was told that this was because although an American, Bob's father had been a pilot with the British and had adopted their style of uniform for greater comfort.

These details were put out of mind by the thrilling days of World War II and Korea, and it was 1965 before I again considered the story. I then sought out Mr. Albert Everett for more particulars. He informed me that two American Aero Squadrons (the 17th and 148th) had been placed on loan to the British to fly Sopwith Camels during the summer of 1918. Further, he had served with the 17th under the command of Samuel Baltz Eckert of the Philadelphia Main Line who was, at that time, on leave from the Sun Oil Company.

Because I lived near Philadelphia at the time, I returned home and put in a call to Sun Oil to see what I could find out. Much to my surprise, Mr. Eckert was still engaged in business and was soon talking to me on the phone. Shortly thereafter I met him at his office where he lent me a copy of a 17th Aero Squadron history by Frederick Mortimer Clapp and wished me well.

Therein began the madness. That book contained an address for every man who served in the unit and I was soon awash in correspondence. Despite what social scientists tell us about American mobility, I found that most of the people I needed to work with were living not far from the hometowns named by 17th Aero Squadron members in 1917. And when they had drifted away, others remembered the family and could tell me where to look. It is through the kind cooperation of many people discovered in this way that this work employs so many diaries, letters, newspaper clippings, photographs, etc.

(George Roland) At that time, Reed and I both worked for a major aircraft company on the outskirts of Philadelphia and my duties often took me into the area wherein he labored. On one such visit (knowing of my interest in World War I aviation) he showed me pictures he had received and asked if I had any idea where he could get them copied. In cold blood I suggested that he let me copy them using my 4X5 Anniversary Speed Graphic. Little did I realize at the time just what I was getting into.

Since I have harbored a lifelong interest in photography, I soon found myself pulling together my equipment from various points of storage, building a darkroom in my basement, and creating a copy stand in my attic. Up there, we were soon involved in major copying sessions. And when we went to the squadron's fiftieth reunion in Dayton, Ohio, in 1968, we took that copy stand along so that we could shoot the occasional picture brought by veterans in attendance. In all, over 500 negatives resulted from this effort.

(Otis Reed) There's more.

(George Roland) In addition to an interest in photography, I have had a lifelong interest in aviation in general (and World War I aviation in particular) and have put together a fairly extensive library of core material regarding the early days of flight. Through this I was able to provide many of the needed source books and to steer the story around historical reefs often blundered upon. My library was frequently instrumental in knitting the tale together when it seemed to be coming apart.

(Otis Reed) Thus we became a team. In the meantime, my association with Mr. Eckert blossomed a bit. Talks continued at intervals and finally he advised me to come out to his estate to examine some papers in the attic. I went. To my astonishment I found a large wooden box containing copies of nearly every paper that ever existed concerning the 17th Aero Squadron. As Mr. Eckert explained it, he had been unsure just what he was to do with the official records after the war and had put them in this crate with the idea that he would forward them as directed by the Adjutant General. The Adjutant General never directed—and they were still there when I came stumbling along nearly half a century later!

Incidentally, I got there at just the right time and, fortunately, extracted the major part of the important material. When Mr. Eckert and I went back to that box, months later, we discovered that Mrs. Eckert (who had died in the meantime) had removed the records and used the container to store tools. As far as I know, the balance of those papers was never seen again.

(Reed and Roland) Early in the effort we located the former adjutant, Dr. Frederick Mortimer Clapp (everyone assured us he was dead), and interviewed him about his official tome, *A History of the 17th Aero Squadron, an American Pursuit Squadron with the RAF*. It was our hope that he could fill in some obscure details. He advised us that the additional information we wanted was most likely available only in the RAF files. This problem was soon under the firm control of Mr. Michael Dickinson of London (whose brother was working in the U. S. at our firm at the time). Michael swore there was nothing he liked better than doing research, gratis, and dug diligently on behalf of the project. Many of the details made available here for the first time come straight from Michael's long labor of love at the Public Record Office in London.

As mentioned earlier, we quickly found ourselves overwhelmed with photographs despite the fact that no official photographer visited the 17th in the field. We were at a loss to account for this until one day we realized that we had a picture of everybody except Lorenz "Larry" K. Ayers. We guessed that he was the photographer, managed to confirm this, and soon he flew in from St. Louis with a large box of pictures for us to work on. It seems that Ayers realized that there ought to be pictures and urged those going on leave to keep him supplied with film. Most of the photographs found in collections belonging to the families of 17th veterans are copies supplied by Ayers and we are all indebted to him.

When, in 1968, the squadron held its fiftieth reunion in Dayton, Ohio, the team of Reed and Roland was there spreading the word that a new history would be out momentarily. Why is it, then, that we are writing this preface in 1995? We can only say, as often did the character portrayed by W. C. Fields when pressed to explain the inexplicable, "Things happened." But all that is past. All i's are dotted, all t's are crossed, and finally the book is done.

We render a fond salute in memory of 17th Aero Squadron friends who went away while we struggled with their story.

Otis L. Reed
George Roland
1995

1

Despair on Two Continents

When the United States of America committed itself to The Great War on April 6, 1917, it had a fair navy, a meager army, and little to speak of in the way of air service. The government was content to pride itself on the possession of some three hundred airplanes of amusing diversity. Mechanics with aircraft experience were few and far between. Officers trained as pilots were rare—and many of them looked upon aviation as a ticket to be punched on the way to more orthodox service. No wonder, then, that initial war efforts included the recruiting and training of people willing to take to the air in defense of the country.

What was to become eventually the 17th Aero Squadron of World War I was part of that story. The 17th was formed—perhaps happened is a better word—at Kelly Field, Texas, on May 13, 1917, just one month after the U. S. entered the conflict.[1] There wasn't a draftee among the disparate group of men who gathered at the assembly point by train from all over the nation. They came flocking to the air service almost as soon as the country declared war; city boys, country boys, immigrants without papers, lads who could trace their ancestry to the Mayflower, strangers, comrades, and relatives—six sets of brothers in the 17th alone.[2] Every last one of them had been encouraged to believe that they were soon to become scout pilots at the front. It was the first of many treacheries that would anger and dismay these eager recruits; to a man they were to become mere supporting players.

The second treachery came hard on the heels of the first. The young recruits arrived to find that Kelly Field was, at best, only an idea. Since America had little air service, this future base was simply a barren plain that seemed a great place to undertake flying. At that very moment a committee in Washington (the Bolling Commission[3]) was at work begging the British and French to tell them exactly what was to be done—a matter of little value to raw soldiers stranded in the middle of Texas.

The intersection of 5th Avenue and 42nd Street in New York City as it appeared in the summer of 1917. Note the men in straw hats, the policeman running the traffic signal by hand, and the quaint cars. The only sign of war in this view is an occasional soldier. (Mrs. John McBride)

One of the six sets of brothers to serve in the enlisted ranks of the 17th. Left to right: Roy Hively, Eldon Hively. (Eldon Hively)

The tent city at Kelly Field, Texas, during facility development in June, 1917. (De Villo Sloan)

The scene at Kelly Field following the July 4, 1917, cloudburst that nearly washed the 17th away. (Eldon and Roy Hively)

So, under the direction of officers who knew scarcely more than they did, the recruits pitched their tents in the heat and dust of Bexar County and began to claw away at the terrain in hopes of somehow turning out an airfield. They constructed the barracks, laid water and sewage systems, and drilled and fought and suffered—and survived. It was a cruel existence: food and equipment came sporadically; the favorite World War I rumor concerning outbreaks of meningitis was worked and overworked; and the nation, which had asked for their help in a great war, seemed to have largely forgotten about them. Then, on the Fourth of July, when it appeared that they were gaining control of the landscape, a cloudburst struck the area, swamping tents, ruining construction, and turning the entire camp into a nearly bottomless swamp.[4] The men of the 17th cursed and gesticulated—and started over.

If no one left for Mexico it was probably because they wanted to see what might happen next. Commanding officers came and went—three of them in three months. It was the third, Lt. Robert Oldys, who finally got them out of the mud that would one day become a major military installation.[5]

The disgruntled men, who had first been known as Company M, then company B, and still later the 29th Provisional Aero Squadron, officially became the 17th Aero Squadron in early August.[6] Shortly thereafter, they happily entrained for Ontario, Canada (as arranged through the Bolling Commission), becoming the first scout squadron to move out under the new arrangement and, it was predicted, likely to be the first scout squadron to land "over there."[7]

They were in for more disappointment. Arriving at Leaside Recruit Depot, they spent the remainder of August unlearning their basic American drill and picking up the British way of doing things. They became past masters in the mysteries of forming fours and pounding ground.[8]

It was during this time that the initial treachery which took place back in May became apparent—not one man was posted to flight school. A lucky few went to the School of Military Aeronautics at Toronto University to become gunners and radio operators; but the rest found that they would become ground crews, servants of the aircraft they had hoped to master. And, as a final blow to morale, the headquarters staff, probably the only cohesive unit in the entire squadron, was picked up and moved 100 miles away to Camp Borden, Ontario, to take charge of the other American squadrons as they arrived.

The Englishmen who inherited the fragments of the 17th found right away that these Yanks took some getting used to. The Americans were not only bitterly disappointed in their lot, they were still, in the words of their official historian, "little more than civilians in uniform."[9]

The problem was twofold. The breakdown in squadron organization had undermined any developing sense of communion or esprit-de-corps. And as a result of their tribulations, these spirited young Americans now held little respect for, or awe of, the military—with consternating results when they came into conflict with the hidebound and tradition-heavy British system.

There were incidents. In later years, Loran J. Cooper, a carpenter with the 17th throughout the war, recalled a typical confrontation. "When Major General Lord Innes Kerr was commanding Camp Leaside, he would come into camp at two or three a.m. and, if the guard did not turn out quite snappy, he would have fire call blown. We would have to turn out in underwear and shoes in the October frost. Then the general would inspect the troops and tents and poke any suspicious pile of blankets with his cane. After several such occasions our medical sergeant got jabbed with the cane, took it away from the General, and threw it into the brush. The English, especially the old professionals, were astonished at such a breach of discipline."[10]

While these problems were being acted out, the men who would actually become pilots in the 17th were entering the air service in a

More tents! These are at Leaside Recruit Depot in Ontario, Canada. (Eldon and Roy Hively)

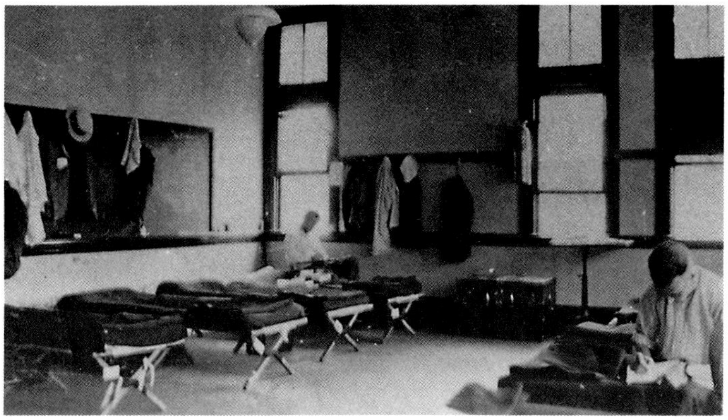

This is the Ohio State medical school classroom converted to barracks for cadets attending ground school there. (Mrs. Gordon Kellogg)

surer fashion, although they too would find it a long and devious way from oath to armed combat. Those with previous military connections (such as service with the National Guard) reported in most cases to Fort Myer, Virginia, the original home of Army aviation. Large numbers of other volunteers were able to simply walk from their college classrooms to training schools established on the campus. Through this, collegiate experience gradually became an official criteria for earning wings.

A distinguished group at Princeton carried this somewhat further. Before the U.S. declared war, Marshall Mills, a well-known alumnus of Old Nassau, convinced many fellow alumni that the nation was on the verge of involvement and that it would not be right for Princeton men to train like ordinary mortals. Accordingly, Mills headed up a campaign that resulted in the purchase of three new Curtiss JN4 Jennies and the hiring of an instructor to train interested students. This Princeton Air Force fared reasonably well (only one plane was ruined in a crash) and Mills took his boys to Washington when the country entered the war to have them commissioned on the spot.[11] It didn't work, and in the summer of 1917 Princeton's finest once again began training in the manner of everyone else. Ironically, they'd get it still a third time before ever they saw wings.

Lying as it did, somewhere between the extremes of Princeton and the military schools, Ohio State (a land grant college) furnished a more typical example of an institution of higher learning gone to war. When called upon to provide ground school services, the college patriotically committed large areas of classrooms and green grass to the military. Billets were a bit harder to come by, however, and many cadets ended up in the medical building sharing quarters with dusty skeletons and dissection sinks.[12]

This much amused the young soldiers, for they were playing their new roles blithely. They went to class day after day studying airplane, talking airplane, and casually insinuating that they were infinitely familiar with flying machines. These poses evaporated suddenly. One day Ruth Law Oliver, an early aviatrix, flew in unannounced for a practical demonstration and startled them into scrambling all over each other in the wildest disorder shouting, "Airplane! Airplane!"[13] It became difficult to posture after that.

The students at Ohio State were a fair sample of the young men coming together for America's first major conflict since the

Three Curtiss JN4-D airplanes belonging to the Princeton Air Force. These were provided by wealthy alumni so that pilots could be trained at the university, then commissioned directly into the air service. This did not happen. (Frank A. Dixon)

William T. Clements was a junior banker when he entered the service. He became a flight leader in the 17th. (Cuthbert Tunstall)

Lorenz K. Ayers finished at the head of his class at aviation ground school, then got entangled in the ever-growing confusion of the times and ended up a ground officer. (Albert F. Everett)

Albert F. Everett had attended West Point briefly and found himself well prepared for the routine and rigors of aviation training. (Samuel B. Eckert)

Civil War. And four of those young men, who would one day serve with the 17th, were typical of this influx.

William Clements was from West Point in the tidewater country of Virginia. Born of an old-established southern family, he was a hard driving and determined young man who, just weeks before, had worn the sedate costume of a junior banker. Fair, of average height, he reflected the strong qualities of leadership so common in old Virginia families.

Lorenz Ayers was from an equally prominent Pennsylvania family. Having just finished college, he'd hardly taken time to stop in at his hometown of Easton before traveling to Ohio and reporting for duty.

Albert Everett represented what had been border states in the Civil War. Everett had grown up in Weston, West Virginia, near the boyhood home of General T. J. Jackson, and, like the general, he'd won an appointment to West Point. But he hadn't Stonewall's luck and had shortly gone down under a volley of mathematics. Now he was looking for his future in the air service.

The broad middle west was represented by Merton Campbell of Wakeman, Ohio, a small town in the endless flatlands around Lake Erie. Campbell was an engineer and a graduate of Ohio State. Bright, gregarious, thoughtful, he had a good sense of humor and quickly became a favorite among the cadets. He played baseball with the same verve he would one day display in aerial combat.

When the Bolling Commission's efforts finally bore fruit, these men, along with scores of others from similar schools, soon crossed the border into Canada to meet the airplane. There they enjoyed

Merton L. Campbell was first an engineering student at Ohio State, and then a pilot trainee. He became a deputy flight leader in the 17th's A flight. (Lorenz K. Ayers)

Curtiss JN-4s on the line in the morning ready for the training flights. (Clinton Burdick)

themselves as the enlisted men never did. They flew, generally for the first time, and found that they liked it.

Harriss Alderman, an orphan from Wilmington, North Carolina, wrote his aunt, "I thought it would feel like I was just flying through the air and could see the ground whirling by, but instead it just feels like you are not moving and the ground seems to be perfectly still and looks like a picture. I am not a bit nervous and the higher the machine goes the safer you are and the better it feels."[14] Some of the others there may not have had the abstract attitude of this cute, pleasant, mild-mannered lady killer.[15] Despite his informal air, Alderman was an experienced soldier who had seen service in the Mexican border disputes of 1916.

These young pilots led fascinating lives. They met colorful Englishmen who had been sent across the seas to train them; the most notable being the stage and music hall star Vernon Castle, who eventually lost his life training Americans.[16] Now and then men did die in the training effort and crashes were common; crashes into trees, into fences, into hangars—everywhere. But somehow all of this became so ordinary as to be hardly noticeable. Writing to his father from Camp Borden in Ontario, Cadet Harold Shoemaker noted that, "...there was an instructor and a cadet burned up here last week...two machines crashed in mid-air yesterday about 50 feet off the ground...but nothing out of the ordinary has happened."[17]

So it went. The cadets risked their lives daily but found it invigorating and challenging. And each looked forward to the day when an instructor would tap him on the shoulder and indicate that he was to take up one of the $15,000 Jennies alone to see if he knew enough to stay alive.

Most had made that trip by the time weather began to force the units out of Canada in late autumn. This withdrawal commenced under the leadership of Major Geoffrey H. Bonnell, the 17th's fifth commander. Slowly, but before too long, cadets and enlisted men drew together once again at Camp Leaside to find that in their short time north they had become a pretty well trained bunch. But if well trained, they were no more tractable. Their final farewell to Canada demonstrated this.

They were ordered to depart on October 12. But since the word was issued a day early, they came up slack for awhile. Accordingly, it was suggested that having no other duties they might jolly well make themselves useful by tending the camp mascots—a large woolly sheepdog named Bruno and a scrawny goat named Billy.

Harriss P. Alderman was a veteran of the Mexican border actions of 1916. (Rodney D. Williams)

An informal group of cadets at Camp Borden, Ontario. Left to right, standing: Walter A. Jones (killed during training in Texas), unidentified, Jarvis J. Offutt, Oliver P. Johnson, Ralph W. Snoke.* Left to right, squatting: Ralph D. Gracie,* Orville A. Ralston.* Asterisks indicate 17th men. (Mrs. John McBride)*

Aerial view of Camp Borden, Ontario. (Mrs. Gordon Kellogg)

The 17th took in the two hapless animals and treated them like soldiers. Billy was deemed unreasonably sober for a proper military man, so they filled him with whiskey after the sun went down and put him away in the mess hall to stagger and butt his way about all night long, setting His Majesty's Air Service back a tidy sum. Critical inspection showed that Bruno badly needed a shave, so they gave him one—one that went from muzzle to tail. When the 17th finally marched away in a morning rain, the allies were richer by one shaven, shivering dog and a drunken goat with "U.S." painted on his sides and a long streamer bearing the legend "17th Aero Squadron" knotted to his tail.[18]

Years later an old soldier reckoned, "It oughtn't to have been allowed." Indeed, many of the things that occurred about then oughtn't to have been allowed. There was drinking and outright drunkenness on the train ride south. Gambling was rife with officers, cadets, and troops, all participating in as near a thing to license as ever occurred in the unit west of the Atlantic.[19]

These problems were the responsibility of Major Bonnell. Geoffrey H. Bonnell was an American who had served with the British Royal Flying Corps as a flight commander, then returned to Canada as a captain to command the 79th Training Squadron. It was only natural that his stock would soar under British-American agreements, so one fine September weekend he popped off to Washington and returned wearing the uniform of an American major. And he returned with a specific assignment soon made known to all. His was the job of forming and commanding the first American scout squadron to go overseas and into combat, and it was to be the 17th Aero Squadron.[20]

This news turned out to be a disaster. The 17th went to Hicks Field, Texas, where it moved toward its apparent destiny amid bitter recriminations and conflicts. Bonnell must have had considerable ability as a commander because Americans hardly ever functioned as flight commanders in the RFC without showing unusual talents. But these skills seemed not to extend to forming and managing a squadron in a situation where so many young officers were contending for a place in the sun. In this environment, the Major soon found himself having to press fellow officers harshly and to pit men against one another in order to fill positions in the squadron's

A group of flying cadets at the School of Military Aeronautics at Toronto University, Canada. Those preparing to depart for Camp Borden, Ontario, are left to right, standing: Ralph W. Snoke, Ralph D. Gracie,* Jesse O. Creech,* Rowland C. W. Blessley, Laurence Roberts,* George V. Siebold, Harold G. Shoemaker,* Walter A. Jones,* Oliver P. Johnson,* Charles W. France*; left to right, seated: Jarvis J. Offutt, Edward T. Comegys, William Hoover, Orville A. Ralston,* Paul W. Loudon. Again, the asterisks indicate those who served in the 17th at some point in its history. (Charles W. France)*

Another informal portrait of a group of cadets at the school of aerial gunnery, Camp Borden, Ontario. Left to right, back row: Paul W. Loudon, J. Harold Myers, William J. Hoover, Ralph W. Snoke, Oliver P. Johnson,* George Siebold; left to right, middle row: Ralph D. Gracie,* Rowland C. W. Blessley, Jesse O. Creech,* Harold G. Shoemaker,* unidentified; left to right, front row: Charles W. France,* Edward T. Comegys, Walter A. Jones,* Jarvis J. Offutt, Orville J. Ralston.* The asterisks indicate 17th men. (Mrs. John McBride)*

command staff. So vast were his problems and so unpopular his solutions that soon a number of officers and enlisted men were swearing that they would never serve in the 17th.[21]

Among those to whom Bonnell made conflicting overtures was a pair of older officers who had already achieved some measure of fame in the world. Frederick Mortimer Clapp, age 38, was a Yale graduate who had received his doctorate from the Sorbonne. He was multilingual, a published poet, and on the verge of an international reputation as an art scholar. His wife Maud had been in the process, when the U.S. entered the war, of making her way back to France to work as a field nurse for a second time. So, of course, Clapp felt it his solemn duty to serve as best he could. He had a discouraging time of it. Military doctors would note his age, look down his six foot two, 120 pound frame, and state emphatically that he would never stand it, that he was undoubtedly a fit candidate for the undertaker. Clapp believed differently and pressed on until a successful conspiracy landed him in the air service. Then he

A flight-line scene showing Curtiss JN4 trainers at Camp Hicks near Fort Worth, Texas. (Ralph W. Snoke)

Frederick Mortimer Clapp, poet, linguist, and art scholar rides a sidecar at Camp Hicks. (Frederick M. Clapp)

settled in, did his duty, and lived to be 90.[22] Bonnell was much impressed by Clapp's skill with languages and ability to make order out of the disorder of paperwork. He implied that he would have Clapp as squadron adjutant.

At the same time, he was posting notices to David Terro Wells. Wells and Clapp were enough alike, although the bent of their intellect was in opposite directions, to have disliked each other without Bonnell's assistance. At thirty-five, Wells was a self-made millionaire. He had gone from his father's grocery store to Cornell where his facile mind and ready tongue had earned him the nickname "Bingo" among students and faculty. On leaving college, he became a reporter for the *New York Sun*, "The Voice of Wall Street," which eventually led him into the brokerage business and his fortune.

It was not this which attracted Bonnell to him, however. While on the Sun, Wells had done a masterful job in covering the sensational Gillette murder trial which was the inspiration for Theodore Dreiser's famous novel, *An American Tragedy*. Indeed, his columns served as part of the research in the writing of the work. Because of this success, Wells had then been sent to Washington to cover the Theodore Roosevelt years. Thus, at least in Bonnell's eyes, the ex-reporter was bound to have connections in the capital that could be useful to a young major with heavy responsibilities. And it is doubtful that Bonnell overlooked the fact that Wells was engaged to the daughter of Major General Edwin Lee Michie.[23]

So the 17th's commander, seeing a need for both men, encouraged them to work against one another for his favor. As a short-range policy it was brilliant; things fairly hummed. As a long-range policy it was disastrous; two such brainy men could hardly be held by such a transparent tack. Soon the pair developed a silent but bitter enmity for each other. To their credit, they never let their personal feelings affect their public or military conduct, which was fortunate. In good time both did become members of the 17th's command staff—long after Bonnell was gone and forgotten. Wells became the unit's supply officer in December, 1917, and Clapp its adjutant in June, 1918.

David T. "Bingo" Wells, who eventually became the 17th's supply officer. He was an ex-newspaper reporter and a self-made millionaire. (Cuthbert Tunstall)

Pilots assigned to the 17th when it transferred from Canada to Texas 1917-1918. Left to right: Jesse O. Creech, Harold Shoemaker, Charles W. France, Ralph D. Gracie, Oliver P. Johnson, Ralph W. Snoke, and Orville A. Ralston. Creech and Ralston later served in the 148th Aero Squadron and Johnson in the 25th. Johnson lost his front teeth in a crash shortly before this picture was taken. (Martin F. Scanlon)

Bonnell had more than a few setbacks. The 17th came down from Canada with eight cadets assigned to it: Jesse O. Creech, Charles W. France, Ralph D. Gracie, Walter A. Jones, Oliver P. Johnson, Orville A. Ralston, Harold Shoemaker, and Ralph Snoke. These budding pilots were soon flying Jennies over nearby Fort Worth and, with suspicious frequency, finding themselves forced down in areas where pretty girls were known to dwell. Not only had they learned to fly, but they were serving as instructors for other cadets who began flocking to the military camp as the Canadian fields closed for the winter.

But eight cadets do not a scout squadron make, and Bonnell saw that if he was to head the first squadron to go overseas, he needed men. So, in his fashion, he decided that he would get the men and all else be damned. He became more determined than ever after Walter A. "Casey" Jones stalled at low altitude and crashed to his death in early November to become the unit's first casualty. At that Bonnell felt time running out and decided to raid other squadrons to find the necessary manpower. The 22nd Aero Squadron, also stationed at Hicks, became the primary target.

By then, Clapp had found a berth as adjutant with the 22nd and was no longer involved in Bonnell's game. Consequently he took great delight in seeing Bonnell rebuffed by the 22nd's officers when he descended upon the squadron and demanded the right to select pilots for the 17th. Enraged at this, Bonnell called for a public showdown. He brought twelve 22nd pilots into the office and questioned them one by one in front of their officers. "Now then," he challenged each in his turn. "You—don't you want to be part of the first squadron to go overseas?" Each replied softly, politely, "No sir," much to his fury.[24]

In the end, Bonnell lost his command over a silly incident. By the beginning of December he had finally managed to get together enough men to have the squadron ready to ship to Europe. While they were awaiting orders, some much needed transportation arrived at Hicks. Bonnell immediately had one of the new cars uncrated and fueled and set out in it for Fort Worth. But he was back shortly with the engine ruined because in his haste he had neglected to wait for oil. Viewing his mission as imperative, Bonnell demanded another vehicle. And, when the officer in charge of the motor pool declined, Bonnell had him placed under arrest. The officer of the day, in turn, carried the tale to headquarters and Bonnell himself was soon also under arrest.[25] And that was the end of Bonnell and the 17th, for a man under arrest wasn't about to go anywhere.

An unusual view of a Curtiss trainer. This picture is thought to have been taken in Texas. (James F. Myers)

An aerial view of Camp Hicks. Casey Jones may have been making the series of aerial views from which this comes when he crashed to his death. (Clinton Burdick)

Major Martin F. Scanlon, a career officer, in flying garb at an unidentified location. Scanlon had seen service in the Philippines and the punitive expedition against Pancho Villa along the Mexican border. He commanded the 17th during its move overseas. (Martin F. Scanlon)

When he finally did arrive in Europe some months later, it was as commander of the 147th Aero Squadron.

Command of the 17th fell then to Major Martin F. Scanlon, an Army regular who had just returned from a brief stint with the 2nd Aero Squadron in the Philippines and was, like all regular officers, eager to get to the front.[26] The squadron left Hicks in mid-December with a full complement, a few of them commissioned and the others tagging along in a sort of military limbo. They arrived at Garden City, New York, on December 23 to find accommodations that made them suspect they might already have fallen into enemy hands. There was a coal shortage, so the barracks were unheated. Food was scarce and indifferent in character. There were inoculations and still more inoculations. And Christmas Eve brought, not carols, but a venereal disease inspection.[27] It was seventeen days before orders to sail arrived.

"Hungry Liz" on the job. Seen here is a state of the art ambulance visiting the scene of a mishap. (Clinton Burdick)

The squadron left Garden City on January 9, 1918, and embarked for Europe on the Cunard liner Carmania. They arrived in Liverpool on January 25, and thus, at least one promise had been fulfilled. The 17th was the first fully trained Scout Squadron, with a full complement of flying officers, to cross the Atlantic—supposedly to go immediately into action.[28]

The unit reported first to Romsey Rest Camp, a spot that made the much despised Garden City seem cheerful. Romsey was a tent city with wooden duck walks spread across mud that oozed up everywhere. There the men soon got into trouble with the strict British discipline. They got hurt. They got sick. They lost their commanding officer when Scanlon went off to Scampton to command an aviation school. And the final ignominy: the 17th lost every one of its pilots.

America's first and finest young scout pilots found that by British standards, they could hardly fly at all. They were to be assigned to various schools in Great Britain to start learning all over again. Worse yet, these schools were already bursting at the seams with Americans. Bombing squadrons and loose groupings of service people had been arriving in England since the past summer. These had posed no problem since they were expected and prepared for.

The chance to travel to Europe was an exciting adventure for these young men. But the escapade was not without peril. This is C. S. Williams of the 17th who died in a training accident April 20, 1918. (Mrs. John McBride)

Group photo of the 17th Aero Squadron officers during training at Romsey Rest Camp, England. Left to right, back row: James A. Keating, Charles S. Williams, Henry C. Starkey, Russell H. Pedler, James S. Ackerman, George Squires, John F. Moffett, Cuthbert Tunstall, George Chritzman, Ralph W. Snoke, Robert A Reese; left to right, middle row: Rodney D. Williams, Charles W. France, Jay I. Carpenter, Oliver P. Johnson, Donald R. Harris, Stanley Hugenin, Robert H. Ellis, Harry Jenkinson, Jr., John W. Baker, Eugene R. Wheatley; left to right, front row: Harold G. Shoemaker, Jesse O. Creech, Orville A. Ralston, Francis J. Connelly. (Ralph W. Snoke)

Then, in September, a shipload of over 200 cadets bound for training in Italy—where Uncle Sam had worked a quid pro quo arrangement—had to be diverted to England because of near civil and military collapse at their destination. So the British got unexpected company and, not knowing what to do with them, stuffed them into the overloaded flying schools, mostly at Oxford.[29] Among these "Oxford Cadets" were the original Princeton bunch who now found themselves undergoing elemental training for the third time. It was all very trying and the school system was disrupted beyond belief by the time the 17th pilots came on the scene.

And that was the last most of the pilots who crossed with the 17th ever saw of the squadron again. Three—Lieutenants Stanley Hugenin, Eugene R. Wheatly, and Charles S. Williams—died in training accidents in England. Four served with the 17th's companion squadron, the 148th—Jesse O. Creech, Orville Ralston, Oliver P. Johnson, and Harry Jenkinson. James A. Keating, while flying with the RAF, become one of the few bomber aces to come out of the war. Two men, Lieutenants Harry Jenkinson and George Squires, were later killed in action and a third, James A. Ackerman, narrowly cheated death two weeks after arriving in France by crashing directly in front of a French first aid station. A Fokker triplane had shot him from behind and ruptured an artery in his left arm.[30]

One high spirited young Lieutenant, however, departed the squadron in unique fashion. On leave in Winchester while awaiting orders, he enjoyed dinner and a bottle of burgundy, then accepted an invitation to join the 18th birthday celebration of a pretty young English lass, named Bubbles, at a nearby table. There he drank champagne until well after midnight which left him no choice but to walk back to camp. Then as he recalled it, "It was a beautiful moonlit night and I thoroughly enjoyed the walk. On the way, however, there was a place with a beautiful English garden with boxwood and rose bushes and I went in to enjoy the scene. There was a three-story house in the garden and it had various window ledges and irregularities in the masonry. I don't know why I did it—perhaps, like Mallory, 'because it was there'—anyhow, I scaled the wall and was nabbed at the third floor by a sergeant of police and two constables. They escorted me peaceably to the gaol, where I spent the night. In the morning I was turned over to the military authorities for courts-martial."

Those proceedings took several months, with the culprit using Major Scanlon as a character witness and getting off with a repri-

James H. Ackerman was an early member of the 17th. He later served in RAF 73 squadron where he was wounded in a fight with a Fokker triplane. (James H. Ackerman)

An unidentified Oxford Cadet sits at the controls of an early flight simulator. (George A. Vaughn)

mand. The situation was made less onerous, he noted, "by my being able to have tea several times with Bubbles."[31]

Meanwhile there developed one bright spot in the goings-on. If the pilots needed further training, the enlisted men did not. A trained mechanic was a trained mechanic and all he needed to function properly was some experience with a specific machine. There was discouraging talk of breaking up the squadron altogether and sending the men out individually to various RAF squadrons. But finally it was decided that the unit would be broken down into three flights and a headquarters detachment, and that the groups would go into the field for on-the-job training on the SE-5 aircraft.*

There was a stumbling block to this, however, since there weren't enough ground officers available to fill all the desired slots. This was solved by persuading Lt. James Bennett not to go to flying school but to come along as commander of C Flight. It was implied that he could learn flying quickly at the front and would probably be an ace before the rest crossed the Channel. It is unlikely that Bennett believed this, but he sacrificed himself to help the squadron stay together.

On the steps of the hotel at Turnberry where the RAF school of aerial fighting was located. Left to right: William J. Armstrong, ___McFee, Frank Dixon, and Raymond Watts. (Frank A. Dixon)

James G. Bennett delayed his plans to become a pilot and accepted a ground assignment as commander of C flight in order to prevent a breakup of the 17 Aero Squadron. He and his flight served with RAF 56 Squadron. (Theose Tillinghast)

The units sailed across the Channel from Southampton on February 9, with a boatload of horses. The eight-hour crossing was not a pleasant experience according to Loran Cooper. "Everyone was sick or had the 'trots' and our privy got washed overboard, almost catching Sgt. Brown and me in the damned thing," said he. "The stack of hard-tack cases fell on us in the hold and I stepped on 'Hard-boiled' Tyrell's Adam's apple with my hobnail trench boots and almost choked him when the boat lurched. I never did tell who it was..." This reticence was wise. Engine fitter Hubert Tyrell was known to be a quick tempered man who would undoubtedly look unkindly on having his gullet walked upon.[32]

Landing at Le Havre, the first American scout squadron to set foot in France quickly scattered to various assignments. Headquarters Flight under command of Lt. Henry McC. Bangs, who had emerged from Bonnell's power struggles as adjutant, was assigned to RAF 24 Squadron at Martigny; A Flight, under gunnery officer Lt. Arthur B. Lapsley, went to RAF 84 at Guizancourt; B Flight, under Lt. Bingo Wells, joined RAF 60 at Ste. Cappell on the Flanders front; and C Flight, with Bennett at the helm, joined RAF 56 Squadron at Baizieux.[33]

They were at war—too much so as it soon developed. They had just reached the point where they were useful to their British comrades when, on March 21, 1918, the German Army began its final desperate push of the war. In a movement that predicted the

See Appendix A for more information on unit assignments.

Wilson "Kid" Marshall goes to glory following a training accident. Laurence Roberts, first pallbearer on the left, described him as "...the best second baseman I ever pegged a ball to." (Mrs. John McBride)

Blitzkrieg operations of World War II, the enemy rose out of their trenches and, behind a withering hail of fast and furious fire, drove forty miles toward the Channel in two weeks.

The 17th was caught smack in the middle of this spring offensive. The flights helped to destroy existing aerodromes and to build newer ones behind the retiring line. Often the Hun was close enough to put them under machine gun fire as they burned hangars and buildings in retreat. These Americans learned first hand what war was about; the camaraderie, the day to day functioning, the fear, and the dispatching of patrols, from which many never returned.

Perhaps most significantly, these Americans—most of them quite young—were seeing first hand what three years of bitter fighting had done to the face of the continent. Private Harry D. Traxler, a fitter with A Flight, reflected almost poetically in his diary on what he perceived.

"This is the most wild, weird country I ever saw. It gives one a creepy feeling even in daylight, parts of villages standing out in the light, brick walls standing like tall towers waiting for civilization to return. What trees the Germans left standing are ones with nothing but bare trunks standing from 40 to 100 feet in the air, the branches being shot off below that. You can see the shells lodged in the trees. By moonlight, the country cannot be described as it has the most deserted look, like a great plague had been through the country...this place which was once 'no man's land' looks more than ghostly—I cannot describe it. It was probably once a most beautiful country for there is still a little evidence of what was here before the war.

A group bound for Italy in the fall of 1917 aboard the Carmania. They were diverted, instead, to England where they seriously crowded the aviation schools. Left to right: Leonard J. Desson, John H. Raferty, Lloyd Ludwig, George A. Vaughn, Jr., Walter Chalaire, Elliot W. Springs, Robert Todd, Donald E. Carlton, Henry B. Frost. Desson, Vaughn, Todd, and Frost wound up in the 17th. Ludwig and Carlton were killed while training in England. (Frank A. Dixon)

Enlisted men somewhere in France during the spring of 1918. Left to right: De Villo Sloan, John B. Douglas, Cecil N. Douglas, Logan T. Johnston, C. H. Mathews. (De Villo Sloan)

"I come upon a little hill or mound and look down on the ruined village of Athies and I wonder how it used to look before the Huns invaded it. It must have been a pretty place once as it is located in a pretty little valley about a mile in length and a quarter mile wide with a nice grove of trees on one side—but it is impossible to guess at the number of inhabitants who lived there and as I sit here it almost makes one want to shed tears to think that the Huns would wreck such beautiful places as these.

"While taking a walk over the country today here in the Somme Valley I see a very level country, almost like the prairie in Central Illinois. The trees are about as thickly grown as they are in the central states...the soil has a yellow color almost the color of clay and the ruins in the distance even look beautiful.

"Ah, France even in ruins you are beautiful still..."[34]

2

Oh, Mother, Put Out Your Gold Star (Your Son's Gone up in a Sop)[1]

It's likely that the world would have heard no more of the 17th Aero Squadron had it not been for Major Harold Fowler who, on May 18, 1918, succeeded Major Thomas S. Bowen as commander of American Air Service units serving with the British Armies in France.[2]

Unlike most Americans traveling to Europe that year, Fowler had friends in high places among the British. A son of naturalized citizens originally from England, the Major had been born in Liverpool during a visit to the homeland and thus laid claim to dual citizenship. And he had been quick to use this situation to involve himself in the war effort on behalf of his Anglo cousins. At a time when most young Americans were just discovering the troubles in Europe, Fowler had already successfully served both the United States and Britain as a secret agent. (So secretive were his doings that ever after, people who professed to know him well could comment only that, "Fowler is famous for whatever it is he is famous for.")

Major Harold Fowler as an officer in the Royal Flying Corps. He had been a secret agent and secretary to the U. S. Ambassador to England prior to enlisting in the RFC in 1915. He transferred to the U. S. Air Service in October of 1917. (Agnes Fowler)

Following that mysterious success, he continued to serve with great distinction in the British Army where he acquired, at the front, a permanent limp that led, ultimately, to a switch to air service. Finally, he found his way into the American Army when the United States entered the war.[3]*

It was Fowler's heart's desire to see the American part of his heritage actively flying at the front in support of the British part of his soul. While the idea was not unique with him, he seems to have been the only one who could make it happen. Within a month of assuming command, he resurrected two American squadrons (the 17th and 148th) and put them to flying in the field with the British 65th Wing. His was not entirely a triumph, however, because he could not furnish the units with the highly successful SE-5 aircraft on which most had trained. He had had to settle for the fractious Sopwith Camel. And while the 148th was to fly the fairly standard 130 hp Clerget powered aircraft, the 17th would have to make do with ships fitted with the feeble 110 hp Le Rhone engine.[4]

But American squadrons would be at the front and that's what mattered. So it was that the 17th Aero Squadron began to come together again for the first time in five months at Petite Synthe, France, on June 20, 1918.[5] The following day, Sunday, their newest Commanding Officer, Lt. Samuel Baltz Eckert, hopped north in a

* *See Appendix B for more information on Fowler.*

The Royal Air Force Establishment SE-5. Fowler wanted the American units to be equipped with this excellent aircraft. Instead they got Camels. (George A. Vaughn)

The DeHavilland DH-9 bomber. This was the type of aircraft flown by RAF 211. (Frank A. Dixon)

Sopwith through a driving rainstorm to meet his unit unknown and unannounced.

By his account, he traveled in the kind of weather that kept those with less pressing obligations on the ground. Having only vague notions about his destination, he picked his way northward along the battle lines until he came to the North Sea near Nieuport, that many-moated, star-shaped city now being visited by modern battle for the fourth year of the war. There he banked west and followed the coastline while studying the flat fields of Flanders for signs of Dunkirk.

Dunkirk was easy. The real challenge came when Eckert had to locate the Bourbourg Canal running Southwest from the city and to follow it to Petite Synthe Aerodrome itself. However, that too went well and he soon saw the field lying in a rough triangle of land bounded by the canal, the main railroad running from Dunkirk to Calais, and a patch of railway sidings.

Samuel Baltz Eckert, commanding officer of the 17th U. S. Aero Squadron at Petite Synthe. (Rodney Williams)

It was an old established aerodrome by the standards of the time (one of the first built by the British). Huge, canvas Bessenneau hangars decorated the edges of the landing field. An enormous sand-bag bomb shelter stood grimly to the east. Farther along were the digs of the RAF 211 Squadron, a bombing unit flying DH-9s, and across from them, the place of his new command. Reportedly, all looked dank and foreboding when Eckert tipped into the wind and landed.

As he taxied toward his destination, two men came running to grab his wings and walk him in, for the wind was up and Camels would flip in a wink in such weather. One of the wing walkers called a greeting and Eckert recognized him at once as Leroy Seney, the A-Flight mechanic who'd been his rigger on SE-5s with RAF 84 Squadron.[6] Eckert took this as a good omen, reasoning that he wasn't going to be totally unknown if A Flight was on the scene.

By almost any standard of judgment, Eckert was the logical choice to take command of the 17th. He was a wealthy Philadelphia mainliner who had graduated from Cornell University in 1908 and, through executive ability, enjoyed exceptional success in business thereafter. Darkly-handsome (a widower, thirty-three, silvery blue eyes, reddish brown hair and mustache), he was not a man to brook much foolishness. Yet there was a wry sense of humor about him that made men like him quickly and respect him instantly.

Eckert was there through long-term planning. As early as 1916 he had decided that the European war would eventually involve the U. S. and moved to be ready by acquiring, with a friend, a Curtiss floatplane with which to pursue flight studies. The two took turns aviating from the Delaware River at Essington just below Philadelphia in an aircraft so feeble that it could only be flown early in the

OPPOSITE: Aerial view of Petite Synthe aerodrome, looking east, as a flight of Camels takes off. The 17th Aero Squadron's buildings are at the center of the right edge of the photo. RAF 211 Squadron occupied the buildings directly across the field. The road at the bottom ran from Dunkirk to Calais. (Samuel B. Eckert)

An unidentified airman stands beside the cowling of what appears to be a Sopwith Pup. The Le Rhone rotary engine is at rest; compare this photo with that of the engine running. (Mrs. Louise Umstead)

morning when the air was cool. They were tutored by a flight instructor, furnished by Curtiss, who knew next to nothing about his art. (To punish Curtiss for this, Eckert and his partner often made their ignorant instructor accompany them on wild flying experiments so that if they were killed, he would be also.) But they became pilots despite these problems, and shortly thereafter Eckert became the holder of U. S. seaplane license number twelve.

Early in 1917, more convinced than ever that American involvement was inevitable, Eckert went for additional instruction at the Curtiss installation at Newport News, Virginia. And when events developed just as he had foreseen, he enlisted in the Army as a sergeant. In due course he was commissioned as a 1st Lieutenant and sent to Selfridge Field at Mt. Clemens, Michigan, to instruct the 9th Aero Squadron bombing unit.[7]

But an overseas command was what Eckert really had in mind. In December of 1917 he arrived in England as commander of the 9th only to suffer the usual fate of American pilots then—he was sent away to flying school. It was during this that he met Harold Fowler, heard that someday there would be American fighter squadrons at the front, and was advised that when this happened, he (Eckert) would one day be a commander.

But before such could happen, Eckert went out to join RAF 84, an SE-5 equipped unit near Bertangles, France. He arrived on April 21, 1918—the very day that Captain Roy Brown shot down and killed the famed Red Baron, Manfred von Richthofen. (Perhaps as an object lesson to himself, Eckert went to view the body, which he found laid out in a nearby hangar.)

While serving with RAF 84, Eckert flew steadily through the fierce fighting mounted to win back the territory lost to the German spring offensive. Then, having been officially alerted that he would soon command one of two Camel squadrons being formed, he went to spend a month with the Camel pilots of RAF 80 at Chateau Thierry—and was not amused. He quickly recognized that the little aircraft was outmoded, quirky, and in some respects downright dangerous.[8]

His reaction was not misguided. Despite a lot of favorable discussion over the years, the Sopwith Camel was hardly anyone's favorite aircraft. It stayed in production largely because it was cheap and easy to build. No small part of the difficulties with the aircraft was due directly to the use of a rotary engine as the chosen power plant. These operated on a peculiar principle; the crankshaft stood still while the heavy cylinders rotated about it. This created, in effect, a ponderous gyroscope that made controlling the little Camel more a matter of calculated perfidy than intelligent response.

The slightest inattention could be fatal. A clumsy bank to the left caused the nose to rise and the aircraft to stall. A heedless bank to the right tucked the nose under and threw the aircraft into a vig-

A Sopwith Camel being run up as the ground crew restrains it. The blur of the rotating Le Rhone engine is most obvious. (Frank A. Dixon)

orous spin. Of course these effects could be avoided by proper technique, but even proper control was unique to the Camel. In performing a steep left turn, the pilot had to immediately apply full left rudder to keep the nose from rising. In entering a steep right turn, however, he did *exactly the same thing* which kept the nose from dropping.

There were other difficulties. Although almost all of the mass of the plane was contained within the first six feet of planform, a well-rigged Camel flew as if it were tail heavy. On top of all this, it was generally understood that any one Camel could be flown through an exercise fifteen times with identical results, then display some unaccountable aberration on the sixteenth try.*

Eckert went away from RAF 80 wondering just how the few American pilots available were ever going to be able to man two squadrons at the front in the face of the probable losses. And he arrived at Petite Synthe on a rainy day, bringing these doubts with him. What was worse, he came as a mere 1st lieutenant when it was planned that he hold a majority. This posed some knotty problems. It put him in the position of trying to deal with the thoroughly traditional British on an equal footing, while clearly being outranked. And it was likely that some of the lieutenants in the 17th might actually outrank Eckert by seniority of commission.

But for good or ill, his was the task of putting together a workable fighting unit. He soon saw that Camels assigned to the squadron were already being delivered to the field by the first pilots on the scene, and that additional fliers were coming in by the hour. And shortly he encountered his staff, a mixture of the old and new.

Bingo Wells was back with B Flight to resume his position as the 17th's supply officer. Wells had suffered two grave injuries while in the field. One night a shell had exploded outside his shelter and sailed shrapnel splinters through his new, tailor-made blouse hanging immediately at hand, thereby ruining what a friend identified as, "The only thing Bingo ever owned that didn't make him look like he came from Cazenovia, New York." A more significant mishap came about during a night-bombing when he tried to dive under a heavy table in the dark. He had missed his mark to come down solidly on the edge of the furniture with his right eyebrow. Within ten years bone cancer developed, dooming him to horrible disfigurement.[9]

Eckert's adjutant was to be the scholarly Dr. Frederick Mortimer Clapp, at last achieving the post he had sought long ago and an ocean away. Clapp was to prove a treasure for the squadron. With several months in the field attached to the RAF 211 Bomb Squadron, he had become a seasoned operator. He knew both the American and British ropes and how to exercise a degree of gentle larceny when the good of the squadron required it. He took a deep interest in everything and everyone; even to looking in on the enlisted men at odd hours to see how they were getting on. At times he would sit and translate the French newspapers for them so they could keep up with events. Little wonder then, that, even as in the 22nd Aero Squadron, he soon became affectionately, but secretly, known as "Daddy Clapp."[10]

Lorenz K. Ayers, late of the Ohio State crowd, was the new armament officer. After graduating from ground school at the top

* *See Appendix C for more information on the Camel.*

David T. "Bingo" Wells again became the 17th's supply officer when it reorganized at Petite Synthe. (Cuthbert Tunstall)

Frederick M. Clapp became adjutant of the 17th. Previously he had been in command of a 22nd Aero Squadron unit attached to RAF 211 at Petite Synthe. (Frederick M. Clapp)

Lorenz Ayers, who succeeded Arthur B. Lapsley as Armament Officer. He is shown here with the camera with which he made many of the pictures used in this work. (Mrs. Louise Umstead)

17th Aero Squadron ground staff at Petite Synthe, June 1918. (Mrs. Gordon Kellogg.)

Lt. Samuel B. Eckert. Commanding Officer

Lt. Frederick M. Clapp. Adjutant

Lt. David T. Wells. Supply Officer

Lt. Lorenz K. Ayers. Armament Officer

Lt Jacob J. Ross. Medical Officer

of his class, Ayers had been chosen, with nine other cadets, to receive special gunnery training along with his flight studies. He was told he would become a flying gunnery officer with one of ten mysterious squadrons expected to fight with the British, as arranged by the equally mysterious Bolling Commission. That arrangement proved to be as mythical as the ten squadrons; Ayers soon learned all about gunnery, but was never able to resume flight training. Commissioned on December 4, 1917, he shipped immediately for France (via England) as commander of A Flight of the 28th Aero Squadron. The unit was assigned to RAF 18 and, finding his duties light, Ayers shortly took up flying as an observer with the RAF. In fifty hours of bombing, photographing, scouting, and balloon fighting, he picked up the distinctive wings of an observer and had been credited with destroying one aircraft and driving another down.[11]

Such were the men who would steer the earth bound fate of the squadron. The story aloft was to be another matter. There were twenty-one flying officers assigned to the squadron, nineteen of them already at Petite Synthe or arriving the same day as Eckert—two to come within the week. Of these, eleven had seen service with the RAF while the other ten came directly from the pilot's pool. This permitted a reasonably good mix and Eckert understood immediately that the 17th was not going to be "Fokker fodder" as he had half feared. Shortly he sat down with the likely leaders and sorted the aviators into three flights of seven men each. The finished roster was as follows[12]:*

**See Appendix D for complete flight assignments and comments.*

A Flight personnel at Petite Synthe, June 1918.

Lt. Weston W. Goodnow.
Flight Commander.
(Mrs. Gordon Kellogg.)

Lt. Merton L. Campbell.
Deputy Commander.
(Albert Everett.)

Lt. Lyman Case.
(Theose Tillinghast)

Lt. Leonard J. Desson.
(Lorenz K. Ayers)

Lt. George P. Glenn.
(Mrs. John McBride.)

Lt. Floyd M. Showalter.
(Lorenz K. Ayers.)

Lt. Ralph W. Snoke.
(Theose Tillinghast.)

B Flight personnel at Petite Synthe, June 1918.

Lt. William D. Tipton.
Flight Commander.
(Mrs. George W. Muller.)

Lt. Ralph D. Gracie.
Deputy Commander.
(Martin F. Scanlon.)

Lt. Frank A. Dixon.
(Theose Tillinghast.)

Lt. William H. Shearman.
(Thomas B. Shearman.)

Lt. Murray K. Spidle.
(Steve St. Martin.)

Lt. Theose Tillinghast.
(Theose Tillinghast.)

Lt. Rodney D. Williams.
(Mrs. Louise Umstead.)

C Flight Personnel at Petite Synthe, June 1918.

Lt. Lloyd A. Hamilton.
Flight Commander.
(Lorenz K. Ayers.)

Lt. Henry B. Frost.
Deputy Commander.

Lt. Harriss P. Alderman.
(Rodney Williams.)

Lt. William J. Armstrong.
(Lorenz K. Ayers)

Lt. Bradley C. Lawton.
(Grace Myrick)

Lt. Laurence Roberts.
(Mrs. John McBride.)

Lt. Robert M. Todd.
(Miles Todd.)

A FLIGHT

Weston W. Goodnow	Flight Commander	Served with RAF 203
Merton L. Campbell	Deputy	Served with RAF 54
Leonard J. Desson	Pilot	Served with RAF 209
Lyman Case	Pilot	From pilot's pool
George P. Glenn	Pilot	From pilot's pool
Floyd M. Showalter	Pilot	From pilot's pool
Ralph Snoke	Pilot	Served with RAF 209

B FLIGHT

William Tipton	Flight Commander	Served with RAF 3
Ralph Gracie	Deputy	Served with RAF 209
Frank Dixon	Pilot	Served with RAF 209
Hugh Shearman	Pilot	From pilot's pool
Murray K. Spidle	Pilot	From pilot's pool
Theose Tillinghast	Pilot	From pilot's pool
Rodney D. Williams	Pilot	Served with RAF 3

C FLIGHT

Lloyd A. Hamilton	Flight Commander	Served with RAF 3
Henry Frost	Deputy	Served with RAF 210
William J. Armstrong	Pilot	Served with RAF 209
Harriss P. Alderman	Pilot	From pilot's pool
Bradley Lawton	Pilot	Served with RAF 209
Laurence Roberts	Pilot	From pilot's pool
Robert Todd	Pilot	From pilot's pool

Lloyd A. Hamilton as an air service cadet. (Grace Myrick)

William D. Tipton, a native of Jarretsville, MD, was one kill short of being an ace when he came to the 17th. Mrs. (George A. Muller)

Weston W. Goodnow was a calming influence among the dashing aviators gathering at Petite Synthe. (Clinton Burdick)

Left to right: Leonard Desson, Lloyd Hamilton, and Theose Tillinghast. Here they are enjoying Eckert's car at Petite Synthe. (Rodney Williams)

Among these, Gracie already was credited with one victory, Tipton with four, and Hamilton with six.[13]

The pilots confirmed as flight commanders through this selection were strong material on which to build a fighting force. 1st Lt. Lloyd A. Hamilton was the sort of man novelists have in mind when they sit down to write a book about World War I flying. Six feet tall, handsome, an excellent athlete who neither drank nor smoked, he was the twenty-four-year-old son of a Pittsfield, Massachusetts, preacher.

Hamilton had dropped out of Harvard Business School to join the Air Service and had been out to the front since March. On April 12, 1918, this exceptional aviator became the second pilot flying for the Yankee dollar to bring down an enemy aircraft. He was already an ace by American calculations when he reported to the 17th and came in on a wave of success that included four victories in the month of June alone. Strangely, Hamilton was known to harbor premonitions of an early death—which most thought only added to his dashing image.[14]

His best buddy, the flight commander for B Flight, was exactly the sort of sidekick a novelist would construct for Hamilton. At twenty-five, 1st Lt. William Tipton of Jarretsville, Maryland, was small, blond, slightly balding, and one of the few men in the war considered by many to be a finer pilot than Hamilton. He spoke with a slight lisp, had no gift for small talk, and was a relentless tease who wilted quickly under similar treatment.

Tipton was bright enough to have entered college at age fifteen, persistent enough to have graduated at eighteen, and fun-loving enough to have done so with atrocious grades symptomatic of just enough work to get by. He knew all about engines and was in the process of applying for a patent on a new type when the war broke out. At that he dropped everything, fudged a bit with his age to assure he would qualify for flight training, then enlisted. Tipton was just one victory short of also being an ace.[15]

Had someone devised Hamilton and Tipton, he would have then almost certainly invented Weston W. Goodnow of A Flight. Like Eckert and Wells, Goodnow was a Cornell man and, like they, older than most pilots. He was twenty-nine; a large bulky man described as perhaps the largest ever to sit in a Camel. Quiet, passive, unexcitable, even-tempered, and the soul of politeness; he was known to everybody as "Goodie." Goodnow had served at the front since April with the RAF 209 without achieving a confirmed victory, but his superiors had found a combination of leadership and prudence in the phlegmatic lieutenant. He was a survivor, and men going out under his lead could be expected to be used wisely in battle and steered from needless risk.[16]

With the flight roster posted, the staff turned to more mundane organizational problems. They found that the squadron was being held accountable for equipment lost in retreat from the German Army; that many of the men had not been paid in weeks; and that serial numbers (a World War I inspiration), having been assigned following the breakup in the spring by different individuals—in different locations—at different times, were incredibly muddled. When Clapp began to look into the matter, he found that fifteen pairs of men in the unit shared the same numbers, and that in two instances, a single number had been conferred on three men.[17]

Also, there was a multitude of equipment to be drawn. This included the squadron motor transport consisting of seven lorries, five tenders, two work-shop lorries, six trailers, two water trailers, four motorcycle sidecars, eight motorcycles, and five Fiat trucks with four Fiat trailers and a large water trailer. As commanding officer, Eckert was offered a Crossley touring car by the British and a Cadillac by the Americans. And while he was more than willing to accept both, he finally settled for the American auto—with white tires.[18]

By now there were Camels everywhere. Seven arrived at the base on June 21; four more on June 23. By June 25, the squadron was up to eighteen, and by July 1 they had reached a total of nineteen, one above their official allotment and the largest number they would ever have. These figures were somewhat misleading, however, in that on any given day anywhere from three to five planes could be expected to be out of service for maintenance. Nor did

The Officer's mess and tennis court built at Petite Synthe. (Rodney Williams)

Sand-bagged quarters for the 17th's enlisted men at Petite Synthe. (Roy Hively)

that total include three other Camels that were generally to be found in the 17th's hangars—the personal buses of Eckert, Fowler, and RAF Colonel J. A. Cunningham, commanding RAF 65th Wing. The first two of these could be borrowed from time to time, but the third was sacrosanct.

During these prepubescent times, some got their first close look at the Sopwith creation. The planes perched nose high about the tarmac, producing a maze of lines, whorls, and angles to amuse and confound the eye. Some of the machines were fairly new and true; others, well used, sat spraddle wheeled and slack.

On the upper surfaces these British machines ranged in color from Khaki brown to near green. Underneath they were buff, an effect produced not by paint but by the aging of clear dope, which was the only treatment ever handed bottom surfaces. The aluminum cowling, which stretched from nose to cockpit, was bare on some, painted on others. All bore the British cockade on wings and fuselage; a red ball surrounded by a broad white ring, which was in turn surrounded by a blue ring. The rudders were striped vertically blue, white, and red going aft. The true voice of the Camel was the twin Vickers .303 machine guns located just forward of the cockpit in the hump that gave the plane its name.

Chinese laborers were hired to do construction work in France during World War I. (Mrs. Gordon Kellogg)

The pilots picked over these cantankerous beasts like horse traders and when one was found to suit, had a distinguishing white block letter painted on the sides of the fuselage for easy identification in the air. That was the extent of obvious individualization for the moment. After a bit of experience, identifying letters were also added to the right-hand surface of the upper wing. Eckert's bus rated a stylized "J," on the sides complete with serifs and flourishes as befitted his position.

By existing American Expeditionary Force orders, American units were also allowed to adorn their planes with a squadron insignia of approved design following their third victory. Since the 17th had no victories yet, the British soon granted them the use of a standard symbol not then being used by any unit in that area—a white dumbbell—to be painted on the sides of the fuselage before the unit began crossing the lines. If anyone thought that strangely appropriate, nothing was said. As things turned out, this was the only symbol ever used by the 17th during the war.[19]

Flying began. Morale was not much boosted when, on the morning of June 24, Eckert's first full day of command, Lloyd Hamilton stepped confidently into Camel C6727 for a brief engine "flip" and promptly overturned and crashed at the far end of the runway. Hamilton was unhurt, but Eckert was left to wonder what would happen to lesser pilots if the best known and most capable

Eckert's living quarters, squadron office, and pilot's ready room at Petite Synthe, protected by the ubiquitous sand bags. (Mrs. Louise Umstead)

The bomb shelter at Petite Synthe. It was reputed to consist of thirty thousand sandbags! (Rodney Williams)

Seen here is a group of German prisoners of war somewhere near Petite Synthe. They were employed in farming. Clapp's unpublished writing contains an account of the British giving the Chinese hand grenades and allowing them to avenge themselves on the prisoners after some Chinese were killed in a bombing raid. (Lorenz Ayers)

aviator in the unit couldn't get off the ground. Two days later, a French Camel pilot crashed to his death on the aerodrome.

Yet accidents turned out to be mercifully rare. The 17th soon found that most often its problems were going to involve mechanical failure. These eventually reached a level where they came to be accepted as normal. "Outside of lots of engine trouble and pressure pumps plus broken lines, our busses in A are all right," wrote Mert Campbell in his diary—presumably with a straight face.[20] "Lt. Case wants a palace instead of an airplane," engine fitter Harry Traxler complained to his diary since, naturally, the weight of all such problems fell on the men who had to keep the planes in order.[21]

Amid all this, Petite Synthe quickly became home. The troops took up a spirited living in the wooden huts along the east edge of the field. The officers set up their mess in a shack near the by-road that crossed the southwest side of the field and added a tennis court in front, which was created by dragging an old cement beam behind a Fiat truck. Eckert's hut served as Squadron office, pilot's room, and reception area for visiting dignitaries.

As at almost every RAF base, the Bessenneau canvas hangars housed the aircraft. In support, the 17th put together an engine shop, carpenter's shop, armory, canteen, and additional technical facilities out of raw materials ranging from dilapidated huts to old airplane crates. Together with a troop of Chinese laborers hired for war work and sent to live by the canal, the 17th strung telephone and electric wires and smoothed out the battered aerodrome roads.[22]

The living was fairly good—although bombing was an ever-present danger from night attacks, which sometimes strayed toward the field from Dunkirk. And the Huns did manage a direct hit on an abandoned shack behind the mess on June 18, A Flight's first night at Petite Synthe. While all the buildings inhabited by the 17th were banked with sandbags, the major defense against such aerial attack was the huge dugout first noticed by Eckert on the day he arrived. As Clapp was to write later, it was, "a vast structure like an oblong, broken-down step pyramid, in the making of which nearly thirty thousand sandbags had been used."[23]

Dr. Jacob J. Ross. A Vermont country doctor turned warrior, he was the oldest man in the 17th. (Mrs. Gordon Kellogg)

This was well used at first, and then less so as people grew accustomed to air raids. Most came to consider the night bombers more of a nuisance than a threat and to suppose that the greater danger lay not in German bombs, but in the falling nose cones from the French "Archie."[24] Despite this, many soon took to gathering on the roof of the dugout to listen to the rumbling of the anti-aircraft barrage and the droning of Gothas in the black sky and to watch the giant searchlights probe for likely targets. Wiser souls avoided the falling nose cones by sitting among trees to watch, some went under bridges. Adjutant Clapp followed the most unusual course of all. Having decided that the landing field was large and he infinitely small, he would go out and lie spread-eagled in the middle of the aerodrome to watch.[25]

Near the end of these teething times the squadron received the one element it had so far been missing, a doctor. Actually three doctors arrived simultaneously. One was a captain and was rejected simply because Eckert felt he had enough troubles regarding rank. From the other two he selected forty-year-old Dr. Jacob J. Ross, a country physician from Vermont who swore he wasn't the greatest doctor in the world but made up for it with work and willingness.[26]

The choice proved to be splendid. Ross was a simple, direct man—garrulous for a Vermonter—who spoke in a high-pitched Yankee twang. He was forever rushing off to the front when his squadron duties permitted, explaining that he wanted to help as much as he could. Besides, he said he could study and participate in more surgery in a month at the front than he would encounter in a lifetime of civilian practice. He soon became "Ol' Doc" to pilots and mechanics alike—this seemingly oldest of all lieutenants. Hamilton helped foster the admiration, for Ross had been a faculty member at Syracuse University when Hamilton was an undergrad student-athlete there.[27]

The good doctor was soon to find, however, that he was blessed with a staff that left quite a bit to be desired. None had ever had any medical instruction. And one, Pvt. James Hartin, was more inclined to mechanics. Eventually this soldier abandoned his post at mercy's office and shifted to engine work entirely.[28]

All of these matters were, of course, secondary to the real business at hand—becoming an active Camel squadron. By the end of the month they had achieved enough proficiency in formation flying and target shooting to begin line patrols and unofficial ventures into enemy territory. They were edging ever closer to that which they had come to do. The cast was complete; the stage was set. Of the twenty-one pilots originally assigned to the 17th Aero Squadron in France, few would last out the summer.

Some of the 17th's finest dressed for flight. Left to right: Lloyd A. Hamilton, Ralph W. Snoke, William G. Armstrong, Bradley Lawton, and Harriss P. Alderman. (Mrs. Louise Umstead)

3

Over the Top

The squadron began abusing the King's regulations almost at once. Since standing field orders forbade a pilot to cross the line of battle before he had been in France three weeks and at the front two—and since enemy planes were seldom seen west of the line in mid-1918, it follows that the 17th should not have engaged the enemy until sometime in mid-July. But that's not what happened. They first encountered German aircraft on Sunday, July 7, 1918, eight days before they were officially to cross the lines.[1] The beginnings were inauspicious.

During this period, the flights were taking turns at leading formation work. On the seventh, Tipton was ahead of fifteen Camels on line patrol, an affair in which they were supposed to fly the lines without crossing. But the Americans were cheating a bit this cloudy morning. Tipton and his men were just to the wrong side of the front and scanning the sky with more eagerness than necessary on a routine patrol.

Camels on the flight line at Petite Synthe. A plume of dust boils up as mechanics hold the planes until the signal for take off is given (Rodney Williams)

Immediately behind the B Flight leader were deputy commander Ralph Gracie and Rodney Williams, both original 17th cadets. Gracie had been at the front since late May and had one victory to his credit. Williams had been out with the RAF since early June but had yet to cross the line because his transfer to the 17th interrupted his service. Like the two leaders, however, he was considered experienced. Not so the remaining members of Tipton's quintet: Theose Tillinghast, fresh from a hospital bed; and Murray Spidle, an erstwhile college athlete from Massillon, Ohio, and late of the pilot's pool.[2] They were green and so acknowledged.

On this occasion, B Flight flew in an ascending "V" with Tipton lowest, a pair immediately above and behind him, and the remaining two up and out still more. Flights A and C trailed along behind, stacked similarly to the left and right, each a thousand feet above the other.[3] The theory of this formation was that the highest rear group could dive in and protect the advance planes in case of attack. A generation later there would be radio to permit coordination as the flight progressed, but in 1918 all communication was by prearranged signal. There was the waving of hands, the waggling of wings, the gunning of engines. And if someone in the rear elements spied an enemy first, he might pull to the front and loose a burst of machine gun fire to alert the others.

None of these things happened, however, on July 7, which was one of the reasons the squadron subsequently dropped five man patrols as being too cumbersome. What did happen was simply that flight leader Hamilton of C Flight spotted two Pfalz scouts chasing a lone Camel a mile below and instinctively tipped over and poured his flight down on the fight. This move was followed in a flash by A Flight and then B Flight. The squadron went into battle exactly in reverse of the formation's purpose.

Just what the outcome might have been remains unknown. Heavy clouds hung over the front that morning and before the unit could descend, all of the combatants disappeared into the mist. This was one of the disquieting oddities of the war to newer pilots on both sides, and the subject of much nervous contemplation. In those

Lloyd A. Hamilton seated in his Sopwith Camel. Notice how the center section of the wing fabric has been cut away to improve visibility. The object on the cabane strut is the wind-driven fuel pump. (Grace Myrick)

pre-radio days it was possible for a pilot to lose contact with even large numbers of friends and foes if required to look away even briefly. What was equally disquieting was that planes could also suddenly appear, unheralded, out of nowhere. And that's what happened next. The flights had flattened out and were reforming when a Fokker D-VII suddenly dropped out of the clouds above and swung into position to the right and rear of Mert Campbell's Sopwith.

How Campbell would have coped with the situation was never resolved. Tipton had gone low in search of the Pfalz scouts and he glanced up just in time to see the German fasten onto the A-Flight deputy commander. Immediately Tipton cranked around and veered up and left to catch the Fokker in his sight. He got off thirty-five rounds into the enemy's side and tail, intent on the kill that would make him an ace. At that, both guns went dead, demonstrating that when the Constantinesco synchronization system employed on British planes failed, it usually failed completely. But thirty-five rounds were enough. Finding himself alone among fifteen enemy craft and under attack from below, the foe dropped away to some clouds 3,000 feet down and disappeared. He was well under control and, although both Gracie and Williams lashed at him before he disappeared, he got away cleanly.[4]

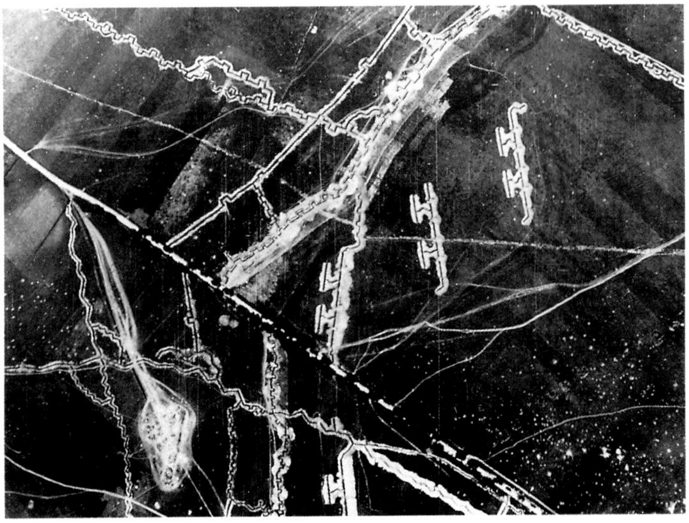

An actual photo of Western Front trenches as seen by 17th Aero Squadron pilots on patrol. There is a camouflaged German Aerodrome at the lower left. (Clinton Burdick)

Tipton was bitterly disappointed. He was more than willing to account for being across the line if he could claim a first for the 17th in their friendly rivalry with the 148th—the other squadron of Camel-driving Americans who were now stationed at nearby Cappel Aerodrome. In truth, both these units were striving to be first to claim a kill for their British hosts. As it turned out, Tipton's problems left the honor to the 148th. On July 13, Lt. Field Kindley of that unit dropped from patrol at 15,000 feet and shot the tail off one of a number of Fokkers scrapping with some SE-5s.[5] This was a full week before the 148th was to enter combat and a week earlier than the 17th would record its first victory.

This mild abuse of official policy gave the Americans a chance to learn much about the area over which they would fight. They saw the front line in detail—where it inched into the North Sea, how it trailed south to Armentiers, how it hooked out and around Ypres and then disappeared south again bulging ever westward to mark the German successes in the spring. They discovered that the extraordinarily straight roads of France and Belgium, generally lined with tall poplars, made maintaining a sense of direction while flying much simpler than it had been in meandering over Britain. They saw the wide, pockmarked, rickrack scars of the battle lines and the dead yellowed areas where poison gas had been loosed in battle. And as the rains began to come with increasing frequency, they saw developing beneath them the incredible mud of Flanders.

Despite these solemn observations, flying was as yet still something of a lark for most of these young men. Hugh "Hughie" Shearman, a handsome blond youth from Chicago, wrote his parents of his adventures shortly after joining the 17th . "I went visiting today and landed at three other Aerodromes. Met a good many boys that I trained with in Texas. Went hedge-hopping for about an hour—chasing the cows in the fields and scaring the women working with the crops."[6]

Another low flier, Laurence "Bobby" Roberts, a blithe spirit from Wilmington, Delaware (with a genuine affinity for apple pie, motorcycles, and motorcycle accidents), also found enjoyment. He wrote, "My first impression of France was not much but is improving very much as I get around and meet people. Flying here is tiresome work except contour chasing. I have been doing a lot along the shore and enjoy it very much. Had a 'conk' on the beach the other day and, with the assistance of two police and two French civvies, I swung my own prop and took off okay. Did not exchange a single word but I talked very eloquently in sign language."[7] Roberts was a former National Guardsman who had served against

Top to bottom: William Hugh Shearman, Harry Day, Oscar Mandel. Horseplay was common among the young pilots of the time. (Mrs. Gordon Kellogg)

Laurence "Bobby" Roberts from Wilmington, Delaware. He learned to wear his campaign hat tilted so in earlier service as a National Guardsman serving against Pancho Villa. (Eric Roberts)

Robert Miles Todd, in typical flying gear, stands by the nose of a Camel. (Miles J. Todd)

Pancho Villa and there learned from cavalrymen to go about with his hat set at a rakish angle.

In their neophyte adventures, pilots were also encouraged to coax their craft as high as possible since that was the stuff of bomber escort. And they learned how cold it is flying along in an open-cockpit biplane at 15,000 to 20,000 feet even in mid-summer. "Our flight commander [Hamilton] had his face nearly frozen," Harriss "Aldy" Alderman of C Flight wrote home after one patrol. "In fact, it's about the same as frost bite and he will have to look like a greased pig for several days."[8]

Most of all, they began to learn the likelihood that at least one of the Camels would run into some kind of mechanical difficulty on every patrol. C Flight's Robert Todd, a young Lieutenant from Cincinnati, (who proved to be both a deadly scrapper and a marvelous reporter) managed to parlay cold temperatures and mechanical troubles into a stirring account in early July. He described his experiences in a letter to his mother:

"We were doing a line patrol yesterday afternoon from seven till nine and I got terribly sick while I was up. We were up about 20,000 feet and my pressure pump froze up on me. I tried working the hand pump for a while but even the washer in it was frozen and I had to give it up. The pressure is for the petrol tank and is very important because the gravity tank will only run for half an hour.

"When you are up high and try moving around a bit or exercising any at all, you start blowing like a fish out of water. It's no joke either to have your hands get freezing cold and not even be able to beat them together to warm them. I have a lot of trouble with my hands. I must have frozen my fingers at one time or another because they are almost unbearable now when they start to thaw out.

"I ran on my gravity tank as long as I could and then gave the sign to the leader that I was going home. We were up above two layers of clouds at the time and outside of the general direction of our side of the lines; I was lost. I glided down until I could see and found out I was about six miles out to sea. I had glided with the wind which I had not counted on and we had been nearly over our camp when I broke off. So you can see how easy it is to get lost. I was taking no chances in landing in 'Hunland' so I kept on trying to see a familiar landmark. It was pretty dark and the tide was up and nothing looked quite the same. To make a long story short, I finally landed at the Aerodrome near Calais and found my directions and finally got home. I had about fifty miles to go against a strong wind and when I landed at 10:30 it was fairly dark. Mighty glad to get home though..."[9]

Pump trouble, gear trouble, engine trouble—trouble came with incredible regularity. Most of the time such difficulties merely caused the pilots to turn home before they were ready. But there were an inordinate number of forced landings and crashes.

Bradley Lawton, twenty-six, had served with RAF 209 in the field since early April and was generally considered a pilot of great promise. But he fell prey to the vagaries of the Camel one bright Thursday morning and all that promise came to naught.

Lawton was a member of C Flight and lost his engine while cruising over the British lines. He used up his altitude in diving to acquire a start and, failing that, had the ill luck to stall at low altitude while dead-sticking to a landing. As his plane smashed into a spot just behind the lines, he was thrown face-first into the butts of

This photo shows how the butts of the Vickers machine guns projected into the cockpit of the Camel. Pilots injured by having their faces mashed against the guns in crashes were said to have incurred "Camel face." Note also the Aldis gun sight. (Mrs. Louise Umstead)

the machine guns, which projected well into the cockpit of the little Sopwith. He came out with smashed cheeks and a lacerated forehead, a combination which RAF aviators had long before termed "Camel face." Lawton tried to carry on for several days despite the pain—even outliving another forced landing on July 18. Finally, though, he had to give it up and was sent to hospital on July 27, never to return to the 17th. He suffered from respiratory ailments the rest of his life.[10]

The results of most crashes were not so grim. Floyd M. Showalter, a quiet loner and deadly gambler from A Flight, unexpectedly got a chance to use skills learned while training in seaplanes with the 45th Aero Squadron at Essington, Pennsylvania; skills learned, coincidentally, at the very spot on the Delaware where Eckert had learned to fly in 1916. Showalter got little more than a dunking when he was forced down with engine trouble in no-man's land just south of Nieuport. Belgians had flooded the area by springing the dikes and Showalter stretched across the water as best he could. But finally he had to plunk into the drink and when the plume of spray died down, Tipton, who was circling overhead, saw "Showie" calmly step from his aircraft and splash away through three feet of water toward the friendly side of the battlefield. Showalter later revealed that he had landed directly on a flooded road and merely followed it homeward. Thereafter, he always wore rubber boots while flying.[11]

A few crashes were directly attributable to enemy gunfire. Frank Dixon, a Princeton cadet who had actually come to the front in June to replace Roy Brown (conqueror of Richthofen) in RAF 209 before coming to the 17th, met his Waterloo on July 12. While nosing around, he picked up a stray bullet through his gas tank and barely managed to make the friendly side of the lines. He went down near a Belgian gun site and was not seen again for several days. And when he got home he was most emphatic that conditions in the sector had delayed him. But since Dixon spoke good French and was notoriously fond of fun and frolic, the pronouncement was greeted with hoots and groans from people who knew him best.[12]

That same day Hughie Shearman's plane was so badly hit by anti-aircraft fire that it had to be stricken from the squadron. Anti-aircraft fire was termed "Archie" by British aviators (a reference to Sir George Robey's hit comic tune, *Archibald, Certainly Not*), and it was making its presence felt to the 17th more and more with each passing day. Robert Todd said it best in a letter home.

"We go over [the lines] in flights looking for trouble and usually find it. If it isn't Hun machines it is Archie, and I am getting to hate the last. The Hun Archie is devilish good and certainly puts your wind up. We'll be tootling along looking for Huns and watching the ground in Hunland for activities when all of a sudden you hear a 'Whoof! Whoof'.

"They get your height the first time but are usually behind you and start to follow you along. Then the chase starts and I am afraid I'll never enjoy a 'catchers' game again after playing it in the air with a Hun Archie battery.

"The only way to keep away from them is to start twisting and turning, changing your course every few seconds. Even then it doesn't work very well and it sure makes you nervous to be doing everything you can with your bus and look behind and see this line of black puffs following you right around, whoofing away. They put some big stuff at us too, some of it being eight-inch. You can imagine what this would do near one of these light machines. Like blowing a feather around a room..."[13]

C Flight's Aldy Alderman wrote about both Archie and engine trouble. "We sighted some observation balloons and started for them and you should have seen them, how they were pulled down. They must have gone down in nothing flat and before we could get them 'Archie' (Anti-Aircraft Guns [sic]—put this in your new dictionary as he is an important thing in our lives) was giving us a morning greeting. We were about ten miles over the lines and our time was nearly up so we went down a bit to be more sociable and to pay our respects in the way of some machine gun bullets into Hunland. When diving, ordinarily we cut off our engine and put it back on again when ready to level out. Well, we went down to about ten thousand, still ten miles over, and when I tried my engine—Blooie! She wouldn't take. Try as I might, she would just tick over. Well, there I was and the wind was dead against me. O boy! O boy! I knew I could glide about six miles, but what good was that? So I began to think of you and her and it and Beach and Lummie and all the rest and even made an effort to sing 'Home Sweet Home.' And to assure me that I was welcome, Archie again spoke up and tried to persuade me to linger a little longer. And I couldn't do much dodging as I didn't want to lose any more altitude than possible. He either felt sorry for me or wasn't very good, for they continued to burst behind my tail. Well, joy of joys, my engine began to show signs of life and soon I was getting along a bit better. But I had lost considerable height and as I neared the lines, tracers began to pick up and I am sure Fritzie wasted enough machine gun bullets to pay

Left to right: Harriss Alderman, Robert Todd, Lyman Case. Taking time out from the war at the beach. Probably near Dunkirk. (Rodney Williams)

The premier fighter aircraft of the German air service (Luftstreitkraft), in the summer of 1918 was the Fokker D-VII. Though of poor quality, this photo is unusual in that we see the plane in flight. Date and location are unknown. (Robert Bowden)

for my petrol. I suppose as we reached warmer atmosphere, my engine felt more inclined to work and I am sure I felt better. Anyway, just about over the lines, she started cooing and buzzing along like a top and it was, to me, the sweetest lullaby ever. And to make a nice show, and to let him know that I wasn't mad—then—I tossed a couple of loops in parting and buzzed along to breakfast. O, it's a great war."[14]

The squadron's occasional and sporadic contact with the enemy increased greatly after mid-July. On Wednesday, July 17, the dusk patrol had an honest dogfight with the enemy and again it was Tipton's B Flight that set the pace. Goodnow and A Flight saw nothing at all in the late evening sky, and Hamilton and his men, while sighting several enemy planes, did not mix with them; the closest they came to contact was when two Pfalz scouts chased Frost back to the friendly side of the lines at about 8:20 p.m. By that time B Flight was wildly dueling with five Fokkers.

The Flights were now experimenting with four plane formations, but B Flight (having lost Shearman in the darkening skies somewhere along the way) was one plane short on crossing the lines. So there were only three 17th planes at 10,000 feet when Tipton spotted five German biplanes a half mile below. He signaled a dive and went for the leader head on, giving him a blast and taking one in return. Gracie sighted on the same Fokker and loosed a hundred rounds from the side, at which a second German got on his tail and rode him down nearly a mile.

A sixth German plane now appeared out of the gathering darkness, a Fokker triplane, which came down on Williams from above. The two exchanged about 150 rounds head on and Williams immediately turned for home with his aircraft marvelously shot up—one bullet actually striking almost dead center in the front plate of his propeller. By that time Tipton had been chased back to the friendly side of the lines by two Fokkers and soon the three 17th pilots came together over Nieuport where they found Shearman waiting. He had mixed it up with two triplanes by himself after losing the formation.[15]

Back at the base, more than a few found time to comment on the condition of Williams' shot-up machine. Williams (small, dark-haired, poker-faced—with expressive blue eyes and a quiet wit) was not considered by many to be the most graceful pilot in the air. But he was daring and determined and showed a knack for being in the middle of nearly every major scrap the 17th fought during his service at the front. In time he would present the unit with so much evidence of hard fighting and narrow escape that any close call would come to be referred to simply as "a Williams show."[16]

The next two days passed uneventfully and Hamilton and Mert Campbell were able to depart for two weeks leave in England. Losing pilots to leave at this stage of the game was a bit of a stretch for the 17th. And things stretched tighter when Doc Ross decided he would have to send Theose Tillinghast away on sick leave. "Tilly" had never really recovered from a bout with pneumonia that had laid him in hospital in June. He went about pale and drawn and exhibited a tendency to black out at heights above 17,000 feet, hardly a desirable trait in a pilot. Ross recommended him for sick leave on July 20, a leave that could not be granted immediately because of the limited number of pilots available. So, Tillinghast went on soldiering despite his health.

Rodney Williams in July 1918. Williams was very aggressive in battle and so prone to the close shave that any incident involving hard fighting and a narrow escape came to be known by his comrades as "a Williams show." He scored the squadron's first victory and probably its second. (Rodney D. Williams)

The only photo of George Preston Glenn discovered is this view taken from a group photo made when he was a member of the 22nd Aero Squadron. Glenn was the first to die in the 17th, on July 20, 1918. (Mrs. John McBride)

Albert F. Schneider. This photo was taken at Soncamp later in the war. Through a mix-up in names, Schneider was erroneously reported by someone to be missing in action in mid-summer. His loyal German-American parents made no inquiry until October when they reported having received letters dated long after his supposed death. (Mrs. Gordon Kellogg)

The day Tillinghast didn't go on sick leave turned out to be a day of both triumph and tragedy for the 17th. The triumph belonged to Williams; the tragedy came to George Glenn, a quiet young man from Lynchburg, Virginia. Glenn had celebrated his 24th birthday on June 21 by reporting to Petite Synthe; it was to be his last.

The 17th was undertaking its first bombing escort on the morning of the 20th, accompanying RAF 211's DH-9 bombers to their targets in German territory. This was exactly the type of assignment Harold Fowler had been dubious about when trying to decide whether to let the Americans accept Camels. In fact, the 148th's William Clements, when he heard of the 17th's assignment noted in his diary, "This is rather bad business, escorting DH-9s over, as they can go higher than we can and are faster at any height."[17]

But as it turned out, the bombing run posed no problem at all. Thirteen Camels went into the cloudy skies between 8 and 8:30 a.m. with deputy commander Henry B. (inevitably "Jack") Frost leading C Flight in Hamilton's absence. Frost, an Oxford Cadet, had served with RAF 210 beginning in early April and, while he had yet to claim a kill, was considered a most likely warrior.

These Americans escorted the DH-9s to Bruges and watched them drop and turn for home. At that the 17th took to scouting on its own and, just short of 10 a.m., came upon a flight of five Fokkers over Ostend. The 17th was at about 18,000 feet with the enemy a good 1,500 feet higher. (This without oxygen!)

The Camels nosed up to meet the foe, at which one Fokker broke from formation and dived after Glenn who was flying Eckert's plane. He fired from short range and then broke away right to escape bursts from Goodnow, William "Army" Armstrong, and Ralph Snoke who were fast approaching. In the midst of the developing mêlée, many saw Glenn dive downward some 5,000 feet, then flatten out and disappear into the cloudy sky below. Although all assumed that their comrade was safe, in reality it would be the last they ever saw of George Preston Glenn.[18]

The fight went on elsewhere—a Fokker fastened itself onto Frost's tail only to be driven off by Todd. Another came at Tipton, guns blazing, then suddenly spiraled down out of control following

Leonard J. Desson was a veterinary doctor from Ithaca, New York, and one of the few married officers in the 17th. He is seen here as a member of RAF 209 in the spring of 1918. (Mrs. Louise Umstead)

a direct blast into the cockpit by Williams. Williams spent no time observing this because, by then, an enemy plane was coming down on him. He did a quick roll and came out slightly to the left and rear of the Fokker just as it began a slow climbing turn. Williams fired a short burst into the cockpit and watched the enemy craft turn onto its back and fall straight down out of control.[19]

The enemy soon decided that enough was enough and broke off homeward. The Camels followed suit and were on the ground by 10:30, full of excitement over William's victory and with ears cocked for the sound of Glenn winging home. By nightfall the 17th had turned to assuming that he was a prisoner of war somewhere.

William's triumph marked the 17th's emergence as a successful combat unit. It also produced the second of the many events that created the "Williams show" tradition. That afternoon when the squadron was examining their morning effort in detail, Tipton asked suddenly, "Who was it that shot that Fokker off my tail?"

"I chased one off just before I got my kill," said Williams.

"Well, you certainly got him too," Tipton reported.[20] Since Tipton could vouch for the first one and reports from the front accounted for the second, Williams had achieved a double victory. But as the paperwork had already been filed, Williams made no additional claim. It was just one of many incidents that would burnish his reputation but obscure his record.

For the next few days increasingly bad weather and a drop in German activities led to quieter times—although both Ralph Snoke (of Davenport, Iowa, and one of the first pilots commissioned in the 17th) and Hughie Shearmen had their planes slightly damaged by Archie on July 22. That day also marked two new arrivals from the pilot's pool, 1st Lt. Albert Schneider and 2nd Lt. George Wise. Wise was replacement for Glenn, who was now stricken from the rolls; Schneider came in to relieve Brad Lawton.

Lawton left five days later, which seemed to precipitate a rash of medical problems. Tillinghast was fated to go, Bobby Roberts was soon sent out for nearly a month, and Leonard Desson—the flying veterinarian from Ithaca, New York—went into a nearby hospital for five days with what was thought to be Spanish influenza.[21] As feared, leaves, losses, and medical problems were rapidly beginning to upset the mix of new and experienced pilots.

It was about then that, someone, somewhere, got the bright idea to try Gotha bomber hunting by night. Both the 17th and 148th formally requested that RAF 65 Wing provide panel and instrument lights for three planes in each squadron. But they were summarily turned down with the reply that "HQ RAF does not wish either of the two American Squadrons to do night flying at this time." However, on July 24, a note from RAF 10 Brigade to HQ explained that, "Some of these squadrons are very anxious to destroy the hostile bombing machines which disturb their rest at night and in view of the fact that the operations of these hostile night flying machines are usually confined to a restricted area, I think that, if approval is given, the Americans will have a very fair chance of realizing their ambition. As this is a purely volunteer request on their part, I respectfully recommend it to the G.O.C. for reconsideration."[22]

While the lights were soon forthcoming, one wonders just who it was that wanted them. Murray Spidle reported scant eagerness for this in a letter home. "I did a little night flying this week as three of us went up and tried to catch the Gothas that raided England, but as usual we missed connections and are happy we did, for it is no fun to attack a machine with as many guns and pilots as a Gotha."[23]

Perhaps the scheme resulted from a lack of other action as July drew to a close. The enemy seemed to have disappeared from the daylight sky and the only real excitement available for several days came on the 30th and 31st.

In the first instance, Rodney Williams went out on a very late evening patrol during which an ambitious enemy pilot fired on him from the incredible distance of 300 yards. That would have been

George T. Wise is shown among a group in front of a gunless Camel during training in England. Left to right: William H. Shearman, Theose Tillinghast, Wise, Oscar Mandel. (Theose Tillinghast)

This photograph is from a document entitled Report of a Gotha Brought Down by French A.A. Fire Near Crochte on the Night of 4th/5th July 1918. The report describes and analyses this G.Va downed near Dunkirk in July. Note the elaborately painted, fire-breathing dragon! (Frederick M. Clapp)

On July 17, 1918, Rodney D. Williams encountered a Fokker DR.-I triplane during the dusk patrol. The two exchanged fire head-on resulting in the strike indention seen here on the front plate of the propeller hub of Williams' plane. (George Roland)

laughable in itself had the burst not hit him—which it did. His plane was so thoroughly riddled that even the center-section bracing wires were swept from before his face. Williams flew home with the wings threatening to come off and stated fixed opinions about any flier who would attempt a shot at such a distance.[24]

Then, on July 31, with the month almost over, five Camels came upon an enemy plane just ripe for killing. It was a German two-seater, and they drove it away just north of Wervieq. Todd told all in a letter home:

"We ran into him just over the lines and all of us dived at him and then split off because of the observer. [Apparently the observer put up a spirited defense with his machine gun while he lasted.] I went down on him again and pulled up close enough to see that the observer was dead but as the machine was going down out of control, we let off and didn't follow him down. Although we probably got him, we get no credit because he wasn't seen to crash and it could not be confirmed. So right then I made up my mind to get the next one or he'd get me..."[25]

The 17th entered August with tails well up and wagging. The feeling was that they had survived their neophyte phase and come through no more likely to be victims than victors. Only one man, Glenn, had failed to return from the repeated tangles with the enemy, and this had been more than avenged by Williams' dual triumph on July 20.

A-Flight's Murray Spidle probably summed up the feelings of all when he wrote, "Well, from all indications, my life is pretty safe now, for if a person survives his first month at the front, he gets by...95 percent are killed in the first month."[26] Such an attitude was being more than a little encouraged by brisk applause from British Command.

Murray K. Spidle of Massilon, Ohio, home of legendary protester Jacob Coxey. Spidle was an excellent flier and equally good at chronicling events. (Lewis C. Spidell)

Still the war was beginning to change the men of the squadron. That astute observer of people and places, Harry Traxler, noted a new attitude in his diary. "Our men show much change since one year and a half ago. At Kelly, we were a bunch of happy fellows. Today we are still happy, but the men have settled down to the steady grind of warfare. No longer do you see the men have sham battles in mess lines, only the occasional joke once in a while..."[27] The enlisted ranks, men who got none of the glory of flying and who often worked far into the night to guarantee serviceable planes, were among the quickest to understand war weariness.

The first day of August was a grand Thursday, dawning warm and hazy with a light wind. The squadron sent up nine planes on offensive patrol at 8 a.m. They rose circling over Petite Synthe, with Goody Goodnow and A Flight in the lead. They climbed southwest and leveled off at 15,000 feet. At that point Frost dropped away with engine trouble and Todd moved to lead C which now consisted only of himself and the new man, Albert Schneider; the boyish first generation American of German descent who had joined the unit just ten days earlier.

All flew toward Tourcoing eyeing the morning sun against the Hun who might be lurking there. He wasn't, but the 17th was much surprised to come shortly across three Fokker biplanes and a triplane circling below them a good ten miles on the wrong side of the line.

The enemy aircraft were flying aimlessly, searching the haze in a careless fashion that gave the impression of play rather than fight. It looked like a well-baited trap and the situation got a stern look-over before the patrol committed to action. By the time the leader was satisfied, the 17th was nearly onto the German airmen who sensed them at last and banked sharply east toward safety. But it was too late. Goodnow went down in a slashing dive that swung the targets back for the following Camels.

Todd dived directly on the triplane and began hammering it from a hundred yards out. True to his word, he meant to kill or be killed and bored in hosing fire directly into the cockpit. The enemy triplane pitched up abruptly as if about to zoom away, at which Todd drew closer and gave the plane a long burst in its vitals. In an instant, the dainty machine gave a sickening wobble to the right and swung away out of control. Todd slapped into a near vertical bank to follow, missed his rudder, and went into a dizzying spin that carried him down a mile and a half before he could recover. As he pulled out he saw his kill tumble wildly, then smash into some trees near Provine.

By the time he got back to altitude, he found that the fight was over. The remaining Fokkers, having been roughly handled, had put their noses down and dived away to safety. The Camel pilots had tried a short chase, then, bouncing about the sky with wild excitement, gradually reformed at altitude.

They went on southwestward hardly expecting anything more, and within ten minutes flushed another covey. Three more Fokkers were spotted above them doing an embarrassing job of trying to hide in the sun. The patrol flicked through their shadows and tipped up to meet them. Before they had climbed far the enemy pilots broke and dived. Gracie of B Flight got on one immediately, ripped a good burst into its belly, and watched it spin down half a mile apparently out of control. By then an enemy had fastened on Gracie's tail and was blazing tracers between his wings. Gracie hauled into a climbing turn and let the foe slip under, where Murray Spidle swung onto its backside in passing. "A very pretty Fokker with a green tail," Spidle described it after he'd killed it with a steady stream of .303s.[28] The enemy went into a right spin, dropped quickly, came under control, then did a very steep dive into the thick haze below.

Now, it developed that there were more than three enemy planes in the fight. One had been truly hidden in the sun and was making his move. At the last possible instant, Shearmen glimpsed the Pfalz lashing out of the glare broadside of the action intent on killing and racing away before he could be intercepted. Shearman cocked his craft so the intruder would fly under his guns and waited to pull a full deflection shot. His burst ripped into the machine forward of the cockpit, which caused it to falter and slide away. Sensing a kill, Shearman dived left and put another burst directly into the cockpit. This time the plane wavered into a sideslip, then fell off into a dive. The young Chicagoan wheeled down a thousand feet watching it dive wildly toward the Allied lines below. He lost it in the gloom at 6,000 feet when he turned back to the fight. But the battle was over. The German planes had all streaked east toward safety and the Camel pilots, low on fuel, turned homeward with swelled heads stretching their helmets.[29]

They had been home three quarters of an hour when Eckert found them holed up in the officer's mess. They still reeked of burnt castor oil (which was added to the fuel to lubricate the engines). They wore dusky, burnt-powder masks that stopped short where their helmets and goggles had ringed their faces.[30] Excitement and euphoria reigned as they rehashed the action and awaited confirmation. And perhaps they drew arcs in the air with flattened palms—for it was a new gesture come to war with the arrival of a new mode of warfare.

When calmer, they would fall to analyzing the capabilities of their enemy. The general opinion expressed by those who knew best was that these were not the number-one German pilots. Flying the newly developed Fokker D-VII biplane (then the finest single seaters in the sky), the German pilots of Flanders often flew as if unaware of their advantage. They regularly allowed themselves to be lured down to the Camel's best dogfight altitude instead of staying high where the Sopwiths had serious disadvantages. They opened fire at too great a distance and generally broke off before they reached most effective range.

These were not just observations made by the 17th. The opinion generally held by most experienced airmen in the area was that these were second-rate outfits holding the line to free sharper units for duty further south. The deduction seems to have been generally borne out by history, but the 17th was soon to discover just how tough even second-rate units could be.[31]

No doubt Eckert was eminently satisfied by August 1. To cap off the three victories of the day, the unit suddenly received two

This is the interior of the pilot's room at Petite Synthe. The people are unidentified. Note the souvenir German insignia and the propeller. (Rodney D. Williams)

Jesse Campbell from Royal Oak, Michigan. Although not related to Merton Campbell, their records got so entwined that Clapp didn't even list Jesse's name among the list of officers in the early squadron history. (Mrs. Gordon Kellogg)

Glenn D. Wicks arrived in the 17th in August 1918. He hailed from Sanquoit, New York, where his father was an Episcopal minister. Glenn was a tall youth of very good humor and a favorite with both officers and men. (Mrs. Louise Umstead)

This trio of aviators wearing the U. S. Air Service uniform was taken somewhere in England during training. Henry Bradley Frost, deputy commander of the 17th's C Flight, is at right. George A. Vaughn is at left. The man in the center is unidentified. (George A. Vaughn)

new pilots, two Oxford cadets. One was Jesse Campbell, no relation to Merton. Jesse was a wide, stocky little man of five and a half feet from Royal Oak, Michigan. He had a frail mustache, but offset it with a thick mop of hair, which he parted straight down the middle and swung back in an generally unmanageable arrangement that usually degenerated into a wild mane as the day wore on. He had yet to see combat but his records spoke well of him and he would shortly become a mainstay in the 17th.

The second newcomer was Glenn Wicks of Sanquoit, New York. Twenty-five, the son of an Episcopal clergyman, and at a shade under six feet he was as tall as Campbell was short. He was lean, clean shaven, and good humored beyond belief. His records also spoke well of him.[32]

All in all, August 1st was considered to have been a truly fine day that called for a truly fine evening. There was much to celebrate that evening—and many willing celebrants in the 17th. Things got even brighter in the squadron when Mert Campbell and Lloyd Hamilton arrived back from leave the next morning. Campbell had spent a relatively quiet time with British kin. ("Aunt gave me a piece of embroidered work made by Grandmother Harris when she was a little girl. Asked that I give it to Mother, who I know will be pleased." he noted in his diary.)[33] Tucked away with relatives, he had little news of other pilots members of the 17th might know.

Hamilton, however, was full of amusing and self-effacing tales regarding the discovery that he had become a growing legend among American pilots still in England. His response was typical Hamilton fare in which the expressed admiration was turned to droll comedy. Later in the day, though, he did an atypical thing. A new plane had just arrived in the squadron and Hamilton laid claim to it. After he'd tried it a bit and had it tuned to his liking he turned to his rigger, George Fellay, with photographs of his father, mother, and fiancee. "George," said he, "Maybe I'm getting sentimental or something, but see if you can find a way to put these in the cockpit." It was a surprising request for the usually unemotional Hamilton, but Fellay soon concocted a mounting out of scrap aluminum and put the small gallery in order.[34]

Changes in Squadron Status—end of day 8/1/1918

A Flight	
Leonard Desson	In hospital with flu.
George P. Glenn	Killed in action.
George Wise	Replacement pilot.
B Flight	
Theose Tillinghast	Slated for hospitalization.
Glenn Wicks	Replacement pilot.
C Flight	
Jesse F. Campbell	Replacement pilot.
Bradley Lawton	Injured and out of the war.
Albert Schneider	Replacement pilot.

4

The Bells of Hell Go Ting-Aling-Aling[1]

With Hamilton and Campbell back, Tipton and Frost began to think of leave. While these events were unfold ing, other members of the squadron left on bomber escort to Zeebrugge. August had been a rainy month in Flanders for some eighty years, and 1918 would prove no exception. The squadron met with little adventure during a two-hour jaunt in a cloudy, drizzly sky. Solid clouding persisted to 18,000 feet making accurate bombing impossible. The sole contact with the enemy came when returning to the lines, as a lone Pfalz materialized out of the clouds and began stalking a straggling bomber. Todd turned on it and drove it off without a shot.[2]

The day was a memorable one, however, for Murray Spidle who had a run-in with the well-known and respected Archie battery at Middlekerke. Because there were so many anti-aircraft guns along the overland route, bombers struggling with heavy bomb loads meant for targets well behind the lines had taken to swinging out over the North Sea at Dunkirk, flying up the coast, and turning in as they neared the destination. Of all the batteries thus to be avoided, that at Middlekerke was generally accepted as the most dangerous.

On this Friday morning, Spidle ran afoul of things when his engine began to falter just as the bombers were making the turn for Zeebrugge. Spidle swung around and was forced to run the Middlekerke battery alone. Although he laid five miles off shore, his plane was pounded unmercifully before he passed out of range.

"You should have seen the stuff they throw up from one of those historic spots (very modern)," he wrote home that afternoon. "They sure do like to get a machine alone and then shell him for all

The 17th benefited from the seasoning many of its pilots received with RAF units. Seen here with RAF 209 are, left to right, back row: Frank Dixon, two unknowns, Ralph Gracie, two unknowns, Bradley Lawton, unknown, William Armstrong. (Frank A. Dixon)

American pilots also benefited from training with many famous British aviators. Seen here, between two unidentified airmen, is Major Edward Mannock who had seventy-three victories when he died about the time the 17th started to cross the line. His grave has never been found. (Samuel B. Eckert)

they're worth. I wish I had the iron simoleon it costs them to pepper up the sky. It's a great life if you don't weaken." said he.[3]

On Saturday the squadron went out on offensive patrol at 7:40 in the morning. There were nine of them, which had become nearly standard now that they had discovered how unwieldy five-plane groupings could be. A Flight was at the point, B Flight slightly to the right, and C Flight on top. One plane from A Flight turned back with engine trouble just before they crossed the lines at Dixmude.

There was no shortage of enemy planes in the sky on that day—they counted thirty as they crisscrossed the enemy territory. Still, it was more than an hour before they spotted a German formation that looked proper for Camels. The target was two biplanes and two triplanes moving along at the same altitude as the 17th about two miles south of Roulers.

Army Armstrong of Philadelphia swung out of the top flight almost simultaneously with a move out of B Flight by Hughie Shearman and each fixed on one of the triplanes. Shearman's target saw him coming and dropped quickly out of danger. Armstrong's move was more successful. He was able to arc swiftly onto the triplane's tail before the enemy pilot spotted him. The enemy pilot came about suddenly, but Armstrong put a short burst directly into the side of the Fokker at which the craft dropped into a steep spiral and spun past Shearman who followed it to 5,000 feet. It crashed into the ground in a near vertical dive.

Mert Campbell was there and rushed to take on one of the biplanes. The Fokker dropped its nose and the two aviators tumbled downward in a long, winding fight that started at 12,000 feet and dropped to 1,000 before a victor was determined. Campbell burned ammunition sparingly, getting off only 400 rounds in the entire conflict while never edging closer to the enemy than 100 yards. At 3,000 feet, smoke began to pour from the Fokker's cockpit and Campbell watched for the signal fires of victory. But they did not come. Instead the aircraft turned on its left wingtip, poised, then crashed into a green field of growing crops.

Merton L. Campbell, the original deputy commander of A Flight, is shown here seated in his Camel. (George Campbell)

Murray Kenneth Spidle was found to be missing after an offensive patrol on the morning of August 4, 1918. It is surmised that he fell somewhere near Dixmude in an area under artillery fire so intense that no trace of him or his machine was ever found.

At that, Campbell flashed overhead and leveled off to survey the situation. He found himself alone with white tracers reaching for him from a road about a mile beyond where lay his victim. Having no taste for this, he joined Shearman who was plying an area nearby and together they left it all behind. They landed slightly behind the patrol, which had just straggled in with the exhilarating news of a double kill.[4]

But Murray Spidle was not among them—and the seven returnees eventually determined that he had last been seen diving on the remaining biplane in the formation under attack. There was little concern at first, but when no word arrived by afternoon the squadron began to seek him out. Hamilton led Schneider and Jesse Campbell on a patrol to look for the missing friend. Eckert got on the phone to wing to see if they had any word. The 148th was consulted, but knew nothing. By nightfall the 17th had sadly concluded that Spidle was probably a prisoner.

No one ever saw him again. Spidle's roommate, Leonard Desson, found everyone still puzzled when he returned from his five days in the hospital. He listened to the story and then, after two days of deep thought and dying hope, quietly burned Spidle's personal letters in their little stove, packed the Ohioan's belongings, and sat down to write the missing youth's parents in Massillon, Ohio.

"Being Murray's roommate, and also one of his very best friends, I take the liberty of writing you," he began. "This letter need not be a source of worry to you, for all things tend to the best." He next described the events of the flight and continued. "One dived and Murray was seen to go after him. From that time he has not been seen. We all figure his chances of being shot down were very small, as all through his fight none of the 'Huns' was seen to open fire. We think that in diving his engine would not pick up again and he was forced to land in Germany. I'm almost positive he did not crash, as the two 'Huns' shot down were confirmed from the front trenches, but they saw none of our machines go down. Knowing he could not make our lines, it is very possible he turned east and landed as far as possible from the front line infantry (which is a very good thing to do if one cannot get over the lines)..."[5]

It seems likely now that Spidle's course was exactly the opposite. Probably he lost his engine and attempted to glide home, carefully trading altitude for distance, stretching harder and harder toward safety. Somewhere in the Dixmude area the game was up, and he smashed down amid the German lines only a few hundred yards from safety; it's likely that he fell in an area being heavily shelled by artillery where man and machine were gradually pounded into oblivion. When his mother searched the area ten years later for a trace of her son, someone recalled a local crash just about the time Spidle disappeared and thought the incident had been recorded in the local courthouse. But, subsequently, the courthouse itself had been ground to rubble, so the trail was gone.[6]

Lloyd A. Hamilton, original commander of C Flight. He is shown here ready for action. (Grace Myrick)

Sgt. Cameron Smith of Fredonia, New York, was a rigger in charge of C Flight aircraft. Although Smith did not support A Flight directly, Goodnow thought so much of his efforts that he recommended him for the Distinguished Service Medal. (Mrs. Gordon Kellogg)

Ironically, the news of the young pilot's disappearance reached Ohio on August 17, a warm lazy Saturday that found relatives gathered at the Spidle home and remarking that the 28th would be Murray's twenty-first birthday. Someone suggested sending a telegram to congratulate him on his majority and they were soon fussing with the details, deciding what ought to be said, and calculating when it should be sent so as to reach him on the occasion. At that, a Western Union boy knocked on the screen door with a brown envelope in his hand.

There was some confusion since it seemed as though the boy had been summoned in error. But gradually it became clear that there was no mistake. It was Washington sending word that Murray Kenneth Spidle, member of the Glee Club, center on the Mount Union College eleven, was missing.[7] His confidence on surviving his first month of combat was misplaced, and from then on he was to be only a name on a memorial wall in Flanders Field cemetery near Courtrai, a man without a grave. His was the only instance of a complete disappearance suffered by the 17th. George Glenn's body was discovered after the war, but no trace of Murray Spidle was ever found.

The unit had time to mull this matter for many days thereafter for swirling fog, turbulent winds, and regular rain now lay over Petite Synthe to keep the Americans close to home. They made a try at escorting RAF 211 bombers to Bruges on August 4, but it was such a filthy Sunday that they failed to meet the formation. The patrol went aloft in swirling fog, bounced about in wrenching turbulence, and finally turned off on offensive patrol to the south. They crossed the lines at 15,000 feet and prowled about in clouding too heavy to permit reconnaissance.

The sky was theirs that morning. The only thing seen in the air was a kite balloon aloft in a clearing near Armentiers, like a dark chip in the drain of an enormous basin. Hamilton swooped for it, but it went back to earth before he could manage a shot.

With that, it became obvious that flight in such weather was dangerous foolishness. The 17th swung back and began to feel cautiously for the soil of Petite Synthe. The last man was down before noon and, reportedly, all stamped into the squadron office ripping the whole affair with notable zest and ability.[8]

Fortunately, there were other distractions with which to while away the time—for there was suddenly much business at hand. By early August, Wing was deep in preparation for an air strike against Varssenaere, a huge aerodrome housing an estimated five Gotha and Fokker squadrons south-southeast of Bruges—about 40 air miles from Petite Synthe. Being the source of the many raids against Dunkirk, it was a continuing thorn in the British side.

While previous bomber visits by British squadrons had failed to diminish the effectiveness of the installation, this raid was expected to be different. Wing now proposed to deliver a death blow in which several Camel squadrons (including the 17th) would devastate the base through low level bombing and strafing, which would then be followed by a series of regular bombing missions.[9] The operation had been imminent for many days and, indeed, members of Wing were cursing themselves for not having taken advantage of the excellent weather on August 1.

The raid on Varssenaere, however, was only one of two pressing matters, for almost simultaneously the two American squadrons were being directed to decamp south where there was soon to be a sudden thrust to regain the territory lost to the enemy in March. It was now definite that the 148th would leave on August 11.[10] Eckert was determined not to be far behind, so he and his staff were busy, especially since Wells had been on leave for two weeks and Clapp was scheduled to depart for two weeks immediately on the supply officer's return.

Such was not, however, the stuff to long delight young pilots and no doubt they were ecstatic to turn from these tedious matters when the skies cleared on the seventh. Hamilton and Mert Campbell lost no time in letting the Germans know that the unit was back in action. Nine Camels set off on offensive patrol, but lost Desson with a bad engine shortly after crossing the lines. The rest watched him go with misgivings for Archie was bad that morning and the missing Spidle was still fresh in memory.

Then soon, they spotted five Fokker biplanes over Armentiers. Campbell made the first sighting of the enemy who was moving over the city at about half the 17th's altitude. He fired a short burst to alert his comrades, then led them in a skillful arc around the enemy flight to where they could descend out of the sun. Within minutes they were diving straight down the blinding beams with the enemy planes in their sights. Soon they saw dark helmets swinging about in alarm and then the 17th was in the middle of the formation spreading havoc in every direction.

Four of the five enemy aircraft fell into twisting dives with Camels following hard after; the fifth darted into some nearby scud and attempted to hide. Todd spotted him, pulled into the mist, and got off two bursts before the enemy made a sudden move and dived away to escape. Ralph Snoke had better luck, although his kill could never be confirmed. He chased his prey down about a mile of sky before he found an opening and put a hundred rounds into the dark fuselage. White smoke immediately began billowing out around the figure in the cockpit and the aircraft continued downward in a steep spiral. Snoke couldn't stay to watch. He lifted back into the sky to engage another foe—and found nothing left to fight.

Campbell had followed his first contact down a winding path much as he had his kill four days earlier. But this time he held his fire, convinced he could close on the enemy. They dropped nearer and nearer to earth with the Fokker dancing to throw off the attacker. Mert finally caught him coming out of a maneuver at 3,000 feet and ripped 75 rounds straight into the cockpit, hitting the pilot. The ship wrenched onto its back and started to whirl down, wheels to the sky.

While he was watching for the crash, Campbell caught a glimpse of another Fokker racing diagonally across his path, seemingly in hope of turning to attack him head on. Campbell lifted his nose and went for the second foe before it could range on him. By the time he'd fired his seventh burst, he had fallen onto the Fokker's tail and was riding him down. One final blast into the ship sent it skidding to pieces in a rolling field. After more than five scoreless months at the front, Campbell had racked up three kills in two days.

The second Fokker had not, in fact, been turning for Campbell at all—it was trying to escape Hamilton. The preacher's son had followed a different plane down to a mile before scoring a significant hit. At his first burst, black smoke poured from the enemy's cockpit and the machine swept into a steep spiral to trace a dirty trail into the clouds below. Hamilton followed, intent on finishing the business, and was nearly finished himself when he met that second Fokker on the bottom side of the cloud. He escaped collision only by pulling over in a half roll, then dropped in behind the second plane, at which the Fokker fled. It dived away only to have the misfortune to run under Campbell's guns.

Following these developments, only Hamilton, Campbell, and Todd were left in the area. Finding themselves caught below the clouds in murderous fire from road and roof-top emplacements below, they set out for home and picked up the rest of the patrol at the assembly point on the friendly side of the lines.

There was one final adventure waiting the patrol. Alderman began having engine trouble on the trip back and elected to land at Petite Synthe with the throttle open. He approached the landing area from the northeast in good style but passed over the grassy

Action at the aerodrome at Petite Synthe. (Rodney D. Williams)

meadow too high and fast. He floated the entire length of the field, crossed Cambrai road, and caught the undercarriage of the machine on the south bank—which threw him skidding upside down on the grassy turf beyond.

The resulting excitement was wild and general. The crash tender raced for the disaster followed by a thundering mob, all expecting to find Alderman dead or badly injured within the broken bird. They scrambled up the road bank, heaved the wreckage upright, and stared in horror at an apparently empty cockpit. Then there was a rustling and fumbling, and an instant later Alderman stood up sheepishly soliciting credit for "one aircraft destroyed."[11]

On Thursday the squadron experimented with four-plane formations while escorting a bomber run to Zeebrugge. The run was perfectly ordinary in most respects. As usual they lost a pilot (Williams) with a bad engine, as usual they took the sea route to the target, and as usual they took a pasting from the Middlekerke battery—but on the way home they got an inkling that perhaps something had been altered in the northern skies. Just above the village of Knocke, seven fighters suddenly appeared in two groups above them and attacked the homeward-bound bomber formation despite the fighter cover.

The attempt was alien to the action of Flanders' foe in the past, and the 17th was nearly caught off guard. The Fokkers swung past the Camels, made slashing attacks on the bombers, then, uncharacteristically, turned back for a swipe at the Sopwiths. At that a general mêlée broke out that involved practically everything in the sky.

Only Army Armstrong achieved anything definite, and his almost-certain victory happened too far from view to be confirmed. The Fokkers had dived in waves, with the first three being jumped by Goodnow and company. Two more swept in immediately, perhaps to take advantage of the confusion, and were engaged by C Flight. At this, Armstrong got behind one and tailed him down, holding his fire until he had his foe cold. His burst struck just forward of the cockpit and an explosion immediately shook the enemy plane. It plunged toward Heyst with thick smoke pouring out around the pilot just as Armstrong jerked into a climbing turn with a second Fokker on his tail. He escaped cleanly and rejoined the formation to find the other Fokkers gone. It had been a brisk, brief scrap, and seemed to show that things had somehow changed.[12]

Back at the base, things had definitely been altered. Eckert had received the expected news that the 17th was to follow the 148th south just as soon as the Varssenaere raid was over—which was tentatively scheduled for August 12, only four days away. This meant that Eckert was now managing a secret raid and a secret troop movement simultaneously. To further complicate matters, the move introduced concerns of protocol. The new assignment would take the unit from the RAF 65th Wing to the RAF 13th Wing and demanded that the squadron formally entertain those who had seen it through its neophyte stages. This was further made imperative by the fact that a dinner was traditionally given after a squadron had achieved three confirmed kills, and the 17th now had four.

Pvt. Roy W. Trezise, a chauffeur attached to B Flight. During World War II he was a Major in the United States Marine Corps and lost his life serving in the South Pacific. (Eldon and Roy Hively)

After much consultation, Eckert decided to schedule the affair for the evening of the 12th, reasoning that the successes of that day would form a nice background for the festivities. Accordingly, letters of invitation were written and passed to Pvt. John Wilcavage, a professional motorcycle racer in civilian life, who set out on a two-day Homeric ride across the face of Flanders.[13] A French chef was hauled in from Dunkirk to hold lengthy wrangles with Clapp as to the cuisine and proper wines.[14] Strangely, amid this planning the Germans suddenly began to give indication of knowing that something was up. Not only did superior fighters mysteriously reappear in the area, but the big Gothas from Varsennaere hit Dunkirk heavily throughout that entire weekend.

Theose Tillinghast left for his long-overdue sick leave on August 9, and on that same day Williams almost left for good. After many episodes in which he seemed to limp home chronically with a plane full of bullets, he had managed to remain fairly whole for a long period of time. He made up for it on Friday. Eight Camels went out at 7:35 a.m., in one five- and one three-ship formation, and an hour later came across a flight of seven Fokkers halfway between Seclin and Lille. The entire patrol engaged at 10,000 feet and Alderman, Shearman, and Hamilton managed brisk but inconclusive engagements. Meanwhile, the others actually pursued the remaining foes all the way back to their aerodrome only to be driven off by Archie and machine-gun fire. The patrol was widely scattered by this scrap and Williams ended up lagging a mile and a half behind. He had just leveled off at 7,000 feet and begun a serious effort to catch up with the squadron when he was set upon by three German aircraft he could not identify but thought possibly to be Siemens Schuckert DIIIs, which were just being tried on that front.

Swooping down from above, the trio dropped between Williams and the rest of the squadron and concentrated on finishing him before others could intervene. To their surprise the spunky farmer declined to run. He swung toward his attackers and engaged the leader so vigorously that the two nearly collided head on. Williams popped over the enemy at the last minute and made a climbing right turn for another try at him. The other two German pilots, confused by his aggressiveness, began stalking to catch the lone Camel in a crossfire. It was a deadly situation. However, after a series of close calls, Williams became convinced that his plane could outperform the enemy's. He wrung his machine through several right turns that brought him into kill position less than fifty yards behind the German patrol leader. At that, he promptly riddled the plane and sent it out of the fight in a steep spiraling nose dive that was later confirmed to have ended in a flaming crash below.

The other Camels had turned back in support by now, but lost the conflict in local clouding just as the two remaining German planes flanked Williams' Camel on each side and began to blast away. One put a sustained burst into the fuel tank, sending a splash of cold liquid up Williams' back. At that, Williams switched to his gravity tank and left the fight suddenly in a series of sweeps from left to right that ended in a vertical spin into the clouds below. While this made it appear that he was fatally hit and on his way to the grave, he actually pulled out a few hundred feet from the ground, consulted his spinning compass, and managed to cross the lines at Bailleau. He soon settled at RAF 213 aerodrome for an inspection of his craft and, although he found thirty-six bullet holes in the ship, he decided the damage was superficial and set off again for Petite Synthe. There he discovered that the main fuel tank held an incendiary bullet that had failed to ignite.[15]

The squadron went on a bombing escort to Ostend Saturday morning, then devoted the afternoon to rehearsal for Varssenaere. At the appointed hour the 17th rallied with British counterparts at 8,000 feet over Fort Maddick, between Dunkirk and Gravslines, and swept through a practice raid on the British Aerodrome at Andembert near Calais. Eckert and Fowler flew with the squadron to observe, as did Wing's Col. Cunningham, who had already announced his intention to fly in support of the 17th on the actual mission.

The rehearsal was deemed fairly successful because there was little else to say about a plan that had already been basically altered. As originally planned, Camels were to initiate the attack in two consecutive waves with the RAF 210th and U.S. 148th going first to strike with bombs at the base's defenses and other targets likely to create confusion on the ground. The RAF 213th and U.S.

Rodney D. Williams wearing a typical "tin hat" helmet of the times following a trip to the front. (Rodney D. Williams)

17th were then to follow close behind, each taking half of the field and going for specific targets. Then the RAF 211 and RAF 218 DH-9 bomber squadrons would appear, an hour apart, and complete the destruction.

Now that the 148th was being ordered away on August 11, it had been decided that RAF 210 and RAF 213 would initiate the attack and that the 17th would follow them alone. This was the plan rehearsed on the 10th. Complaints were few with the execution. It was believed that the Camels had come in too low for safe bombing, so safer altitudes were prescribed. Also, it seems that some RAF squadrons were flying more than three flights per unit, making it difficult for pilots in the rear to see the leaders. Accordingly, the units were obliged to move into an unfamiliar zigzag pattern to increase the visibility from back to front.[16]

And that was that for the moment. The following morning, nine Camels set out on offensive patrol with Hamilton and Gracie carrying bombs to demonstrate technique to those with less experience. Schneider and Williams were soon back with engine trouble, but the rest went on to tangle briefly with a pair of two seaters near the lines. When those had escaped, the patrol turned for Armentiers where Hamilton swung down and planted his bombs directly onto a busy road. Next they proceeded to Lille, where Gracie unleashed his payload on what appeared to be military billets. He then started back to the formation, but spotted a kite balloon near the lines and made for it instead. It was reeled down before he could engage and he banked about to return to his comrades. At that he found three Fokkers racing out of the sun toward him.

The enemy craft were between him and his patrol who were unaware of his predicament. His enemies spread out and began to stalk the lone Camel pilot, convinced that he was theirs for the taking. Immediately Gracie was flipping wildly about to keep them from getting a shot, diving and whipping his Camel into the incredible right turns that no other plane could follow. He twisted and turned inside his tormentors and gradually, very gradually, edged toward the lines. Certain that they were chasing a dead man, the Fokkers did nothing rash. They pursued him back and forth at their leisure west of Armentiers. But when they apparently had him cornered for the kill, Gracie unexpectedly tipped into a steep right bank and spun into the haze below. The Fokkers raged after him, but overestimated the Camel's rate of descent in a spin and shot on past him. And by the time they came about, their prey was gone. He was down following the contours of the countryside in the ground haze and drawing considerable, but inaccurate ground fire. He could still see the deadly trio hunting the skies for him as he crossed the trenches and headed home, forty minutes behind the rest of the patrol.[17]

Gracie had been forced back Saturday with a dud engine; Sunday morning he'd almost gotten himself killed. Perhaps to rid himself of a growing uneasiness, he immediately became a part of the afternoon bombing run to Zeebrugge. The assignment was what, in a later war, was to be known as a milk run and probably did much for Gracie's jangled nerves.

That night the pilots went to bed early in anticipation of the raid on Varssenaere and mechanics prowled the darkness and fussed with balky machines. Then—nothing happened.[18] Word came that the show was mysteriously postponed until the following morning, weather permitting. Instead, the 17th was to provide escort on a bombing run to Bruges. What no one anticipated was that this change would be the root cause of additional changes when the raid finally occurred.

On this substitute bomber run, the 17th flew three four-plane flights similar to those they had fielded a week earlier. Shortly after the DH-9s had dribbled their payloads on the perennial target, four Fokkers came up to contest the intrusion. They drove in from the flank, then thought better of it and turned aside when the Camels headed toward them. At that, two enemy planes, camouflaged in broad patches of black and cream, suddenly appeared and pounced on a DH-9 at the rear of the formation. Several of the escort planes turned for the attackers, but only Shearman and Williams managed to engage. Shearman got into a advantageous position as one of the attacking duo passed below in firing at the bomber. He got off a burst as the Fokker moved past his sights, then whipped around to fall behind it for a second burst at about 50 yards. Holding this position, he sent in another 150 rounds before the Fokker fell away from its attack, tilted over into a nose-dive, and went spinning into the ground haze.

The second Fokker, in the meantime, had been driven off by the combined fire of Camels and Bomber, but Williams got after him and did his best to see that the miscreant paid for his sins. The pair went east in a terrific race that carried them clear out of the area and over the electric fence that the Netherlands had erected to keep the warring powers away. At that Williams concluded that he wasn't to have this prey short of Berlin and turned back toward the North Sea.[19]

Ralph D. Gracie takes a rest while training at Camp Borden, Ontario. (Mrs. John McBride)

Ralph W. Snoke is seen here in a snapshot taken at Petite Synthe. (Rodney D. Williams)

Harriss Alderman points to his bullet-pierced Camel after a patrol. The arrows locate some of the holes in the fuselage. (Mrs. Louise Umstead)

Williams caught up with what was left of the formation after the fight and pulled in behind Gracie and four other Camels. But, as they were moving toward Ostend, he spotted what appeared to be a Camel, or perhaps two, being chased by a Fokker some distance below them. He signaled to Gracie and started a dive toward the action, then noticed after dropping a bit that only one comrade had followed. Pulling up to investigate, he found five biplanes dropping out of the clouds west of Ostend and heading for the remaining Camels.

He raced to get back in formation before the scrap began but could only watch in horror as one of the Camels went down from a rear attack just as he arrived. It was Gracie, his run of foul luck having reached an ultimate conclusion. Apparently he was in the midst of turning tightly to lead a counterattack when a burst of fire struck his plane and a shower of bright clean splinters swept by from the upper wing. Probably he slapped the stick forward to unload the weakened span, but it was too late. In a flash of buff and brown, the wings folded up about him, and the deputy commander went flapping, spinning, tumbling into the sea two miles below—the third member of the squadron to die.

It all happened so suddenly that only Williams and Schneider saw it, for now a major scrap broke out with the attacking Germans. Obviously superior to any the 17th had run into before, the squadron was to learn much later that the black aircraft (with black-and-yellow-checked tails) encountered that day were part of the highly regarded Marine Jasta 2 from Steenbrugge, just south of Bruges.[20]

This quickly became a fight for dear life. Williams mixed with one scout, caught him in a hammerhead stall with his prop barely turning, and downed him. He saw Snoke under attack by three enemy planes who were getting it their own way and raced over to help his comrade. As he approached, the three foes thought better of things and pulled off, whereupon Snoke turned back for the lines and raced away from Williams. That seemed odd since the remaining Camels still had more than they could handle, so Williams went after him thinking that perhaps Snoke had been hit. Williams soon noticed with increasing mystification that whenever he pulled up to his friend to cover him, Snoke would make an obvious effort to shake him off.

The truth of the matter was that Snoke, while not hit, was flying blind. His own plane was out of commission that morning, and he had borrowed Showalter's for the run. Unlike Snoke's Camel, Showie's had no windscreen and the borrower had been obliged to fall back to wearing goggles. But they played him false. Throughout the mission they fogged with such regularity that he spent most of his time trying to wipe them clear. This was no condition in which to engage in combat and thus he now sped for Petite Synthe under the impression that Williams was a Fokker trying to score.[21]

With Williams and Snoke out of the fight and Schneider having been driven away, Todd, Alderman, and Armstrong were all who were left to deal with the five German planes. The enemy began to lash into them with vigor. Armstrong hammered one heavily as it under-ran the formation, and obviously damaged it. It limped away from the fight. Alderman fell on another and sent it off in trouble. At three all the odds were apparently equal. But appearances were deceiving in that with Alderman's last burst, both of his guns fell silent and refused to clear.

The Germans discovered this shortly, and made Aldy their primary target. Todd and Armstrong were determined to protect their friend, and the fight became a five plane tangle revolving around the toothless Camel. Finally the Germans pressed Alderman beyond the ability to evade, at which Armstrong played the top hand; he interposed his Camel between friend and foe. A checkertail ripped a burst straight through Armstrong's fuel tank filling his back with debris, puncturing his chest, and lodging bullets in his right arm high up near the shoulder. Armstrong wavered off, weak with shock and injury.

That left the protection of both men to Todd. He flashed wildly around the excited enemy trying to keep them from his friends. But the German pilots were not to be denied. They forced Todd aside, caught Alderman in a stall and sent him side-slipping, well damaged, toward the sparkling sea below.

That accomplished, they turned their attention to Todd and proceeded to shoot his plane to ribbons. They boxed him again and again only to see him limp from under their sights, damaged but still flying. It seemed only a matter of time until he was finished—and then the enemy broke off. The fight had drifted too far across the lines for safety's sake, so the foe turned for home where, no doubt, they filed claims for three kills. It would have been an honest mistake. Alderman was down, Armstrong was faltering so badly that it seemed inevitable that he must crash, and Todd's aircraft was so battered that he should have been finished in any reasonable application of the odds.

But the odds didn't hold. Armstrong and Todd wallowed on toward Petite Synthe with the wounded Philadelphian slumping deeper and deeper into the cockpit, and waggling the stick in a semi-conscious state. Todd hung close to him hoping for the best. He was wild with rage at the loss of his roommate, Alderman, and growing more and more doubtful about Armstrong's chances of getting down safely.

There was already plenty of excitement at Petite Synthe when the pair swung into view. The crash tender was pulled up where Snoke had completely destroyed his borrowed plane by smashing headlong into the base incinerator in landing. Somewhere a bit of Archie or a stray bullet had slashed a tire on his machine and he'd ground-looped the moment he touched down. People were dragging him unconscious from the wreckage and uncovering his injuries for examination even as Todd and Armstrong started down.[22]

With only one useful arm, and that the one normally occupied with throttle and spark, Armstrong could only blip the engine and watch the sod rise to meet him. The fast running engine began to lay down a blue haze of castor oil, and the men on the aerodrome scattered to safety as they realized he was coming in downwind. There was no way of advising him of his danger, and he probably couldn't have done anything about it anyway. He came lower and lower, drifting along the field toward the RAF 211 hangars where several DH-9s were drawn up for service. At last he settled with a heavy crunch directly onto the back of one of the bombers. His prop shattered on impact and the engine began to wind to a scream. Somehow Armstrong killed the ignition before dropping his head in submission. When the horde of rescuers reached the tangle of aircraft, they found him just barely conscious, still snugged to the wicker seat by his Sutton harness.[23]

By the time Todd landed and could come to his side, Armstrong was on a stretcher and being carried away. Recognizing Todd, he asked weakly what had happened to Alderman and the distraught young man, speaking now in grief and anger, the vision of Alderman's Camel spinning down toward the water vividly in mind, blurted out, "They shot him down in the sea."

The loss of his comrade weighed heavily on the wounded Armstrong. He was rushed to Queen Alexandria Hospital where surgeons dug a harvest of bullets and fuel-tank fragments from his chest and arm. When he was rolled out hours later, dazed with pain and ether, he spied flies circling his head and in his confusion took them for Fokkers and began mumbling weakly, "There they are, Aldy. We'll crash the last God-damned one of 'em."[24] His golden eyetooth glinted behind his purple lips as he spoke and he feebly moved his injured right hand about under the crisp white sheets in an effort to bring his bed to bear on the elusive flies.

Left to right: Walter B. Knox of the 148th U. S. Aero Squadron, William J. Armstrong. (Lorenz K. Ayers)

Morning brought him to his senses and yielded a pleasant surprise; the much mourned Alderman lay in the bed beside him. Aldy's plane had been hit in the tail and a single bullet had gone through structure, bracing, and fuel tank and then (nearly spent) had wormed its way into the lower part of his hip. The impact was akin to being kicked by a horse and almost knocked him out of control. He'd slipped down certain that he was mortally hit and that the draining petrol was his life's blood leaking away. Still he managed to cross the lines, make his way to the beach beyond Nieuport, and land safely. Belgian soldiers appeared immediately and arrested him as a suspicious character; but the matter was cleared up shortly and he was whisked to the hospital. Now he had the bullet that struck him in his tunic pocket as a souvenir.[25]

These were events of momentous consequence. The loss of Gracie, Snoke, Alderman, and Armstrong, all pilots scheduled to participate in the Varssenaere raid, required a great deal of replanning. The arrival of a new pilot, Harry Helmar Jackson, a boyhood friend of Shearman's, only added to the disquiet, for he represented the one thing Eckert had feared most since taking over the 17th. Jackson simply wasn't ready for combat duty. He had thirty-five flying hours, like most men sent to the front; he'd been to the good schools. But there was evidence that somewhere someone was hurrying to fill the pilots pool as fast as it was emptying. Jackson was as honest as he was green. He admitted himself to be no master of the Camel and allowed that he got lost a good bit.[26]

Eckert had not guessed it would come to this so soon. There was nothing he could do but make reassuring sounds and vow silently to hold the boy in reserve as long as possible. He expected to give Jackson every chance at local flying before committing him to the fray.

In the meantime, there was a dinner to host. Clapp, who had postponed leave repeatedly, got a chance to join his wife in Paris and went away nominating Wells to oversee the event. Because the weather forecast looked promising, the Varssenaere attack was now firmly on track for the morrow and many could not get away from duty to attend. Still, several distinguished guests did show: RAF 211's Major Reid held the Military Cross; as did Harold Fowler; Major Bell of RAF 210 held both the Military Cross and Distinguished Service Order; and Wing Commander Colonel Cunningham also attended. As is common with higher ranking officers among the British regulars, Cunningham held no decorative honors as yet, but he would win a Distinguished Flying Cross before another day was out.

Whatever pall remained from the day's cares faded quickly. The evening bill of fare was too spectacular to fail at lifting the spirits. Mert Campbell declared it to be the most excellent meal he had eaten east of the Atlantic. And good food demanded good drink since, as Ayers was to recall years later, "The 17th Squadron was

Left to right: Howard Knotts, Harry H. Jackson, Howard Burdick. Jackson was assigned to the 17th on August 12, 1918, the day Ralph Gracie was killed and Harriss Alderman and William Armstrong wounded. Ralph Snoke was injured in a crash following the same action. (Clinton Burdick)

never one to allow impending assignments to interfere with pleasures of the moment."[27]

Down on the flight line, mechanics labored over the machines and prepared for Varssenaere.

Changes in Squadron Status—end of day 8/12/1918

A Flight

Ralph Snoke	Injured. In hospital.

B Flight

William Tipton	On leave.
Ralph Gracie	Killed in action.
Harry Jackson	Replacement pilot.
Murray Spidle	Killed in action.
Theose Tillinghast	Ill. In hospital.

C Flight

Lloyd Hamilton	On leave.
William Armstrong	Wounded. In hospital.
Harriss Alderman	Wounded. In hospital.
Laurence Roberts	Ill. In hospital.

Private Frank J. Zoubeck from Kenosha, Wisconsin. He was a fitter with B Flight, and an excellent diarist. (Eldon and Roy Hively)

Flight Office-Headquarters of the RAF 211 across the field. (Rodney Williams

5

Varssenaere and Points South

Instructions to the Guard, Bulletin number four, line item six, dated July 2, 1918, stated explicitly that, "The sentry on duty from 4:00 a.m. to 6:00 a.m. will call the bugler at 6:15 a.m." It was a strange order and the subject of much grouching—directing, as it did, the man just relieved from duty to perform additional duties. That problem was of little concern on the morning of August 13, however. Petite Synthe had twitched with activity throughout the night and was alive with preparations for the raid on Varssenaere by 3 a.m. Long before the sentry with the odd duty was posted, flashlights winked into cockpits and lighted the way for busy men scurrying about the tarmac in nervous anticipation.

Had the weather of the 12th held, there would have been little need for torches. The waning three-quarter moon did not set until nearly 2 a.m. and the twilight before dawn began at 2:30. It approached being one of those nights in Flanders during which one can sit outdoors and read almost till dawn without artificial illumination.[1] But the weather didn't hold. Those working saw the sky gradually close over with heavy clouding and half expected to hear that the attack was again postponed. But no such word came.

The pilots were up and stirring by 3:30, more than one finding that he hadn't been as temperate as hoped during the festivities the night before. Eckert and Wells were among those first about. They checked and rechecked details and attended Colonel Cunningham who had crawled into a borrowed cot and spent the night with the 17th.

Soon the pilots began to drift about the field in small groups, well awake by now and aware of a sharp edge of excitement. By 4 a.m. they had breakfasted and garnered a final briefing about the target.

From the 17th's standpoint, the most important changes resulted from their losing four pilots the previous day. They'd expected to put fifteen planes in the air—sixteen if one counted Col. Cunningham, who planned to fly with the Americans until the grand formation turned for the target area. At that, he would rush back with information needed for launching the bombers on schedule. But, of course, the 17th would now be able to send up fewer than anticipated. B Flight was particularly in bad shape. With Tipton on leave in England and Gracie dead, Williams, Dixon, and Shearman would have to go it as a threesome.

With only eleven experienced pilots left to him, Eckert now had to bow to the insistence of George Wise to be included in the raid although he had barely been in France three weeks. Wise had been across the lines a half a dozen times already—he'd actually made his first trip within a week of his arrival at Petite Synthe—but Eckert hadn't wanted him out for anything as demanding as Varssenaere might prove to be. Now there was little choice. Eckert stuck him in with A Flight, put Williams in charge of B, and let matters proceed. With that, the 17th was putting up every able-bodied pilot available except Wicks, Jesse Campbell, and Harry Jackson (the first two had each crossed the lines for the first time the evening before; Jackson had been with the squadron less than 48 hours).

It was amid such considerations that action commenced. In the gathering dawn came voices calling, "Switch off," then "Contact." Immediately engines began to cough and sputter to life and shortly the field was alive with cacophony. Chocks were pulled and mechanics strained to hold the little planes until all was ready. Finally the brown Camels began to waddle across the turf and lift into the air, each burdened with four twenty-pound bombs and 1,200 rounds of ammunition. Shortly the last ship disappeared into the misty sky and the ground crews turned away to the waiting mess halls.

Eckert had a pet superstition that was at play this day. He'd flown a Camel bearing the letter M in RAF 84 squadron despite earnest advice not to do so; he had been informed that associating one's self with the thirteenth letter of the alphabet meant certain death. Having survived repeated near brushes with the Grim Reaper while flaunting this emblem, Eckert had become convinced that for him the number thirteen was a good omen—his lucky number. Now he was sending up thirteen pilots, counting Cunningham, on the thirteenth day of August, in his thirteenth month of commissioned service.[2] He expected good things.

This notion soon got a nudge when all were startled by the sounds of a Camel coming back to the field in distress. It was Williams, forced down with a broken connecting rod before he had reached the rendezvous point. It was a most unfortunate turn. It deprived the mission of a hearty fighter and it left Dixon and Shearman to proceed without a leader.

In the meantime, the squadron flew on. They went south of Dunkirk to Bergues and began climbing to altitude through the clouds. At 6,000 feet they leveled off with the bright morning sun glinting off their bracing wires and formed up. A Flight was leading, the two planes of B Flight followed at a hundred feet higher, and C Flight closed the rear a hundred feet higher still.

All turned north and flew along the Bergues-Dunkirk canal as best they could and soon came to where RAF squadrons 210 and 213 were already assembling. The liaison was effected without difficulty and in a few minutes a coherent formation was heading out to sea. Lt. W. E. Grey of RAF 213 was in command and fired a red parachute flare to let everybody know that the condition was go.[3]

The 17th wasn't the only squadron with problems. After all, these were Camel units. Both the British squadrons had planned to put eighteen planes in the air. But RAF 210 had lost five on the way (two crashing on takeoff), and RAF 213 saw two turn back with engine problems.[4] Still, drawn together finally, the strike force made a respectable armada of forty-two planes.

Six miles off the coast they swung nearly into the sun and began to follow the edge of the North Sea toward Ostend. They went in columns with the two British units flying abreast half a mile apart, RAF 210 standing out to seaward. The 17th followed a mile behind 210. They flew well throttled down because there was one more rendezvous to achieve before proceeding to strike. It had been decided that RAF 204 would fly above all, guide the formation to the target, then sit overhead during the attack to see that nosy Fokkers did not break into the game.[5] This depended on RAF 204 arriving on station and in formation before the armada arrived. The strike force soon spotted them where expected at 10,000 feet. The leader of RAF 204 spied the approaching formation, saw that it was in order, and led the protective force down from altitude to a position directly in front of the fleet.

As the formation turned inland and settled en route, Col. Cunningham drew off and recorded the time. Now he had done his part. He watched Camel after Camel pass, then turned home. Within minutes he encountered a new element in the game. About three miles off the coast he saw a German two-seater loafing along below him apparently headed for Ostend. Several things must have occurred to him at once; that this plane might be on its way to report the heavy activity in the area; that he should do something to prevent that happening; that he was a man with a message and ought not to risk losing the information.

Whatever came to mind, Cunningham reacted like a fighter pilot. He swung to approach the enemy out of the sun and bored in noticing that both the pilot and observer had their eyes fixed inland. They were still watching when his first burst tore into their plane and knocked the engine out. Two heads swung as one, then the enemy pilot wrenched his plane into a steep dive for the shore with Cunningham close behind him. The German seemed to have but one thing in mind—stretching for the shoreline. But he had no chance with his engine out and an excited Wing Commander on his tail. The plane went down, flattened out, hit the water with a mighty splash, and turned turtle some 300 yards off shore. The pilot and observer were clambering out from under the wreckage as Cunningham resumed his journey wild with joy. By 5:45 a.m. he was back at Petite Synthe yelling excitedly as he tumbled out of his plane, "I got a Hun!"[6]

Meanwhile the attack force was continuing its ten-mile run from Ostend to Varssenaere, dropping 500 feet a minute to bring them on station just right. Shortly they began to sink into the clouds again. They pitched and wallowed, losing sight of other elements of the formation and, from time to time, each other.

The two members of B Flight were doing their best to look like an important part of this strike force despite their lack of numbers. Then after a dip through some thick and violent clouding, Dixon emerged to find himself alone in the murky sky. His first thought was that Shearman had gotten lost. His second thought was that perhaps he himself had gotten lost. This seemed more likely, for if it were not so, where was the rest of the formation? He flew on for awhile hoping to catch a glimpse of the missing fleet.

The loss of Williams had left Dixon with no leader, something he hadn't expected. What was more, he realized that he had never really known where Varssenaere was. He knew approximately where he was, and his compass would lead him back to the general area of Ostend, but what then? He began to wish he had paid more attention to briefing. But that wasn't really his style. Ordinarily he was content to understand what job needed doing and then to go and do it without fussing much with the details. Once, in England, while awaiting assignment to the front, he'd been asked to deliver a Camel to London. He was actually geared up and on the way to the plane before dropping a comment that he hadn't the slightest idea where London was. He was turned around quickly and given a specific briefing.

But now there was no one to brief him. He droned along hopefully for a few minutes, then turned back. As the coast brought thinner weather, he identified Ostend and loosed his bombs in that general direction from 6,000 feet. With that there was nothing left to do but go home.[7]

By then the rest of the formation was arriving at the enemy field. RAF 204 turned the following fleet so it was attacking from due north, then climbed away to circle above and repel intruders. The remaining pilots stared ahead to find confirmed the layout they had been studying for days. Here was a vast field slightly more than a quarter-mile square. Its former use had left it patched in color and etched with abandoned roadways until it blended nicely into the meadows and grain fields around it. There the resemblance ended. Varssenaere held hangars galore for housing Gothas and Fokkers, an incredible complex of workshops and living quarters,

OPPOSITE: This aerial view of the German air base at Varssenaere, home of Gotha G-Va. bombers and numerous fighters, was taken at 11:30 a.m., BST the day of the raid. The aerodrome was located west and south of Bruges. (Public Record Office: Air 1/85/15/9/208, photo no. 4156; D6146, London, England)

This chateau was living quarters for flying officers at Varssenaere. It received a direct hit that destroyed parts of the upper story. (Public Record Office: photo no. Air 1/2121, D6467, London, England)

and a liberal sprinkling of narrow nosed anti-aircraft batteries. Off to the right of the attacking planes (east, and not really on the field itself) was base headquarters, an ornately ugly chateau of red brick and stone with a long tree-lined roadway pointing like an arrow to its door.

Fokker biplanes were lined up on the aerodrome with mechanics working with them in preparation for flight. German pilots stood by, probably bantering about the coming mission. No doubt they looked up curiously, unable to comprehend the aircraft overhead. In an instant, the British were triggering their guns and the matter stood revealed. Men scrambled in all directions, some away from the carnage—some into it.

The two RAF squadrons were still leading abreast. They swung down to 500 feet and began unloading their bombs. RAF 210 hit the juicier targets on the eastern edge of the field; RAF 213 contented themselves with the meager pickings to the west. And as they bombed, the squadrons kept up a killing gunfire, walking bullets ahead of them, striking equipment, mowing down men, sowing the seeds of ruin all over the base. Finally, they flicked over the

One of the buildings severely damaged by the raid. Careful examination shows numerous wrecked aircraft and parts. (Public Record Office: photo no. Air 1/2121, D6468, London, England)

southern edge of the field and flew straight ahead for a mile as the mission plan directed. Their part of the action was over except for joining RAF 204 overhead in providing cover.

Ninety seconds after the British units passed, the 17th came swooping in with unlimited license. The place was a minor hell before they began. Intense white phosphorous fires burned in gun emplacements. Five Fokkers were blazing on the field and a sixth had vanished in a bomb strike. Captain M. E. Paley of the 210th had scored a direct hit on a petrol dump, igniting a fire that was to burn throughout the day. Smoke and dust boiled up everywhere.

Goodnow led Case and Wise into it. They flew past the hangars heading for their assigned objectives—the machine shops in the southwest corner of the field. They went along firing at Fokkers lined up below their course. Two were already burning. A third caught as the trio lashed it. Then they were past and closing on the shops at 200 feet. All twelve bombs fell among the buildings and flames spurted up as they passed over.

Mert Campbell followed, leading Showalter and Desson as a second element of A Flight. They came in slightly east of Goodnow's track and turned on the hangars and the headquarters building beyond them. Campbell and Showalter dropped all their bombs on the hangars and went for the chalet, guns blazing. Desson placed his bombs on the ugly headquarters building—at which point his engine began to falter. Realizing that something had put his fuel pressurization system on the bum and having no wish to land among those he had just been trying to slay, he pumped the hand pump for all he was worth to pressurize the tank and circled to join RAF 204 overhead.

C Flight was racing not far behind with Shearman of B Flight tacked on. Hamilton hit the smoldering hangars with all four bombs despite the heavy smoke. Todd was just behind and some fifty feet above Hamilton. He laid his bombs right on the chalet which now began to burn. At this Shearman nearly lost sight of the targets. He swung out over the center of the field to get a better view of what was happening, then slipped back across and dropped bombs on what looked to be billets east of the hangars. Schneider put two on a hangar, then placed the rest on machine-gun emplacements that had suddenly come to life and begun hosing fire toward the attackers.

By now the base was a burning mess, but the Germans were beginning to realize their best hope of survival was to fight. It was good reasoning but bad timing. Bomb-free, the Camels were now wheeling back for low level attacks. They packed together and came back from the south at altitudes and speeds that blurred the orderly patches of green meadows and golden ripe grain below. They were below the height of the hangars now, all but rolling their wheels on the enemy field.

C Flight was after the headquarters building again. Hamilton, Todd, Showalter, and Campbell sailed up the long driveway with the tall poplars towering above them and poured concentrated fire into every opening. By their side, but across the trees, Goodnow,

These buildings were barracks for enlisted men serving at Varssenaere airdrome. They are visible in the lower center part of the aerial view. (Public Record Office: Air 1/2121, photo no. D6467, London, England)

Schneider, Shearman, Wise, and Case were after those rushing to organize some defense. Shearman caught a man running for a machine gun nest and sent him sprawling. Schneider swung on an enemy pilot scrambling into a Fokker and gunned him down. Case and Shearman traveled up the field firing into every aircraft that crossed their sights.

They crossed over the broad road that marked the north edge of the field just as Hamilton's bunch banked away from the chalet and turned for the tarmac. By now enemy mechanics were swinging wildly on propellers, trying to start some engines. Hamilton raced south into this situation and fired into the first aircraft with a running engine. It burst into flames and burned on the spot. As they came on, Todd saw a pilot settling into a machine and attacked it so heavily that the man jumped out and ran for cover behind a hangar. Todd banked around the building the other way, dropped to fifteen feet and watched. When the man appeared at the corner, he gunned him down in a heap.

The attack had lost all coherence. Planes were zooming, dipping, banking about. Everyone sought his own amusement. Hamilton made a circuit of the drome peppering at will, then came around again and fired at a row of Fokkers, setting fire to the third in line. Wise was whirling around and around. He and Schneider teamed up and went along blazing into the collapsing hangars. Off to the east Showalter was doggedly pounding nearly 600 rounds into the chalet. All were in constant danger of collision. A pilot breaking out of the smoke from the north would find himself on a collision course with one breaking into the smoke from the south.

It must have seemed the maddest mêlée from the ground, with brown and buff aircraft whipping out of the opaque smoke and coming on like so many angry, deadly hornets. Bullets kicked up from the turf from every direction; men went down in fear and injury. Dead and wounded graybacks lay about from one end of the field

Robert M. Todd with his Camel. Others involved in the attack were awed at his ferocious and daring performance at Varssenaere. (Theose E. Tillinghast)

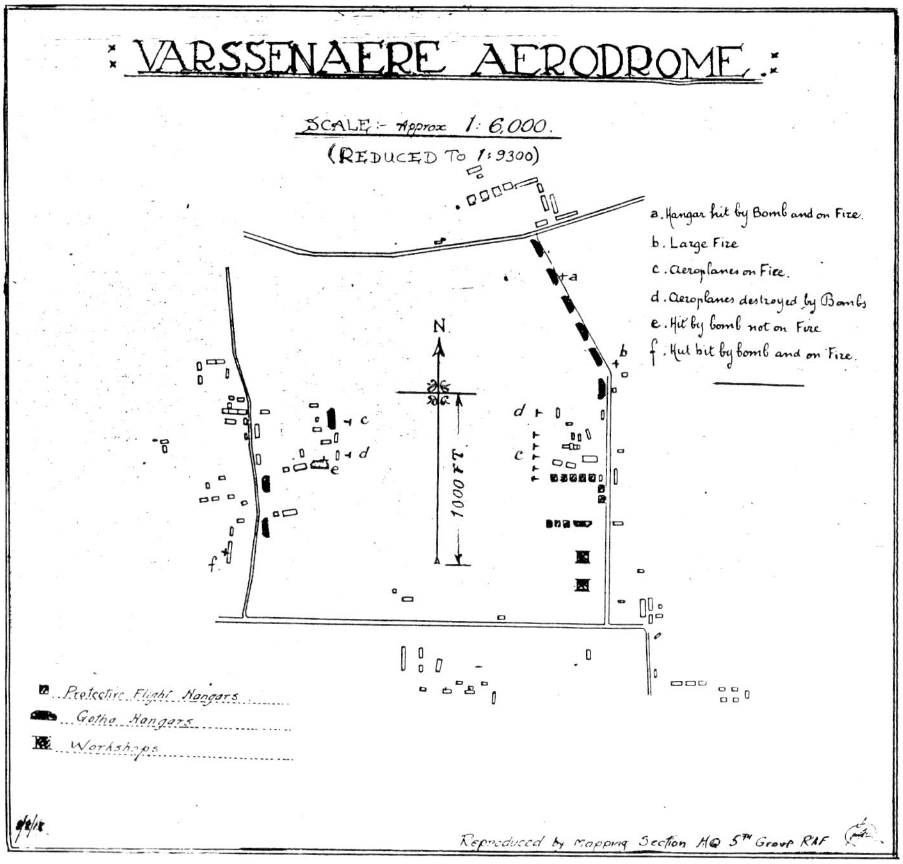

This map of the times assesses the damage to Varssenaere as a result of the raid. The 17th was allowed a claim of eight to fourteen planes destroyed for their part of the effort. (Public Record Office: Air 1/62, London, England)

to the other. No doubt many more were out of sight beneath the rubble.

Then it was time to leave. The 17th began to buzz west in ragged groups. They went for home via the inland route staying low and strafing random targets that caught their fancy. The anti-aircraft batteries to the west got first notice. Soon the Camels were driving a convoy of six lorries off the road in a sweeping dive from nearly nothing to virtually nothing. As a final hurrah, they fired a general salute—then swept across the lines near St. George.[8]

Soon then they were trickling into Petite Synthe to a scene almost as mad as that left at Varssenaere. Everyone was out. Everyone was wild. A quick look showed that the cost of the day's work would be no more than a lot of patching. And apart from Desson's blisters from miles of pressurizing his gas tank, not a man was injured.

Before giving over to complete joy, the 17th waited to see how the bombers made out. Oddly enough, nothing else touched Varssenaere that day. RAF 211 dispatched five planes to strike the aerodrome an hour after it was calculated the Camels had hit, but two were forced back with engine trouble, and when the other three arrived in the area they found enemy planes gathering so closely that they went on and struck Snelleghem aerodrome two miles south instead. When RAF 218 arrived in the area two and a half hours later, they were so heavily pressed that they swung about and unloaded on Ostend.[9]

But those raiders reported their help really wasn't needed. They were convinced by the heavy smoke that things were unwell at Varssenaere—and they were. The attack proved to be a stinging blow and a splendid success. The 17th came home claiming six aircraft destroyed. In time the RAF would grant the squadron eight to fourteen. And in October, intelligence was sent along that the attack destroyed twenty Gothas, demolished eighteen to twenty Fokkers, and killed thirty-six flying officers and one hundred and twenty enlisted men.[10] All this was achieved at the cost of a few yards of fabric.[11]

It had been their most successful effort and it was over by 8 a.m. Little happened for the rest of the day. Eckert saw that the new man, Jackson, got in a couple of flights to hone his skills. The hard-gambling, teetotaling Showalter took Wicks and went off to bring up two new planes. Williams fussed with his machine in hopes of never again missing sport because of malfunction. And the rest stood down—and perhaps drank a bit too much.

But even as the unit celebrated, a new era was dawning—one that would prove more terrible than that just passed. On August 10, the British had launched a drive to regain the northern territory lost to the Germans in the spring. The German push had not rolled forward in a steady line, but swept along irregularly as terrain and defenses permitted. As a consequence, while the line remained unchanged at the North Sea, it bulged far out along the Somme River and created a military hernia susceptible to strangulation.

A view of Varssenaere aerodrome taken on August 22, 1918, at 1:15 p.m., BST. There is a new railroad siding near the enlisted men's quarters probably to deal with rebuilding. (Public Record Office: Photo no. Air 1/2004, D6347, London, England)

This situation had not been dealt with previously because the means were not at hand. But now things had changed. British strength had grown in the north and driving Allied troops in the lines around Paris had pulled enemy defenders away from the Flanders area. So now, the British were preparing to press forward suddenly between Arras and Amien.[12]

The 17th Aero Squadron was to be a part of that. With a month of action and the impressive Varssenaere success to their credit, they would depart Petite Synthe with honor on Friday, August 17. But before going they had some final flings. On August 14, for the first time, they downed three German planes in one encounter. But again, they lost two comrades in a single mission—one in a bizarre incident. Ironically, the 14th was also the day that receipts for George Glenn's personal effects arrived in the squadron office. By then it seemed ages since that friend mysteriously disappeared one day in Eckert's plane.

The Camels lifted off at 10:30, twelve planes strong in four three-plane formations—perhaps something suggested by the affair of the day before. The cast was the same as that of the previous morning except that Wicks and Jesse Campbell, now on their second trip across the line, were given the places of Showalter and Wise.

The run was an interesting one; escorting the RAF 211's DH-9s on a picture-taking sortie over the Varssenaere target area, to be followed by a bombing raid on Bruges. Wing was apparently feeling foxy and sent the formation to the target over land rather than out over the sea, a ploy that was quite successful. The bombers droned along under their escort without opposition and soon turned north on a line that would take them to their tasks.

While the enemy seemed not to be out in force that day, they were out in vengeance. The convoy was at 14,000 feet, in sight of the still smoldering Varssenaere, when Fokkers of the 1st Marine Feld Jasta suddenly came swooping in.[13] Six of the aircraft were the familiar biplanes; a seventh was a Fokker monoplane, a machine new to the front. The Americans had neither the time nor inclination to study this peculiar devil and turned their full attention to

Lyman Case died two days after the attack on Varssenaere in a collision with a Fokker D-VII flown by Flugzeugmeister Karl Goldenstedt of Marine Feld Jasta I. (Theose Tillinghast)

William Hugh Shearman in his U. S. Signal Corps Air Service uniform. He was killed on August 14, 1918. (Thomas Shearman)

Left to right: Harry H. Jackson, Howard C. Knotts. Officers who joined in mid-August got there just in time to move to Auxi-le-Chateau. (Clinton Burdick)

protecting the RAF bombers. It seemed a relatively easy task as the outnumbered enemy at first contented themselves with diving toward the formation and pulling up when about 200 yards above it. This obvious attempt at drawing the Camels away from their charges did not work.

The photographs that RAF 65th Wing wanted were recorded and a course set for Ostend before the phony action stopped. And it stopped most unintentionally. One of the enemy planes made a thrust from behind the formation, coming in deeper than any had dared previously. Wicks, no doubt much excited at this first taste of combat, realized in fascination that the Fokker would become vulnerable to his fire as it completed its arc. Accordingly, he watched as the German looped in. Then with a sudden flick of stick and rudder he turned his Camel onto the Fokker. Williams, too, had noticed the adversary's precarious situation and sent a brief burst into the Fokker's tail just as Wicks was completing his turn. But it was the minister's son who made the kill. He put a short burst right into the cockpit just as the Fokker passed before his sight.

Then occurred one of those brief unexpected moments that linger forever in the memory. The German pilot, much later identified as Flugzeugmeister Karl Goldenstedt, was mortally hit and made no further attempt to fire or fly.[14] His plane continued on its looping turn, flashed over Wick's Camel, and swung into A Flight—which was still proceeding on course with the bombers. Wick's thrill of triumph turned to one of horror as he watched the doomed Fokker collide almost soundlessly with Lyman Case's plane.

It was over in a flash of color. The Fokker's left wing cut directly across the little Camel's fuselage and both planes immediately slapped over and started down. Case's aircraft was completely out of control and flailing to the ground, a broken thing. The German pilot's descent was slower but just as inevitable. There was no fire. No smoke. Just the plummeting of two machines, dropping ever more swiftly, growing smaller and smaller. And like an exclamation point of sorts, there was the left lower wing torn from the Fokker twirling over and over as it followed its proprietor to the grave. "Poor old Casey," Mert Campbell would lament to his diary that evening, "he was a full out chap and right with you in everything."[15]

The collision broke the pseudo-truce. Machine guns began to stammer in both groups. The Germans tore through the defending Camels with abandon and made for the bombers and soon the fire of the observers was added to the fight. One of the DH-9s scored a kill almost immediately: Lt. H. M. Moodie sent a Fokker down in a field just southwest of Varssenaere as it made its first pass over his bomber. Hughie Shearman pounced onto one's tail and began pursuing it straight down. A foe came awkwardly at Jesse Campbell, Todd, and Hamilton and they put him away for keeps. "It wasn't much of a feat," Todd confided in a letter, "because the poor boob flew directly in front of three of us and we all had an excellent shot at him. It was impossible to tell whose bullets reached him first so we split him up between us."[16] Thus both Jesse Campbell and Wicks had scored on their first real taste of combat.

While Jesse Campbell was earning his spurs, his namesake, Mert, was having difficulties. He'd managed to isolate a Fokker and had him all to himself. He dived neatly onto the craft's backside and was instructing the pilot in the approved manner when both guns suddenly went dead under his thumbs. As he turned his attention to that, he saw his prey roll over onto its back and drift down out of the fight. He never saw it again for he was busy with his guns. He had complete stoppages in both weapons, and when he pounded the crank handles to encourage the bolts to go into battery, nothing happened. He was north of Bruges, unarmed, and in big trouble.

He detailed his situation and how he resolved it in his diary. "While trying to clear my guns, two more hopped on to me and after a couple of minutes of fighting I tried to locate the formation, but it was nowhere to be seen. I then went west wiggling to the best of my ability with both Fokkers pumping lead at me as fast as I could listen to them. I was just behind Bruges at the time and those lines were miles away. I had vertical gust up [British slang for extreme terror] for a while, but gradually calmed when I found that I could play the game with both of them. My old engine was doing 1300 and thereabouts all the way out. I was afraid they would get me when I was changing from one bank to another. I lost 12,000 feet going to the lines. The closer I got to the ground, the safer I felt for the Huns cannot play the game down there.

"I came over the trenches doing verticals, right off the ground, with every machine gun in the sector firing at me. Maybe I didn't sweat those twenty-odd minutes coming out of Hell. I expect the Fokkers thought I was going to crash when I got down to the ground, but nothing like that in my family. I might have been scared but not sufficiently to make me crash. The reprobates left me at the lines, being too poor sports to come over. After I crossed I throttled down my engine to about 1050 to let it cool off, as it had been badly overworked. I certainly did heave a sigh of relief at my escape, for that is what it is, no more or less. It is no pleasant sensation to have jammed guns with Huns on your tail. I got only scattered bullets over my machine but the spars in three planes were shot through which meant changing the planes. None came near the cockpit which surprised me greatly."[17]

Campbell got back to base ten minutes ahead of the others and watched from the tarmac as they came home to roost. There were only nine. The men searched the sky for a tenth dragging behind. But there was nothing. Shearman was missing, last seen on the tail of a desperately diving German who seemed dead in his sights. They cared not to admit him dead, of course—Lyman Case was enough for one day. Finally accepting the fact that he was not going to return, they turned to the hope that he was somewhere a prisoner. That was the theme of Eckert's letter to the Shearman home.

Not so with Harry Jackson, however. The presence of a boyhood friend had been one of few pillars he found to cling to in his uneasiness. Now that that pillar had crumbled less than 48 hours after his arrival on the scene, he immediately dispatched a letter homeward expressing his belief that Shearman was dead. His letter arrived before Eckert's, and it was from the Jackson family that Shearman's parents heard of their loss.

Still, on the basis of the commander's encouraging missive, the Shearman family dared hope. Consequently, shortly after Armistice Day, Eckert received a joyous letter from Mrs. Shearman:

"We are delighted to report to you that we have learned that my son, Lieutenant Shearman, is a prisoner of war at Rastatt, Germany. On October 24 he was reported alive but seriously wounded. Nothing as to the nature of his wounds were given so I fear he will be unable to help himself in any way when peace is at last declared.

"I hope there will be an opportunity given to some of his friends or members of his squadron to look after him and help him to return to us at the earliest date.

"It seems wonderful after all those months to again hope to have my boy Hugh."[18]

It was all a ghastly error; by November 11, 1918, Shearman had been dead and in grave 728 at Bruges Cemetery nearly three months; lying beside his comrade, Lyman Case.[19] And the sad truth was, fortunes of war being what they are, by the end of the conflict there were few in the 17th who could remember either.

The squadron knew them well on August 14, however, and thirsted for enemy blood in repayment. In addition to the three claimed by the squadron in the morning, Hamilton sent a Fokker spiraling down after a brief encounter on evening patrol (although he declined to claim it because he considered its antics suspicious).[20] And Todd recorded another unofficial kill the next evening. Following a wild but inconclusive scrap with some adversaries during bomber escort, he found himself separated from the formation and took up with a wandering Bentley powered Camel from RAF 210 for mutual protection as they headed homeward.

They were floating along blissfully, never expecting trouble, since, as Todd wrote his sister, "All of us had gone down on about a dozen Huns and we had run them down to their own aerodrome, so we thought the sky was clear of them. Just as we were about to cross the lines we heard this loud put-put-put, and looking around saw this Fokker about fifty yards behind us and firing to beat the band. We both turned to the right and went after him..."[21]

The Bentley had a power advantage and got off his shot ahead of Todd, but the Fokker nosed straight up to allow the British craft to pass under and, momentarily, out of the fight. The maneuver was a costly one, however; the German plane suddenly stalled and began to drop in a near vertical dive. Todd was on him in an instant, with his throttle chopped and the stick well forward. He began firing from about 150 yards out and closed to within fifty yards still blazing. He fired one continuous burst that lasted through a 3,000-foot dive. There he had to pull up finally as the Fokker began to plunge straight down. After that, Todd could not find the prey crashed or flying.[22]

Hamilton also niggled the foe a bit that evening. He was heading for Petite Synthe when he spotted a brace of Drachen lofting about at the end of 5,000 foot tethers just behind enemy lines. Hamilton said to anyone who would listen that he considered balloon fighting extremely dangerous and he counseled all to avoid it if possible. But his actions were nearly always otherwise. He seemed to have a fascination regarding the sport and now he made a move on two of them.

Lloyd Hamilton beside a Nissen hut at an unidentified location. He led C Flight in crushing low level attacks during the attack on Varssenaere aerodrome. (Grace Myrick)

Albert F. Everett joined the 17th the day Shearman was killed. This detail is from a later picture. (U.S. National Archives SC39372)

John F. Donoho also arrived on August 14. He is remembered as a most cheerful fellow, which is evident from the photograph. (Lorenz K. Ayers)

He flew along, oblique to the bags to fake the observers regarding his intentions. Then as the two came into line, he banked hard right and dived directly for them. There was a sudden yawing as the ground crews began desperately to reel-in and all Hell broke loose in the air around the Camel. Intense machine gun and anti-aircraft fire searched that corner of the sky. As Hamilton came closer he saw that the Drachen were protected by small balloonets about eight feet in diameter intended to keep attackers at a distance.

Hamilton had no Buckingham ammunition aboard and had to depend on his sparklets (tracers) to do the job. But they weren't up to it. He fired at the first bag, saw it tugged out of range, and turned on the second. He got off two good bursts before it too was pulled away. At that the little Camel was pitching about in a surf of ground fire and Hamilton had to pass over and abandon the project for another day.[23]

But that was the last opportunity for those targets. By the time Hamilton landed, the squadron was packing for the move south. Thursday, August 16, was spent seeing that all planes were airworthy, arranging the motor transport, and sorting supplies and belongings that were to be taken on the sixty-mile journey.

There was major concern in the orderly room when a flood of replacement pilots suddenly arrived just as the paperwork was being throttled to a stop. Jackson had arrived on August 12. The 14th brought both Albert Everett, the ex-West Pointer from the Ohio State bunch, and John "Jake" Donoho of the Princeton contingent, and the 15th brought three men who alone could have created a clerical nightmare at the best of times. All were 2nd lieutenants and all were named Howard.

The oldest of these, Howard Bittinger, was a first-generation American of Swiss descent. He was a quiet, good-looking man of twenty-four and a nephew of the American Expeditionary Force's purchasing agent (Charles L. Gyer) at Berne, Switzerland.[24] The other two Howards, Lts. Burdick and Knotts, were nearly inseparable comrades destined to play major roles in the 17th.

Howard Burdick, at twenty, became the youngest officer to serve with the unit. He was a small man, the son of a wealthy Brooklyn financier. Lively and extremely good looking (dark hair and blue eyes), he was almost the complete extrovert and manifested in his every activity a devil-may-care attitude that would cause much comment among older pilots once he crossed the lines. He'd been a long time getting to the front—nine months—and he was anxious to try his hand at the big game.[25]

That Burdick's closest friend was Howard Knotts seemed to prove the old adage that opposites attract. The only child of a U. S. Attorney in Springfield, Illinois, Knotts was big, blond, reserved, and well aware of the dangers of aerial combat. At six feet two inches in height, he towered over his buddy, and most others in the squadron for that matter. But the twenty-three-year-old pilot was the twin of Burdick in intelligence and determination. It had taken four tries and a nose operation to admit him to the air service and put him at the front.[26]

The new men introduced themselves around, unpacked a bit, then almost at once repacked and prepared to join the exodus to the new station; a bit of grassy meadow on the Somme called Auxi-le-Chateau—Auxi for short. At first it seemed the squadron might not depart as expected, for as late as 11 p.m. on the 16th, the orders to move had not arrived. But then a dispatch rider roared up bearing the word.

Now they were ready. The nearby Chapeau Rouge bar had been visited and celebrated. The Continental Hotel in Calais had seen

Left, Howard P. Bittinger, center, John A. Myers, and an unidentified officer. Bittinger was one of three "Howards" who came to the 17th on August 15. Myers joined the 17th two weeks later. (James F. Myers)

Howard Burdick wearing the mixed RAF/U.S. uniform in the field. (Frank A. Dixon)

Howard Knotts the third Howard. Also a member of the Toronto group, he would prove to be one of the staunchest pilots ever to fly with the 17th. (Mrs. Gordon Kellogg)

them last. Supposed sweethearts had been kissed good-bye and there was nothing left to do but go.

And so they went at nine the next morning, with Eckert flying lead. And they left behind only Army Armstrong, for Alderman departed the hospital to make the trip with the unit. He was unable to sit in a Camel, so he made the journey south in Eckert's Cadillac, a conveyance he deemed most suitable. As the unit moved out he lolled back on his uninjured ham, elevated his feet, and took charge of viewing the scenery.[27]

Meanwhile the Camels rose from the tarmac and formed up in a double column behind the Commanding Officer for a life different than any known to them. It was the first time Eckert had had an opportunity to scout the lines with a force behind him and he led them generously about the front, implying later that for a time he had been more or less lost.[28]

His act was good enough to convince Mert Campbell. After they had crossed Hesden three times from various directions, Mert drew out and set off for Auxi alone. He found the town easily enough, but could not locate an aerodrome that fit the given description. Finally, he landed at the RAF 205 field near Conteville. There he found that no one had ever heard of the 17th Aero Squadron and settled down to lunch and advise his hosts.

Shortly, Major Fowler, who had been flying the move with the unit and had also lost faith in Eckert's sense of direction, flew over, saw Campbell's plane and settled in thinking he was there at last. The British set another plate and after lunch loaned the pair a lorry to search out the squadron's location. By that time, of course, Eckert had led the rest of the squadron to the new field and the faithless had to endure many a laugh.[29]

The Americans were heartily greeted by the men of RAF 6, an RE-8 squadron already housed at Auxi. But the hosts reportedly seemed puzzled. These Americans had British mannerisms and slang—"bus" for airplane, "Archie" for anti-aircraft, "Get the wind up, breeze up, or gust up" for varying degrees of fright, "petrol" for gasoline, and "gone west" for being killed. But they gave things strange inflections. And their uniforms were unique in any circumstance, having become strange combinations pieced together from both the American olive drab and the British powder blue. Perhaps most shocking to the proper British military was the condition of their flying boots, which had obviously started life as the RAF hip-length model, then been hacked off roughly at the knee. It was a practice some had adopted at Petite Synthe (much to the consternation of Wing) and one that would become even more prevalent in the 17th when pilots discovered that the leather tops made excellent straps for lashing down the two-man tents they were now to live in.[30]

The new base was on rising ground to the southwest of Auxi-le-Chateau along a road leading to Crecy. The aerodrome was a grassy meadow surrounded by fields of ripening grain. There was a small wood to the east running right up to the back of the hangars. All about was gently rolling terrain, full of villages and pleasant sights—unless one went too far east. Should one get that indiscreet, one found a land sadly damaged, abused, outraged; for this was the front door to the battlefield.[31]

Despite the bucolic air, the Americans would find life to be more difficult here than at Petite Synthe. Local water was not potable and drinking supply had to be trucked in from miles away. They would miss the comfortable barracks to which they had become accustomed. And the entire area was found to be infested with yellow jackets and earwigs, pesky creatures that had taken

Capt. (later major) James T. B. McCudden, V.C., D.S.O. & Bar, M.M., Croix de Guerre, with the Vickers FB16D fighter he test flew at Joyce Green, England, on June 22, 1917. Many Americans met and flew with McCudden during training. Ironically, he was killed in a flight accident at Auxi-le-Chateau about a month before the 17th was posted to that station. (Rodney D. Williams)

over when the population of the Somme went away to let the war pass through.

Still, the 17th now had a feeling of being out on their own and away from the bothersome hands of commanders located too close for comfort. Thus it came as a shock when later in the day Brigadier General C. A. H. Longcroft and Col. P. H. L. Playfair of 3rd brigade RAF (their new commanders) dropped in unannounced. But as it turned out, it was merely a show of good will. The two wanted the Americans to be properly and courteously received and even arranged to stay on hand until the ground elements of the unit arrived.

That happened at 5 p.m. The trucks rolled in handled by men unable to make a suitable military display. They were dirty, exhausted, choked by dust—and poisoned! They were poisoned so badly on canned beans that twenty of them would have to be hospitalized within the next four days.[32]

That was most inauspicious and must have set Eckert to considering. They were on a new and unfamiliar front where they were soon to switch from high altitude efforts to trench strafing. (This always meant long casualty lists. No doubt there were knowing glances among the older warriors when the order went out for armored seats.) The southern German was said to be tougher, and Brigade commanders had already confirmed that the remains of the famed and respected Richthofen Circus (now commanded by Hermann Goering) was stationed at Bernes—not far away.[33] While on paper the 17th was at full strength and ready to take on new assignments (indeed, one of the reasons that the 148th and 17th had been moved south was Major Fowler's insistence to the RAF that the Americans were capable of doing more than had yet been asked of them), the facts were something else again. One of twenty-two pilots assigned to the squadron was on leave, one was unable to sit in a cockpit, and six had never crossed the lines or seen a Hun. That left fourteen to pull all assignments at a time when assignments were sure to be plentiful. And with a mass poisoning at hand, the unit was as short of mechanics as of pilots.

These had to be troubling considerations. Within days the 17th Aero Squadron would encounter its worst week of the war.

Changes in Squadron Status—end of day 8/20/1918

A Flight	
Howard Bittinger	Replacement pilot.
Lyman Case	Killed in action.
John Donoho	Replacement pilot.
B Flight	
William Tipton	On leave.
Howard Burdick	Replacement pilot.
Harry Jackson	Replacement pilot.
Hugh Shearman	Killed in action.
C Flight	
Henry Frost	On leave.
Harriss Alderman	Present. Unfit.
Albert Everett	Replacement pilot.
Howard Knotts	Replacement pilot.

Sopwith Camels on the line at Auxi-le-Chateau. No. F2141 (second in line) was Howard Burdick's "bus." (Frank A. Dixon)

Frank Dixon is seen here performing his ablutions in a camp basin typical of the equipment used by air service troops in the field. This picture was taken when Dixon served with RAF 209 in the spring. (Frank A. Dixon)

6

Late Days of August

The 17th's days of familiarization and practice at Auxi-le-Chateau were soon over, for with the launching of the battle for Bapaume, on August 21, the squadron drew immediate assignments. They were ordered to provide escort for the RE-8s of RAF 6 Squadron, also at Auxi, and to commence bombing and strafing sorties of their own. This presented Squadron Commander Eckert with a bit of a puzzle. Many of the new pilots whom he was now required to put into the air had not yet been in France three weeks as was required by standing orders, and few of the available pilots had had a chance to fly the lines and learn the layout.

Assignment of the Camels to support RE-8s was not without irony. If the Camel was the trickiest scout plane at the front, the quirky RE-8 was surely the most treacherous. A hold-over from 1916, it had been proven to be virtually unsuited for any aspect of the current war. Good-humored British pilots had nicknamed the RE-8 "the Harry Tate" because of its supposed resemblance to that music hall comic, but it had quirky characteristics that Camel drivers knew well; it was notoriously hard to fly because of heavy stick pressure and it was quick to drop into a fatal spin. And it went the Camel one better—it was a flamer.[1]

The 17th soon saw this for themselves. Shortly after the squadron's arrival at Auxi, one of the RAF pilots asked Pvt. Alfred Haig to go up with him and make weight for a practice test. Haig was on ambulance duty and couldn't go, but he did help the officer load a large bag of sand aboard for ballast. Minutes later, the young flier was lying burned to death amid the wreckage of his ship. The fire following the crash was so intense that the pilot's skin was actually seared away and later, in the interest of educating his untrained crew, Dr. Ross was able to give a quiet anatomy lesson using the remains.[2]

At Auxi-le-Chateau the 17th was placed in support of an RAF RE-8 unit. Here an RE-8 is seen in its usual mode—being trucked back from the crash site. (Frederick M. Clapp)

Still, a determined warrior could do considerable damage with a Harry Tate if someone would keep the Fokkers off his tail—and that was to be part of the 17th's duty. The inaugural show was a noon bombing run to Cambrai—fifty miles off and twenty miles within some very hostile territory. Howard Burdick, who had been discovered to be an extraordinary pilot, was the first of the new men to cross the line. He was tucked into B Flight amid Tipton (just back from leave), Williams, and Wicks. Goodnow led A Flight with Mert Campbell, Showalter, and Wise. Hamilton had Jesse Campbell, Todd, and Schneider.

They found the enemy waiting for them just short of the target. Tipton was the first to spot them lurking at 13,000 feet, a thousand feet above the Camels. He signaled, then climbed to meet the lead Fokker as it began its dive. He and the enemy blazed at each other head-on briefly, at which his opponent ducked under to go for the easier RE-8s. Tipton rolled, got behind his foe, and quickly closed, gunning the Fokker in the backside. Immediately he heard an ominous putt-putt-putt from behind and swung about to find two Fokkers sitting on his tail. Tipton broke right as a shooting, swinging quartet of fighters passed to his left. Showalter had fallen upon one of the Fokkers and Williams was chasing the other.

Showalter picked up his man as Tipton dived past. He immediately brought his ship to bear and fired a burst from 300 yards out, too far to do more than scare an enemy. This it did. The Fokker abruptly half rolled to the right and dropped into a steep dive. With that, he was doomed. Showalter followed for about a thousand feet repeatedly riddling the tail until the aircraft fell into an uncontrolled spin. Meanwhile, William's opponent had taken a respectable burst, stalled, dropped left, and went down in a very steep dive.

But there were more enemy aircraft. Hamilton signaled nine additional planes hidden in the sun. Strangely, as he went for them they dived away as if to avoid the conflict. But the preacher's son got among them and singled out a victim. He swung onto him at about ten or twenty yards distance and followed along peppering the plane with gusto. They went down more than a mile in this fashion with the Fokker pilot making no successful effort to free himself. Hamilton pulled off at 5,000 feet when the German plane began to smoke and Todd subsequently saw the hapless foe splinter into a field below.

The main fight raged now directly above the bombers. Mert Campbell had rushed into the new batch of Fokkers and saw his intended victim maneuver about and above him, a situation not to his liking. He did a half loop, rolled out on top and climbed sharply toward the Fokker firing at its underbelly. As he closed on his target, though, his plane began to stall and he had to kick into a turn to avoid conking. The Fokker dived out of his line of fire in an erratic sideslip.

Then suddenly, as often happened, the skies were completely clear. When the bombers reached their destination and unloaded their bombs, the Fokkers lost interest and headed home. By 1:30 p.m. the 17th had returned to Auxi where the new man, Howard Burdick, reported that he had, "Fired at a couple with no success."[3]

This foray hardly confirmed the message that had been carried to the 17th by their sister outfit, the 148th, that this was a more savage breed of adversary than were to be found farther north. But those who knew how to read events were not comforted on hearing that Tipton had framed foes in his sights three times only to see them fly away.

For the second mission on August 21, the squadron drew a late afternoon bombing show—with the Camels to be the bombers. Flights A and B went off around 5:00 p.m., and soon came upon the railroad station at St. Leger to find it aswarm with activity. They immediately strung their bombs along the track, and it was believed that Goodnow hit the station itself. C Flight was not long behind. They too hammered the railway and turned for home. But C Flight was not to reach Auxi without incident: on the way back Hamilton spied a balloon lofting about just behind the front. Since the Camels were carrying Buckingham incendiary ammunition, the flight commander waved for an attack.

Moved south to be a part of the British drive on Bapaume, the 17th was furiously busy from the day of arrival. Lloyd Hamilton is seen here at a calmer time when he was associated with the Avro trainer in the background. (Grace Myrick)

A view of the hangars at Auxi-le-Chateau. (Frank A. Dixon)

Todd went with him while Jesse Campbell stood guard. The two attacking Camels swooped level with the balloon while lashing it with machine guns. Almost from the start it was being tugged away by the ground crew. The observer took to his parachute and heavy ground fire rose to meet the attackers. For a time nothing seemed to be happening. The bag sank lower and lower. Then, at 200 feet, it burst into flames and flashed into oblivion. The Camels streaked westward under heavy fire.

All this would have greatly impressed Howard Knotts, the second new man to be sent across the lines that day, had he been there. But he was not. He had lifted off rightly enough with C Flight, but half an hour later he got lost when the formation crossed the lines at Bapaume. He was searching the air and noting landmarks that he might need later when, suddenly, he discovered that everyone had vanished. One minute he was among friends—and the next he was alone.

Angry with himself, Knotts began to prowl the lines watching for the squadron's return. Soon he saw planes making off toward Auxi and joined them with a happy wave. At that, the fifth aviator in the formation turned and machine gunned Knotts in the nose—that splendidly reconstructed nose that had four times denied him entry into the air service. He had, of course, blundered into a nest of Fokkers looking for action. With the kind of fearless anger that

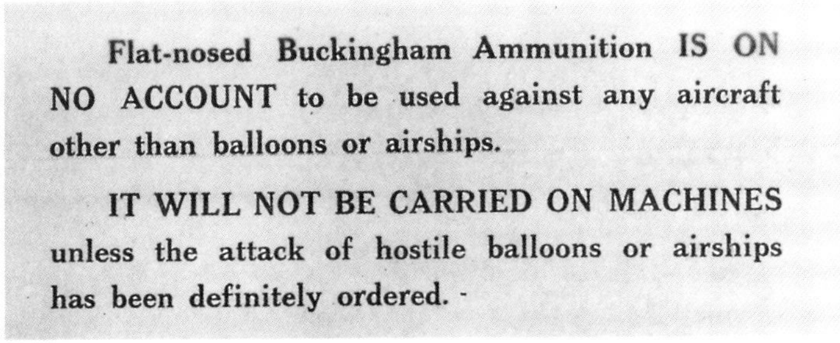

Flat-nosed Buckingham Ammunition IS ON NO ACCOUNT to be used against any aircraft other than balloons or airships.

IT WILL NOT BE CARRIED ON MACHINES unless the attack of hostile balloons or airships has been definitely ordered.

This printed notice was posted in the cockpit of RAF aircraft, where a pilot could readily consult it when in doubt. The incendiary .303 ammo was developed by J. D. Buckingham of England. (Samuel B. Eckert)

Robert M. Todd achieved a Fokker kill on August 22, 1918, during an offensive sweep against targets of opportunity following bomber escort duty to St. Quentin. This was the day after he and Jesse Campbell shared a balloon kill. (Miles Todd)

was to mark his combat career, Knotts turned on his attacker, gave him a long burst in diving past, and scooted for home. On his way he rendezvoused with C Flight who were much puzzled by his bloody countenance.[4]

The last plane was down by 7:40 and Knotts drew laughs and drinks at the mess. Later Doc Ross hauled the fledgling warrior off for a tetanus shot—which could sometimes be worse than the wound itself. Still, it was a night for celebration. In its first active day on the new front the 17th had, without serious casualty, wrecked a railroad connection and downed three Fokkers and a balloon.

Probably as a result of his serious losses the previous day (the 148th had downed four Fokkers as well), the enemy proved a bit more cautious on Thursday, August 22. But the 17th was up and spoiling for a fight. Neither one of the fledgling Howards was available that day. Knotts was nursing his nose (stung by the Boche) and Burdick his eye (stung by a yellow jacket, swarms of which were loose at Auxi that summer). This gave the squadron a chance to reintroduce Jack Frost, who had just returned from leave, and to send out Jackson for his initial look.

The first assignment was to accompany the RE-8s on a bomb strike at St. Quentin. This was a dull affair without a Fokker in the sky. As the bombers turned for home, the Camels swung away for some private hunting. Shortly they discovered balloons standing over the peat bogs south of Bray by the murky waters of the Somme. Tipton was in the lead and he went down with Williams in tow. The pair dropped amid steady shelling from the ground. Years later Williams reported that it was the noise that impressed him most on this occasion. "It was deafening," he recalled. "Bursting flack, the howl of the straining engines and struts, the clatter of machine guns...finally our bullets ripped the top of the balloon. I could see it start to burn in the holes like the jets of a gas stove. Then the whole thing exploded."[5]

In the meantime a dozen Fokkers happened by and came down to look in on the fun. Shortly five of them got amid the Camels. Todd and Hamilton pounced on one together, then Todd had to roll off to escape one on his tail. He immediately picked up another diving past and settled in behind him, guns pounding. Hamilton, in turn, lost the original target, spotted the Fokker that had attacked Todd and went for it. He followed it down to 1500 feet before his guns went silent—at which he slunk away homeward. It was a wild fight in which one seldom saw the result. Todd pursued his target for several hundred yards before losing him in the general mêlée, but Tipton later reported seeing the Fokker scattered over a quarter mile of the terrain below.

Wise was there and downed a German. He got suddenly head to head with a Fokker and poured a good burst into it at point blank range at which it stalled and fell over sideways into a dive. Before Wise could see what had happened, two Fokkers began to pepper him from behind and he had to take refuge in the reforming flights.

The Germans also began to retire, although before it was all over, Frost and Jesse Campbell managed to mix it up again with several Fokkers at 14,000 feet. Campbell's plane was well shot up in this encounter. When he had limped back to base, it was discovered that both the cabane strut to the right of his head and one of the body spars had been severely chewed away by bullets. The damage was so substantial that the craft was sent to depot for repair.[6]

By that afternoon things grew calmer. Bittinger got an actionless baptism on a patrol that turned up nothing of interest but the reporting of four large fires near Archie-le-grand, probably the result of bombing and strafing runs by the 148th earlier in the afternoon.

In addition to starting these conflagrations, the 148th had gotten two Fokkers that day to hone a bit the rivalry that was already growing between the two such similar units stationed so closely together. It was never to be an open rivalry, or even generally acknowledged, but it was there. At that moment, the two stood about head to head. They were nearly equal in strength, although the 148th had slightly faster planes powered by 130 hp Clerget engines. And they were about equal in victories—if one disregarded the eight to fourteen planes the 17th had been allowed in the Varssenaere attack. It is probable, however, that although they had been south longer and had fought fiercely every day, the mental state was better in the 148th. That unit had not yet lost a pilot; they had not seen Glenn drop into the sea, Spidle circle into oblivion, Gracie drop from between his wings, or, most especially, Lyman Case flailing to his death completely out of control.

But, all in all, the 17th felt fairly cocky by the end of Thursday. And Bobby Roberts came back that happy day. He arrived late in the afternoon with yet another tale of motorcycle mishap on his lips. First being ordered north, he had actually passed the squadron without knowing it. At Le Havre he was then ordered to backtrack to Auxi and, while awaiting the final word, had borrowed a Harley

Sopwith Camels lined up on the field at Auxi-le-Chateau. The raging battles engaged in by the 17th from mid-August to mid-September took place miles to the east beyond the line of trees seen here. The aircraft second from right is Eckert's personal plane. (Mrs. Gordon Kellogg)

to look over the town. "Had a slight crash," he noted in his diary. "Knocked down two English officers and scratched my hand."[7]

Strafing sorties began the next day—on Friday the 23rd. By then it had become evident that the present attack was driving the Germans from their gains in the spring and that they were drifting toward the rear. Accordingly, the British decided to punish them as they went.

On this day the 17th began habitually to get the view of the war seen previously only at Varssenaere. The flights went out in waves, four planes at a time, each plane carrying four 20-pound bombs and plenty of ammunition. Flight A went first at 11:30 in the morning. Showalter and Wise followed Goodnow right and left with Mert Campbell above and behind. They crossed the lines and headed for a known ammunition dump in the Combles area. Within half an hour they were diving on their target as ground fire grew thick about them. The little ships bounced up as one at bombs away, except that Showalter's bomb control fouled after he unleashed his first. He went away with three still aboard.

The patrol pulled up, saw the terrain disappear in boiling clouds of earth, then turned north looking for strafing targets. Presently they came upon the Albert-to-Bapaume road in the vicinity of Warlencourt and found a horse transport. Wise went down first, his Vickers blazing, and saw the drivers scatter to the fields leaving their frightened, dying beasts behind. Showalter moved a little farther down the road and dropped in on lorries traveling in groups of three a few hundred yards behind the horse-drawn vehicles. He was about to concentrate his full efforts on them when he noticed that Goodnow had uncovered a balloon and was going after it. He swung to help and the two of them pounded away until the bag was down out of reach.

Mert Campbell, meanwhile, had lingered at a thousand feet to look the situation over. He probably saw little not already under attack. But there was something in the sky, something he never suspected, something swift and deadly coming out of the sun. A lone Fokker swung down suddenly, rattling and swerving, raking the Camel broadside from prop to tail. It was too fast, too sudden for Campbell to do anything. Bullets smashed into his plane and into his body and he tipped over into a steep, unending dive. He crashed belly side up in the fields below.[8]

The Fokker was gone before anyone could react. Shocked, Campbell's companions broke off and made for the lines. It seemed incredible that Campbell could have gone to his death as a result of a sneak attack; he had been out trench strafing with RAF 54 Squadron before joining the 17th and knew the ropes better than most. And yet, in the end he'd fallen victim to inattention. They had gotten entranced by the ground war and forgotten to scan the air. It could have been any one of them, but it was Mert Campbell whose time was up, the sixth member of the squadron to die within a month.

Jesse F. Campbell. Three weeks after Campbell joined the unit, he and Todd took on and destroyed an enemy observation balloon during a late bombing patrol. (Mrs. Gordon Kellogg)

Flight A went out on August 23 to bomb and strafe east of Bapaume. After unloading his bombs, Mert Campbell fell victim to the ubiquitous "Hun in the sun." Seen here is a notice of his loss and a picture of the second of three graves occupied by him. (George Campbell)

The flight reached Auxi just as the second wave was forming for takeoff. Tipton led his flight to an area about five miles south of the region where Campbell lay dead and found a concentration of lorries halted along the Bezertine Le Petite and Martinpuich road. Tipton, Dixon, and Williams dropped down to 200 feet along the northern end of the column, raining bombs on the enemy as they went. The flight leader put all four right on the convoy. The other two hit it with three each: one of Dixon's bombs stuck in the rack and would not come free; Williams saved his fourth for a gun emplacement he spotted off to the side. He struck it soundly and then circled firing into the emplacement to keep it out of action. In the meantime, Dixon and Tipton used their fire to chase scurrying figures out of the dust clouds raised by the bombs and to kill them as they ran.

B Flight arrived home to the glum news concerning Mert Campbell about half an hour after C Flight had taken off—with Hamilton, Schneider, Todd, and Jesse Campbell—for their first crack at this new game. Hamilton led into the same area just worked over by B Flight and found several transports now moving south along the Courcellette to Bapaume roads, not toward the major throughway, but into the Martinpuich-Le Barque road, which paralleled it about a half a mile to the south. Campbell and Schneider split away to strike this traffic, while Hamilton and Todd went for the major column heading east toward Bapaume.

They went in separately. Todd dropped all four bombs on a grounded balloon he spotted near the intended target. Hamilton unloaded his directly on some horse transports. Then both began to sweep back and forth across the road, machine gunning anything that moved.

In the midst of this action, Todd suddenly became again the relentless killer seen at Varssenaere. He dropped lower and lower in placing his fire where he wanted it. Spotting a driver running desperately along the road for the safety of the ditch, he was on him in seconds and spitted his body in mid-leap. He next caught sight of a machine gun crew swinging into action and dropped almost to eye level with the frantic foe before blasting away. There was a momentary heavy exchange of fire and the enemy pitched away dead. Todd circled and came back to ruin the weapon as well.

By this time he knew that his Camel had been well riddled by ground fire and that he was low on fuel, so he popped up to join Hamilton who had watched the entire performance in awe. They were considerably east by now, within three miles of Bapaume. Below them the side roads were choked with troops who had learned that day to avoid the major roadways under attack by the 17th. With some satisfaction they headed for Auxi, picking up Schneider and Campbell along the way.[9]

The exhausted fliers ate, then sagged into their cots for fitful sleep while the mechanics readied their machines.

Soon they were at it again. Flight A led the evening patrols, with Snoke flying behind Goodnow in place of Mert Campbell. They flew due east, along with Showalter and Wise, then banked

Another view of Sopwith Camels at Auxi-le-Chateau. The white dumbbell insignia assigned the 17th by the RAF is clearly visible here. It was painted on each side of the fuselage. (Note: the other U. S. Squadron, the 148th, was assigned a white triangle.) (Rodney D. Williams)

off south toward the area already so hard hit during the day. By now they were striking a full five miles beyond the Courcellette-Bapaume road hit by C Flight four hours earlier.

Following a course south of and parallel to the major Albert-Bapaume Road, they soon found an ideal target; eight trucks halted at the intersection of the roads from Ligney to Baulencourt and from Gueudecourt to Bapaume. It was an incredible stroke of luck. Whether the convoy had stopped to debate directions or simply selected this conspicuous spot at which to eat is unknown. Whatever their purpose, it was soon lost in bomb blasts.

All four Camels dropped to 1,000 feet and flashed toward the vehicles; the bombs commenced to fall even as men on the ground began to scramble. Goodnow and Showalter put all of their bombs directly on the crossroads; Wise came right behind and unleashed three, holding one in reserve. Snoke went for another target after noting that his mates had done incredibly well. At the last instant, he spotted a second knot of five trucks parked by a side road a short distance ahead. He hit this new target with the same success enjoyed by his comrades. One bomb actually struck directly between two of the trucks, severely damaging both. As the quartet of Camels swept away from the smoking, burning confusion to reorganize for a strafing run, Wise found a likely place for his fourth bomb, a shed off to the side of the road, and scored a direct hit without even changing course.

Strafing proceeded methodically from a thousand feet. Figures scampered about on the ground and blazed back at the attackers. Snoke went back to his previous target and peppered the remaining enemy repeatedly. Showalter came upon a balloon floating close to the ground and raked it heavily without success. Then he uncovered half a company of infantry skulking down a side road and methodically executed them amid a hail of return fire.

Finally, the Camels drew off short of fuel and ammunition. Wise was back first despite pausing to engage a machine gun nest near Eaucourt, which had hosed away at him. Goodnow and Showalter came in next. And Snoke didn't get home for nearly half an hour after that.[10]

By then Tipton, Dixon, Williams, and Wicks had departed for their evening strike—at which Williams would put on his strangest show. The trouble started when Wicks failed to depart as planned; no sooner had the formation got into the air than his engine quit. Cool as ever, he sailed straight ahead to the inevitable crash, never wavering. He went down with a full load of bombs and ammunition, yawed to a dusty halt, and in seconds walked away uninjured.

With Wicks gone the formation was already one plane light when shortly they fired on some enemy trucks. At that Williams found that his guns were barely working, but concluded that the mission might be scrubbed if he also turned back. Typically, he decided to go on. Except for bombs, he began prowling about an unfriendly sky in a relatively harmless Camel.

He was soon wondering if he hadn't made a mistake. Flying at 4500 feet directly east of Bapaume in a layer of mist that drastically limited visibility, the trio came suddenly under a patrol of Fokkers two miles up. These were the first German planes the squadron had seen the entire day. Williams saw them at once and, jockeying his throttle, pulled up alongside Tipton to point them out. Tipton nodded and the three Americans awaited the attack. All figured they were in serious trouble, but only Williams knew how serious.

Glenn Wicks with a Camel. During the busy times of late August, he went down with a full load of bombs on takeoff. Fortunately, all bombs remained aboard during the ensuing forced landing and Wicks walked away unscathed. (Mrs. Louise Umstead)

Surprisingly, though, the Fokkers ignored them. Shortly it became apparent why when eleven British SE-5s appeared to the west at about the same height as the Fokkers. The two patrols were moving back and forth a little more than half a mile apart with the Camels sailing below and between them. Under these new conditions, Tipton was more than willing to make a move. He began to lead his flight in long climbs toward the Fokker formation followed by steep dives down and away. The 17th repeated this performance several times, but the Fokkers were too wise to give away height to the SE-5s. Finally, after noting that five of the enemy had disappeared into mist where they were undoubtedly waiting to catch the Camels unawares, Tipton gave up the game and led his companions off to the southwest—past Bapaume—to the area visited so repeatedly that day.

There they found the hunting still good. They spotted six lorries moving in convoy on the Martinpuich-Le Barque road, just east of Eaucourt and moved down to 500 feet to extend their greetings. At that, copious machine gun fire rose from the surrounding area. The aviators ignored it to go for the trucks. Tipton released all four bombs at once and scored a telling hit by upsetting one lorry in the path of the others. Williams came right behind him and then discovered that his Bowden control was hardly working; only half of his payload dropped. Right behind him, Dixon put all four on the target.

The Camels pulled up and around for strafing. Williams was, of course, useless in that venture and had no business remaining on the scene. But perhaps reasoning that things could hardly get worse, he decided to stay in. Spotting what appeared to be a machine gun emplacement, he swept back into the heavy crossfire to try his remaining bombs on it. The plane bounced upward when he yanked the control and he shot the stick over, thinking to come around to view his handiwork. Then, as he was nosing across, there came a spattering all about him and something struck him a heavy blow in his right hip. He realized instantly that he'd been hit.

Williams banked off sharply and headed for home still carrying his fourth bomb. His reaction was instinctive, done before he tried to make assessments. But he soon saw that he was in deadly trouble. The bullet embedded in his hip had pierced the corner of his fuel tank in such a manner that the fuel streaming out was being whipped into his face by winds lashing about the cockpit. He tried side-slipping to avoid the bath and deflecting the spray aside with his hand, but neither worked. Of course there was a fire hazard; drenched with fuel as he was, death was certain should the slightest spark reach him in flight or upon landing.

The solution hit upon by him was of the sort that had enabled him to survive many a Williams show. He transferred the spade grip to his left hand and began working his right arm aft between the seat and fuselage toward the damaged fuel tank. This was an awkward and painful business for a wounded man, but at last his searching hand found the punctures. With that, he thrust his fingers into the openings until the spray diminished, then ceased.

Rodney Williams in full flying gear. On his last patrol he continued into enemy territory in a badly malfunctioning Camel and came away so severely wounded by ground fire that he was invalided out of the war. (Rodney D. Williams)

His situation was now improved, but not by much. He was flying along wounded, sitting side-saddle in the cockpit with his right hand buckled behind him, and with only his left hand free to operate the stick and throttle. And he immediately found adjustment necessary, for the engine was beginning to run rough. This meant that the wind driven fuel pump was out and the pressure in the tank was dropping.

Working coolly, he chocked the stick with his knees and used his free hand to advance the fuel adjustment knob a bit. Then he set to work on the manual air pump, at which the engine picked up and smoothed out. He was moving along satisfactorily now and had time to evaluate his condition. There was blood enough to indicate that he was well hit, but the excitement of the moment had so far served to keep him alert.

By now he was safely across the lines and guessed he was still some twenty-five minutes flying time from the base. That would mean a lot of pumping to keep up fuel pressure, which could mean significant weakening on his part, which might mean a botched landing and death by fire. He saw that he would have to preserve his strength and decided to rely on his reserve tank once he was sure he could make Auxi. He tried the reserve tank and found it working—one of the few things that had gone right on that flight. Good enough! He went back to the main tank, pumped the air up to an acceptable level once again, and settled himself to the task of getting home.

For some time Williams performed well considering his physical condition. But eventually he saw that he was beginning to fade. As an old Camel hand, he knew that it would never do to pass out in the air. There were no mysterious tales of a Camel drifting down to a passable landing unassisted. One either flew it or crashed.

What he didn't realize, though, was that he wasn't headed for Auxi-le-Chateau. He was several degrees off course and flying so low that he couldn't really tell. True the landmarks were not as he expected them, but he thought that perhaps he was not quite so far along as he had imagined. And it seemed to be getting dark; the light was strange, abstract, misting, and fading. He finally realized that this was a result from his wound and made a concerted effort to rouse himself. It was becoming more difficult to concentrate, to stay in control. It would be easier to sleep, to rest...

Suddenly he saw something that gave him a start. It was the aerodrome of the RAF 3 Squadron near Feinville. He knew now that he had been flying off course and, incredibly, his first thought was to correct and head for Auxi. But some decisions are best made by providence; his engine began to sputter again. At that he resigned himself to landing and switched to the reserve tank. He banked, got a look at the wind sock, and moved into position for the descent. It occurred to him that he had better make it good the first time.

Williams leveled out and watched the turf rising to meet him. His right hand was still stuck in the fuel tank and he was doing it all with his left. He punched the blip switch sporadically and the engine sputtered and belched. The airspeed dropped; everything looked good through the mist growing before his eyes. He had just a bit longer to go. Now! He pulled his right hand free from the tank and at last had the proper hands on stick and throttle. He killed the engine and hauled back on the control. The little Camel flared, rode along on a cushion of air momentarily, and then was down in a perfect landing—jostling lightly as it rolled across the rough sod to a stop.[11]

It was midnight before word reached the 17th. RAF personnel had taken Williams from his plane poker-faced and, "still partly conscious," as they described it. He was off on a series of moves that would take him to England and completely out of the war.[12]

Rodney Williams had given his last show on that stage.

Changes in Squadron Status—end of day 8/23/1918

A Flight	
Merton Campbell	Killed in action.
B Flight	
Rodney Williams	Wounded. Out of the War.

Aircraft rigger De Villo Sloan (Left) is shown with two unidentified Companions. (De Villo Sloan)

A camel is towed with its tail skid on a dolly as the pilot, Robert Todd, reports on his patrol to the C.O. (Rodney Williams)

7

The End of Nearly Everything

Having lost two men in one day, the men of the 17th were in somewhat of a distraught state on the morning of the 24th. One of the most openly affected was Lloyd Hamilton who took a dim view of his chances. "They'll get me," said he. "They'll get the lot of us."[1]

This opinion was not new to him. Everyone knew that Hamilton fully expected to die in combat. But his current forebodings were so strongly upon him that they had to have an unsettling effect on the squadron. He was among their most able and respected leaders. If he thought all were to be lost, it just might be so.

And the war would not wait for rationalization. Saturday's assignment, once the weather cleared, was among the trickiest yet. The 17th and 148th were to cooperate in the continuous bombing and strafing of an area ten miles wide and five miles deep northeast of Bapaume. By now the enemy was pulling back through that city and the Camels were to strike them every twenty minutes as they went.

This group of vaguely identified airmen has two members of the 17th among its number. Left to right: Merton L. Campbell, "___ Mason from Detroit", Henry B. Frost, "Andy from Chicago," Reed Landis, an unidentified new Zealander. (George Campbell)

Since Fokkers had been scarce the day before, it was decided to launch in units of two from each squadron. The main problem was to mate the capabilities of the groups to achieve the desired result. This wouldn't be easy since the 148th was located eight miles closer to the front and had slightly faster Camels. As it worked out, finally, the brunt of the labor fell on them; the 148th would make eighteen strikes to the 17th's eight.[2]

The first 148th Camels rose at 12:45 p.m.; Hamilton and Jesse Campbell of the 17th were to follow along shortly. Things seemed to be going nicely at Auxi until the signal for takeoff was given at 1:10 p.m. Then, Hamilton did not respond. His ground crew had seen him fuss about with his controls and instruments as he awaited the signal and then, uncharacteristically, lay his head down on the gun butt padding. He stayed that way, resting, perhaps praying, perhaps merely steeling himself for the ordeal. In any case, for the first time ever, this superb pilot missed his signal.

Finally, rigger George Fellay made his way forward along the fuselage and shook the unmoving pilot by the shoulder. Hamilton looked up slowly, glanced about, and understood.[3] In a moment he was away, gathering speed and lifting off with Jesse Campbell behind him. They were only a bit late, but the second pair of 148th planes were already in the air.

When Hamilton and Campbell passed north of Bapaume, the smoking results of the 148th first attack on Ecourt St. Mein was visible to their left. The second wave from that unit dropped down and began hunting just as the 17th duo chose to strike some transport moving east a few miles out of Lagnicourt. Even as the Camels dropped to unleash their bombs, a third pair of 148th Camels was crossing the line while Frost and Schneider were rising from Auxi in the second 17th effort. The synchronized attack was in full swing.

Hamilton and Campbell made short work of the transport. Then as Hamilton pulled up he spied a balloon at about a thousand feet. He headed for it at once with Campbell backing him eagerly. They had no Buckingham ammunition aboard (it was illegal to carry it in ground strafing) and they had to depend on tracer bullets to fire the

Lloyd A. Hamilton rests on a flight of porch steps, probably at his home. He died August 24 while attacking a balloon with Jesse Campbell. Hamilton had a weakness for balloon fighting despite repeatedly warning others against it. (Grace Myrick)

bag. This meant that they had to go closer and stay longer to get results. Hamilton's fire was taking effect even before Campbell began shooting. Still, Campbell got in 150 rounds at close range before the balloon burst into flames and plummeted from the sky.

Campbell veered away, then realized with horror that Hamilton was continuing down, down, down, obviously out of control. The flight leader was probably dead from ground fire before he hit; dead and burning in his ship with the pictures of his father, mother, and fiancee mounted before his unseeing eyes.

It was a bitter and astonishing blow for the 17th—linked as it was with Hamilton's mood of the morning. Campbell returned with the news just as Goodnow and Showalter were taking off in the next wave of the attack. He tromped about the office chain smoking and relating the story to others listening in stunned silence.[4]

The blow was twofold for Eckert. Not only was there the personal loss of Hamilton, but the day's activities were now imperiled early in the game. It was expected that flight leaders and deputy flight leaders would spearhead each attack. Now, with Todd grounded with a dud aircraft and Hamilton dead, C Flight was left leaderless. The 17th was badly crippled just that suddenly.

Hard decisions were going to have to be made, but the war was not going to wait. Even as Campbell's short legs carried him back and forth across the squadron office, Frost and Schneider reached the target area. The pair spied a fleet of some forty lorries densely packed together and heading for the forks of a road northeast of Queant. Frost hit the convoy with all four bombs. Schneider, however, could not drop then, but after fiddling with his Bowden control, managed to strike a railroad station and train near Vaux Vraucourt. Goodnow and Showalter came along about then and dropped on some more passing transports.

It went on almost to monotony. By the time Goodnow and Showalter turned for the lines, Snoke was approaching in his first trip as Deputy Flight Leader for A Flight, with Wise just behind him. They were bent on penetrating the target area and boring into the lines at Courcell when Wise suddenly swung away and flew to the south. Snoke watched him go in some confusion, then decided that he must have been hit by ground fire. Snoke banked about, waved to his departing comrade, and went on east seeking a target. He bombed some guns and gun crews and attacked two balloons that refused to burn. When he got home he expressed the opinion that Wise probably had engine trouble and was down somewhere west of the lines trying to call in.[5]

Wise was indeed down with engine trouble, but he was hardly trying to call. The rash young man from Washington, D.C., had banked away from his leader not because he'd been hit, but because he had decided to attack a balloon he saw swinging about south of their intended course. Never lacking in confidence, he felt

Four Allied airmen pose for their picture on release from captivity. Left to right, standing: Robert M. Todd and William Tipton of the 17th. Left to right, seated: George T. Wise of the 17th and Oscar Mandel of the 148th. During the action on August 26, Tipton shot down two enemy planes to firmly establish his role as an American ace. (Miles Todd)

he could fire this target and then pick up the mission where he'd left off. So intent was he on trying his hand at balloon killing that he never saw Snoke's parting wave.

It didn't go well. Within minutes he was caught in raging ground fire. The sausage was well placed and well protected; still, he got it in his sight and did manage to set it afire. Then, all of a sudden, his little ship shook with a serious hit. Machine gun fire had spanned the cockpit, shattering the prop before him and holing the fuel tank behind.

He came about instantly and chopped the engine, which was threatening to tear loose from its mounts. The lines were nearby and he tried for them but soon saw that he would never make it. Resigning himself to landing among the enemy, he began to look for a decent place. He finally spied a spot and soared along amid considerable ground fire. At last he dropped in an unexpectedly easy crash among the German support trenches. The enemy came along shortly to gather him up and he became the first man in the squadron to become a prisoner of war.[6] With that, the 17th had lost their fourth man in two days.

Still the aerial barrage continued. The 148th had sent three additional waves into the area since Wise had gone down. By then (4:30 p.m.) Frost and Schneider were in the air for a second run—which occurred simultaneously with yet another duo from the 148th. And the 148th got in two more waves before Snoke and Showalter went off at 6:00. By the time they turned for home the twelfth wave from the 148th was in the area and Tipton and Wicks were crossing the lines on the 17th's penultimate effort. Then the final 148th strike came on the scene followed shortly by Todd (flying Eckert's plane) and Dixon.[7]

With that the day was over at last and the enemy had suffered much. But there was a butcher's bill. Word came that the 148th had lost their first pilot to the war; Lt. Marvin K. Curtis went out on the 4:45 wave and had not reported back.[8] The 17th had, however lost two men; and perhaps Hamilton would have to be counted as more than one. His skill and example was the sort of thing that made a squadron tick. So great was the sense of loss that even a full week later when the monthly report was filed with Wing by the Squadron, Hamilton's name was left off the list, a significant slip, perhaps indicating a subconscious desire.

Eckert's problems had certainly mounted as the day wore on. Accordingly he sent word to have all unserviceable aircraft repaired by morning and dispatched Goodnow to take Knotts, Roberts, and Bittinger on line patrol as a refresher.

Naming a successor to Hamilton was a delicate task, and since it involved sanctification by the 28th Headquarters of the American Air Service, getting a nominee confirmed for the next day's work was impossible. A little quiet canvassing among the pilots and staff settled the matter locally: Frost was deemed the best candidate and his name was forwarded with a request for immediate attention.

By the following morning twenty planes were again ready for combat and Wing was clamoring to know what was going on in the direction of the Hindenburg Line. Sam Eckert made a decision to lead this parade himself. The rationale behind the decision—and one was needed since squadron commanders were not supposed to cross into combat zones—was that orders appointing Frost as C Flight Commander had not arrived as expected. Having placed his name in nomination, Eckert did not feel justified in sending him without confirmation. Nor could he bring someone over from the other flights to pinch hit; both deputy leaders in A and B were new at their jobs.

And there were other problems. Willie Tipton had spent the last hours of the previous night packing Hamilton's gear and editing his diary—closing him out for good. In doing this he rapidly sank into a state of depression much akin to the lost feeling his best friend had suffered hours before his death. Thus, B Flight was in a leadership crisis of sorts.[9]

So Eckert decided to captain the ship abroad as well as at home. He led them away at 11:10 a.m. into a warm hazy noonday sky. They went to 10,000 feet and soon crossed the lines. Shortly they passed the German support and communications facilities and passed over the territory (now hidden by cloud cover) that they had pounded so energetically the previous day. As they came upon Bapaume they tested their guns, at which Bittinger found his not working and turned for home.

After a time they were in the clear and saw that traffic was still heavy along the roads to the Hindenburg line. Periodically they would see planes from the 148th still bombing and strafing. Soon they were farther east than they had ever been before, but the skies remained clear. They approached Cambrai and ascertained that the suppositions of the British high command were well-founded; the Hindenburg line was still strong and growing stronger. After brief observations, the flight turned for home.

When back over Bapaume and amid more familiar and comfortable territory, they suddenly spotted two German observation planes working the area. All went down in a rush—ten planes on a mere two. One of the DFWs immediately dived east and went so low there was no opportunity to fight him. What resulted then was a comical situation in which the remaining DFW, well-flown and defended, managed to turn the 17th's strength against them. For several minutes the Camels kept getting in each other's way. Then Burdick raced in and got off a good burst at the German but couldn't score. Bobby Roberts swung out of a turn and found the enemy dead in his sights—and his guns went out. And on and on. Then the gods of war showed a poetic bent; Sam Eckert, the Squadron Commander who shouldn't have been there, came in on the two seater with a telling burst from his Vickers. The enemy plane wobbled and pitched down eastward—at which the Camels headed for home.[10]

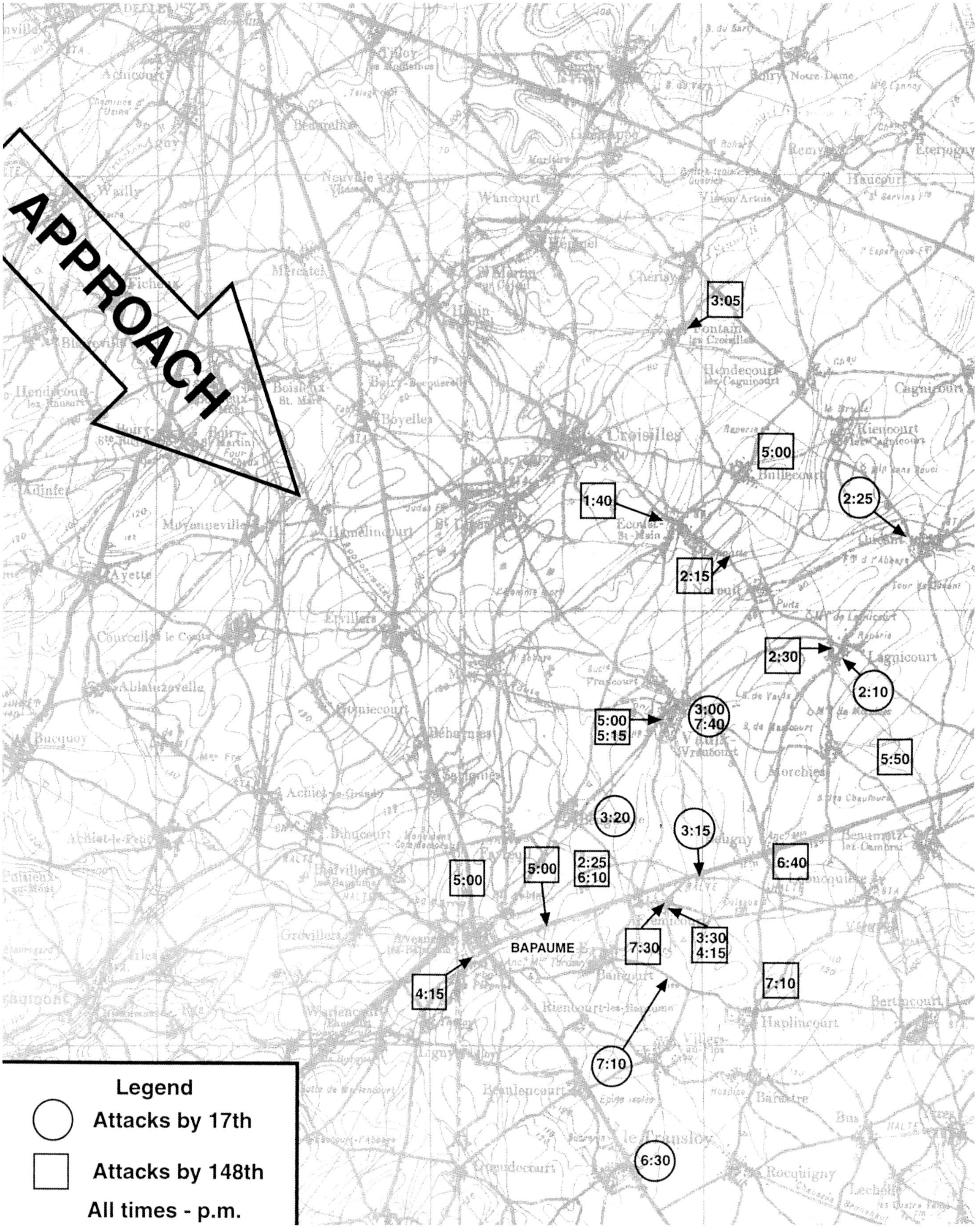
APPROACH
3:05
5:00
1:40
2:25
2:15
2:30
2:10
3:00
7:40
5:00
5:15
5:50
3:20
3:15
6:40
5:00
5:00
2:25
6:10
BAPAUME
7:30
3:30
4:15
4:15
7:10
7:10
6:30
Legend
Attacks by 17th
Attacks by 148th
All times - p.m.

Major Fowler poses in front of a Camel during one of his visits to the 17th. (Lorenz K. Ayers)

The squadron came home to find Major Fowler making one of his periodic visits, this time to learn what they had seen across the lines and to check the status of the unit. The good natured banter surrounding Eckert's successful day led, eventually, to talk of Hamilton and his probable fate. It was an unfortunate turn for the conversation to take in Tipton's presence. He was obviously no longer himself and growing increasingly morose as the day wore on. He sat apart from others, rising from time to time to wind the phonograph in the mess and to play a record that he seemed not to hear. He would not be drawn into conversation. It was a dangerous state that could only be waited out.

Tipton did not go out with the evening patrol; neither Doc Ross nor Eckert was anxious to see him in combat again until his emotional state improved. Todd took out B Flight in his stead with Jackson, Burdick, Dixon, and Donoho.[11] Flight C went out under Frost since Fowler had urged it and assured Eckert that his confirmation was pending. He led Campbell, Schneider, and Knotts, the latter celebrating his twenty-third birthday and openly pining for a kill to mark the day. Flight A put up Goodnow, Snoke, Showalter, and Bittinger.

They went east and penetrated the lines north of Bapaume at which Donoho left them, having been instructed to do a little exploring on his own and return to base. The squadron was in the midst of test firing the guns when anti-aircraft fire picked them out and began chewing away at them. Shortly, Todd headed home with his pressure pump shot away.

Knotts got just about as far and then found himself lost again. He was systematically working his way through the Archie when he suddenly realized he had turned himself all about and was no longer with his comrades. Not only that, but the sky was suddenly filled with aircraft. There was a flight of Dolphins from the RAF 87 at 6,000 feet, a flight of five Fokkers just below them, and various elements of the 148th at the bottom of the stack. The latter were the only Camels that Knotts could find on the scene, so it was plain that his patrol had gotten completely away from him again.

This was ample excuse to turn for home. But that wasn't for Knotts. Since he wasn't a member of any of the contending formations, he decided to sit tight and see what happened. It didn't take long. The Dolphins suddenly swooped on the Fokkers, which in turn spilled down on the Camels. Knotts was craning his neck to look at the action when one of the Fokkers broke through and arced in his direction. Knotts rolled to meet the foe, coming up to within twenty yards of him before firing. He got away two bursts and saw the dark German helmet pitch around in the Fokker cockpit. The enemy plane did a nip up and plunged straight down a full 2,000 feet with no attempt being made to recover. It smashed and immediately burst into flames. It was a kill, a clean kill, in front of numerous witnesses—and a most unusual birthday present.

Almost simultaneously, Knotts spotted another Fokker coming down out of the fracas, but it posed no threat. It was spinning out of control and went on to crash next to his own kill, a victim of Henry Clay of the 148th. But now a flight of German two-seaters was fast approaching at 2,000 feet, balancing the odds somewhat for the remaining three Fokkers. Knotts went up to join the main battle and almost immediately found himself with another Fokker dead in his sights. But his second birthday kill got away when his

OPPOSITE: A map of the pounding raids engaged in by the 17th and 148th on August 21, 1918. As shown here, by having better planes the 148th carried the brunt of the effort. (The Waller Design Group)

Howard C. Knotts in training as a member of the 182nd Aero Squadron. He made his first kill during the evening patrol on August 25 as a member of C Flight. (Mrs. John B. Dixon)

guns went out of action. Prudent at last, he withdrew and headed home.[12]

That night the drinks were on Howard Knotts. Even Burdick had to ignore his self-imposed rule of abstinence in the face of the enemy and drink to his friend.[13] It had been the easiest day the squadron had seen since coming to this front and morale seemed once more on the mend—except for Willie Tipton.

It would prove to be the lull before the hurricane.

Monday, August 26, started out perfectly for war weary pilots. The day came on gray and rainy with gusty winds which began at dawn and grew stronger until they were blowing into the east at seventy to eighty miles an hour.[14] What it all meant was that there was little likelihood of anyone being sent on patrol.

It was a day for splashing across the tarmac to chat with the Harry Tate pilots who would be leaving the next day for a spot closer to the retreating German lines. Or perhaps it was a day for writing letters or playing hearts, a game that was sweeping through the unit like an epidemic. Best of all, it was a fine time to catch some much needed sleep. It should have served Tipton well, but from the start he sat the lazy day away in the doldrums with his big, slightly balding head in his hands and a dead cigar in the corner of his mouth.

The otherwise general good feelings improved even more when a couple of old familiar faces reappeared. Clapp was back from two weeks leave that had provided a marvelous break from the war. His wife, Maud, had obtained leave from her field hospital outside Paris, and through the kindness of friends, the couple were able to spend their time at Versailles. It was the perfect respite for an art scholar.[15]

Tillinghast was also back, to the surprise of many who had convinced themselves that he was out of the war for good. People would, in fact, go on for years shaking their heads about the delicate state of poor Tilly's health even though he was now fully recovered. The cure had been simple—a long distance hike across Scotland.[16]

The general happiness that day even extended into enlisted quarters. All but two planes were in flying shape, and nothing could be done about those. The newest craft, number C3351, needed sighting in at the firing range, something that could not be done on such a day; and number C1627 required a new inner tube which was not available. There was nothing to do but stand down and relax.

Elsewhere, however, events were unfolding that were about to put an end to this bliss. At Wing there was concern that nothing was happening from the Allied side of the lines. Reports indicated that the German skies were somewhat active and Wing felt they should be opposed. This ignored the fact that strong winds were blowing into the east, which would present serious problems for friendly planes trying to get home. Nevertheless, Wing made a decision to get on with the war.

The 148th received the astonishing news first; they were to start out in waves, commencing at 1:00 p.m., and continue the pounding of the rectangular area east of Bapaume.[17] Two planes were aloft on schedule, followed by four more at 3 p.m., and another four half an hour later.

They flew into a much altered situation. For the last few days the Camels of the 17th and 148th had been going out in small patrols, then breaking apart to attack targets at will. The maneuver had been singularly effective in pointing out to the Germans a specific need for more air cover in support of troop withdrawal. Accordingly, Jagdgeschwader III, an element equivalent to a British wing had just moved to an aerodrome at Aniche, ten miles due north of Cambrai. This unit was composed of Jasta 2 (commonly called "Jasta Boelcke" in honor of its famous leader—now dead nearly two years), Jasta 26, Jasta 27, and Jasta 36. Additionally, the old Richthofen Circus, Geschwader 1, was also in the area with Jasta 4 at Escaufort, and Jastas 6 and 11 stationed at Busigny—villages about fourteen miles southeast of Cambrai.[18] These were all seasoned squadrons filled with battle-wise veterans well able to make the most of opportunity.

Somehow, Wing seemed totally unaware that these changes had occurred over three days. The reality of it unfolded with the arrival of the 148th over the enemy lines on August 26. Jagdgeschwader III was making its first foray in the area precisely as the three o'clock flight of four Camels arrived on station. Just what happened then is not entirely clear, but within minutes a cloud of Fokkers came roaring down on a lone Camel flown by the 148th's George Siebold and swarmed about it like vultures. For some reason the other Camels did not recognize the craft under attack as one of theirs and turned off, leaving their companion on his own.

By then the 17th had received word from Wing that some trench strafing Camels from the 148th were in trouble out beyond Bapaume and that the unit must hurry to the rescue. This was no sooner said than done. It was Tipton's turn to lead the patrol and by 4:25 he was guiding a flock of eleven Camels due east ahead of the seventy- to eighty-mile per hour winds.

Two never made the lines; Wicks turned back with a dud engine; Jesse Campbell dropped out with dead guns. The others—Goodnow, Snoke, Bittinger, Tipton, Todd, Jackson, Dixon, Frost, and Roberts—formed up as best they could at 6,000 feet and streaked for the battle at a ground speed of some one hundred and forty miles an hour. They sailed into the area north of Bapaume just in time to witness the last desperate moments of George Siebold several thousand fcct below.[19]

Simultaneously with their arrival, those in the rear of the formation spied a large number of additional Fokkers over Queant heading their way and fired warning shots to alert Tipton to the danger. But they were unsuccessful. The 17th had been sent to help Siebold and the Camel below was all Tipton had eyes for. In a flash he went into a steep dive with Todd and Snoke following close behind—and then the rest. Even as they swooped to the rescue, Siebold spiraled to the ground and a fiery end. At that instant the other Fokkers came spilling down. The 17th had flown into an almost perfectly laid trap and suddenly found themselves embroiled in one of the largest dog fights of the war.

It was a spectacular and colorful confrontation, one that men in the trenches on both sides abandoned the war to watch. Nine Camels and some thirty Fokkers went at each other while drifting ever deeper into German territory. The 17th was up against Jasta 27, who flew dark gray Fokkers with red and white stripes painted vertically behind the cockpit and chordwise on the center section; "Jasta Boelcke" flying black and white camouflaged Fokkers with white tails; and a number of unidentified green and yellow-checkered planes.[20] These brightly colored killers flashed handily about the brown and buff Camels and it was every man for himself.

Todd later wrote to his parents, "Tipton and I were leading the show and are both responsible for getting into the trap the Huns laid for us. There must have been thirty of them in the flight at least and for a while I thought they were all after me. I finally managed to get a breath and pick out a Hun that was shooting up one of our fellows, and then dove on him. But I couldn't hold my machine steady very long because I'd no sooner dive than Huns would dive on me, so I contented myself with doing every stunt I knew and firing whenever I got a chance, which was every second at least."[21]

It has not been determined exactly how many planes went down in the fight, but it seems likely that six from each side ended up in the fields below. Years later, much of the combat was deciphered and many of the combatants paired. Jackson was the first to die, shot to death and crashing almost immediately, dead on his third venture across the lines. Bittinger, the new man, went next. Two Fokkers dived out of the east after the thin blond youngster and found him an able scrapper. Lt. Noltenius of Jasta 27 later wrote in his diary, "He maneuvered so smartly that it was nearly impossible to close in. Finally, when he flew straight for a moment, to run for home, Lt. Klimke and I got behind him and he plunged down burning."[22]

In a short time Bobby Roberts joined the dead—machine gunned to death in the air and crashing toward Cambrai, the first victim of Lt. Fritz Heinz of Jasta Boelke.

Even the incomparable Tipton fared badly, although he managed to pick off two attackers and sent them to their graves before bullets disabled his dancing plane. Eventually an explosive bullet reached the carburetor of his Camel stopping the engine cold and sending a shower of metal particles into his legs. He settled his Camel near Beaumetz-le-Cambrai and was taken prisoner at once. The Germans tried frantically to move his plane out of the area by truck to save it from shell fire, but the effort was a fiasco. With every movement the Camel would roll off the machine and fall to the ground to the sounds of splintering wood, ripping canvass, and the raucous laughter of the limping, bleeding Tipton.[23]

Todd nearly escaped. He was caught in the middle of the swirling mass of Fokkers and had driven one down under his attack. "This couldn't last forever, though," he later wrote. "My ammuni-

Harry Jackson was killed a little over two weeks after joining the unit. The best assessment of his plight was that he was sent into the field before he was ready. (U.S. Army Records Center)

Howard P. Bittinger was a member of A Flight for less than two weeks before being shot down and killed on August 26. He was the second to die that day. (U.S. Army Records Center)

Laurence Roberts returned from the hospital on August 22 and was in action with C Flight only four more days before being killed. He was a victim of Jasta Boelke. (Mrs. John McBride)

tion in my right gun giving out and my petrol tank being hit at about the same time. So I dove out of it and switched onto my gravity tank and started for the lines at about five hundred feet above the ground and two Huns taking turns shooting at me from behind. Not to be outdone, the Huns on the ground tried their hand at it and I gave a wonderful exhibition of a mad dog being chased by a crowd."

He still had a chance; he was flying Williams' resurrected D6595 and it was conceivable that he was about to pull a Williams show. But a bullet found his gravity tank and the Camel plunged down like a stone. "I went sailing over the trenches and could see the Huns standing up firing pistols at me as I went by," he wrote. "And then I hit some barbed wire and over I went on my back." He hung there upside down for an instant fumbling with the Sutton harness, then fell onto the French soil under the wreck. A party of Germans came out shortly and cut the wire so he could creep back to their trenches with them.

He found the troops in the trenches (near where Tipton had also come down) to be cordial if not friendly. "The captain was mighty nice to me and instead of being killed as I expected, I was given cigarettes, offered food, and treated nicely," he wrote home. "Then I walked across the fields to brigade headquarters and was taken in to five German officers. Here was where I received my first impression of German 'sportsmanship' and really commenced to hate the Huns with all my heart. I was kept standing holding my flying suit while they compared my things with some others that belonged to Frost, and while they insulted me for half an hour."[24]

So Frost was down too, shot blind and with both legs broken in the resulting crash. He died that night at the main dressing station at Boursies.[25]

The remaining three Camels emerged from the battle as lone elements, each with no one but himself to call upon. Goodnow had

Of this quartet of Oxford Cadets, none survived the war unscathed. Harold K. "Buck" Buckley and Donald E. "Kid" Carlton were killed in training accidents in England. Walter "Charlie" Chalaire was wounded in action while flying with RAF 202 Squadron. Henry B. Frost was shot down while flying with the 17th and so severely wounded that he soon died. (Frank A. Dixon)

dived from the formation immediately as the attack began and was soon entangled in a cloud of green and yellow Fokkers that swarmed around and above him. He sorted out the possible targets, then went for one directly above his craft and sent a long burst into its underside. The Fokker dived away immediately, but Goodnow was able to stay with him and put in a second burst at about twenty-five yards.

Suddenly there was a pounding of Spandaus behind him. He banked hard, rolled and turned under his attacker, and shook both him and a second attacker that was on his tail. He sighted a third enemy craft behind those two at a lower altitude trying to come up under him if he pursued his initial course. Goodnow went at the new adversary head on, firing continuously and holding his Camel on a collision course until the German slid under. The three planes were now firmly behind him, banking, swerving, sending tracers his way; actually driving him out of the fight. He was more than glad to oblige them and went winging homeward to become the first plane back to Auxi with the tragic news.

Snoke also suffered from the green and yellow plague. He had gone down as steeply as Tipton on one of three Fokkers pursuing a Camel—probably Frost's—and had placed a hundred rounds into its wings and tail. He was only ten yards out when he fired and the effect was startling. The plane yawed over and went flopping down, obviously finished. But the embattled Camel also fell from the sky at the same time.

Snoke couldn't watch. He'd become the target for several other Fokkers and set about shaking them with a steep climbing turn. He then nosed over and fired several bursts into one of his pursuers as it passed under him, then kicked away from the area and straightened out to look things over. At that—the war went away again. It seemed impossible that such a massive dog fight could just vanish, but there wasn't a plane to be seen. Satisfied to accept the impossible he turned west for the lines.

His escape was not to be that easy. As he later wrote, "Before I could reach the lines, two Fokkers dove on me from the front. They were shooting and I returned their fire. To avoid a collision, I pulled up and they went under me, but turned and were on my tail. They really shot up my Camel."[26] Snoke used every known trick in the book and a few invented on the spot to evade the enemy duo. Then a wad of bullets tore out the right rear cabane strut by his head and the whole Camel went slack in his hands. At that moment there were three men in that bit of sky who figured Snoke was a dead man.

From then on there were no smart maneuvers to ward off thrusts. Snoke swung his head like a weather vane to single out the most imminent danger so he could side-slip, ever so gently, away. The Camel wobbled strangely even through these gentle tricks and it began to look like a toss-up as to whether the Germans would gun him down or if the plane would simply come apart and drop him to his death.

As he was dwelling on this unpleasant consideration, the shooting stopped. Looking about, he found that he'd crossed the lines and the Fokkers had given up. So far so good. But he was still far from safety. He headed his ship for Auxi, passing up opportunities to set it down at other available bases. It was now just a matter of skillful flying and luck, and A Flight's new deputy flight leader had both at his disposal.

Heavy winds buffeted his wings and he watched closely for signs of disintegration. But it never came; Auxi slipped up under him and he was shortly letting the ship slip gently over the trees behind the shops. He sailed skillfully into the eye of the wind and searched for the exact moment when he could chop the throttle and roll onto the aerodrome. For the first time that day the wind was in his favor. His ground speed dropped to nearly nothing as he sunk lower and lower and then was down and rolling to a stop as the wings drooped low about him.

So it was that he and Goodnow stood before their agonizing comrades in the hushed squadron office and unfolded their tale of woe. But even as they recounted the horror, one final dramatic moment was to be played out. A distant sound came—and then over the trees appeared Dixon, hedge-hopping homeward to safety.

Dixon had managed to down two Fokkers in the battle before breaking away. As he had gone down in the diving attack, a flash of yellow and green passed in front of him and he let go an immediate burst. The enemy wrenched upside and plunged away pouring out black smoke. He then spied another Fokker chasing a Camel lower down and continued his dive in that direction and got on the unsuspecting German's tail from about 75 feet away. The enemy craft dived straight down, never pulling up.

By then he was extremely low and drawing heavy ground fire. He took strenuous evasive action to protect himself, but that precluded him from gaining altitude. So he went bouncing westward into the wind, struggling away from the enemy guns. It grew hazy and misty as he flew and he was often lost before finally struggling home.[27]

Dixon's return sounded just the slightest cheerful note to the crestfallen and shocked squadron. Many thoughts were running through the minds of those who had stayed behind; Eckert had sent his men out to die before, but never in such numbers; Wicks and Campbell felt that they should have been there for they might have made a difference; even the newer pilots were disconsolate through half suspecting that they might have fared better than Bittinger and Jackson.

Probably the hardest hit of all, though, was Clapp who had returned from leave to find that too many had gone west in his absence. The loss of Roberts added a cruel personal touch, for now all the 17th pilots he had known with the 22 Aero Squadron—those cheerful young men who had first called him "Daddy Clapp"—were gone. Glen, Gracie, Case, Roberts—all gone now.

In little less than a week on the new front, the 17th had downed sixteen German planes and wreaked untold damage by bombing and strafing. But it had cost ten pilots: six of them dead, three in enemy hands, one in the hospital and out of the war. Among the missing were the flight leaders and deputy flight leaders of both B and C Flights.

For all practical purposes, the 17th Aero Squadron no longer existed as a fighting unit.

Along with Goodnow and Snoke, Dixon was one of three pilots to return from battle on August 26. Up against distinctly marked green and yellow checkered planes, he scored two kills before managing to slip away after losing contact with the others. (Frank A. Dixon)

Frederick Mortimer Clapp returned from a two-week leave with his wife near Paris to find the 17th's pilot strength reduced by ten: six dead, three prisoners, and one hospitalized and out of the war. (Lorenz K. Ayers)

Four officers of the 17th who were most active when the unit prepared to rebuild. Left to right: David Terro Wells, Weston W. Goodnow, Lorenz K. Ayers, Ralph W. Snoke. Deputy Commander Snoke shot down one Fokker during the major battle of the month, then was forced from the fight with a badly damaged Camel. (Eldon Hively)

8

The Changing of the Guard

So badly frayed was the thread of continuity by the events of August that the 17th Aero Squadron now to rise from the ashes of its predecessor would scarcely resemble that which had gone before. Accordingly, throughout the day of August 27 the personal effects of the previous cast were carefully examined for minutiae that might prove painful to families, and then directed elsewhere to make way for the arrival of new players.

Over in the squadron office the staff was engaged in a careful weighing of the general situation. Two pieces of new correspondence were on hand. One was the order officially confirming Frost as C Flight commander. By that time, Frost was dead and buried. The second letter, a note from 13 Wing, had come in the night before. It read:

"Dear Eckert,

"I was extremely sorry about your losses tonight. You seem to have had no luck since you came to me, but I hope it will improve now.

"Your fellows have done exceedingly well, and I am quite sure that it was because they were so stout-hearted that they got pounced on tonight. They all put up a very good show.

"I have not put you down for any work in orders tomorrow, and would like you to get in as much practice as you can.

"Yours,

P. H. L. Playfair"[1]

The news had reached Wing even before the 17th called in its sad report, for the spectacular dogfight and the resulting grisly downpouring of wrecked British and German aircraft on the afternoon of the 26th had sired a tale that quickly spread along the front.

Not being scheduled for duty was a bit of a bad joke, however. In truth, some of those leading the 17th were wondering how they would ever get back to work. A study of the original flight roster was painfully revealing:

OPPOSITE: Harold Goodman Shoemaker. He was one of the first pilots commissioned in the early days of the 17th and had four victory with RAF 74 while flying an SE-5. Although known as a hot pilot, he had difficulty transitioning to the Camel. (Mrs. Lois Shoemaker)

The stalwart Weston W. Goodnow was the only flight commander left to the 17th as the end of August drew near. (Mrs. Gordon Kellogg)

A FLIGHT

Weston W. Goodnow	Flight Commander	To duty
Merton L. Campbell	Deputy	Killed 8/23/18
Leonard J. Desson	Pilot	To duty
Lyman Case	Pilot	Killed 8/14/18
George P. Glenn	Pilot	Killed 7/20/18
Floyd M. Showalter	Pilot	To duty
Ralph Snoke	Pilot	To duty

B FLIGHT

William Tipton	Flight Commander	Captured 8/26/18
Ralph Gracie	Deputy	Killed 8/12/18
Frank Dixon	Pilot	To Duty
Hugh Shearman	Pilot	Killed 8/14/18
Murray K. Spidle	Pilot	Killed 8/5/18
Rodney D. Williams	Pilot	Wounded 8/23/18—out
Theose Tillinghast	Pilot	To duty

C FLIGHT

Lloyd A. Hamilton	Flight Commander	Killed 8/24/18
Henry Frost	Deputy	Killed 8/26/18
William J. Armstrong	Pilot	Wounded 8/12/18
Harriss P. Alderman	Pilot	Wounded 8/12/18—unfit
Bradley Lawton	Pilot	Injured—out 7/26/18
Laurence Roberts	Pilot	Killed 8/26/18
Robert Todd	Pilot	Captured 8/26/18

Only six of the original pilots were still available for duty—and the sole remaining member of the original C Flight (Alderman) was unfit. And even this did not tell the whole story for the original list had not included George Wise—arrived July 21, captured August 24; Harry Helmar Jackson—arrived August 12, killed August 26; or Howard Bittinger—arrived August 16, also killed August 26. The 17th had lost eighteen pilots in about six weeks.

A current roster compiled for audit on August 27 was hardly more cheering:

A FLIGHT	B FLIGHT	C FLIGHT
Weston W. Goodnow	Frank Dixon	Howard Knotts
Ralph Snoke	Theose Tillinghast	Jesse Campbell
Floyd M. Showalter	Glenn Wicks	Albert J. Schneider
Leonard J. Desson	Howard Burdick	Harriss P. Alderman
		Albert Everett

By this it would seem that the squadron was at about half strength; but even that was not the case. While A Flight was in fair shape, there was growing dissension; Goodnow's tactic of holding his formation tightly together in fights had paid off in lives preserved, but some thought this cautious approach led to few victories. Ralph Snoke, who now became deputy commander, was one who thought this.[2]

In B Flight there was little depth. Wicks had not been at the front a month and, despite his kill on the 14th, was not considered a seasoned pilot. Tillinghast had just returned from sick leave and was an almost unknown quantity. Burdick was new.

Frank Dixon, however, was seasoned to command and he was immediately offered the deputy flight leader's spot if he wanted it. Dixon didn't care much one way or another but leaned toward taking his scheduled leave in England instead. His mind was made up that very day when he took his ship on a practice flight to check repairs on the previous day's damage. He raced away in a routine takeoff, but as he lifted into the air observers saw something drop from the plane, bounce, and go careening away like a whirligig. Dixon had lost his left wheel and part of the axle. A flare went up to warn him that something was wrong and a man ran onto the field holding a spare wheel with the letter L painted on it so he would know specifically what the trouble was.

The message got through and Dixon turned it into a private quandary. Hating paperwork, he debated whether it was best to crash on the aerodrome and fill out involved reports, or to put the Camel down softly in the fields and perhaps get away with a mere crop damage account.

Passing over an oat field northwest of the aerodrome, he decided that crops looked softer than turf and chose the latter. It was a mistake. He sailed almost to earth in apparent success; but the standing crop began to brush against his undercarriage, then flail at it, and finally to twine about the components. His flight came to a sudden and immediate end when the aircraft nosed down and snapped over on its back.

The damage was extraordinary considering the relatively minor nature of the incident. Although Dixon walked away unhurt, hardly a piece of the Camel survived. With that, the pilot stumbled through the ruined oats with his mind made up. He was off to England.[3] There was still a vacancy.

Over in C Flight, where only one man could remember the thrilling days when the squadron reformed at Petite Synthe, there was little that could be done. Alderman had not suitably recovered. Schneider, who had been with the 17th since mid-July, was considered an excellent pilot but not thought especially good at scout work. Everett, who had come into the field ill and had not recovered as expected, would soon leave for hospital. Jesse Campbell had been at the front only twenty-seven days and Knotts had yet to complete a fortnight in France.

It was apparent that new stock was needed. Amid these troublesome considerations, the squadron soon began trolling for additional leaders with which to bring the unit back to life. And since

When the 17th needed restaffing after the August disaster, Eckert called on his former commander at RAF 84 Squadron for assistance. Left to right: Capt. Andrew Frederick Weatherby Beauchamp-Proctor, a South African ace who finished the war with fifty-four victories, and Maj. William Sholto Douglas. (Samuel B. Eckert)

there was little in reserve except untrained talent, Eckert began by looking in other squadrons.

One of his first moves was to phone his old unit, RAF 84, to talk to William Sholto Douglas, a man already well into a career that would make him one of the most famous British military leaders of the century. Eckert was after a pilot he'd met briefly before leaving that unit—a slight, blond, quiet youth from Brooklyn by way of the Princeton air force. He was George A. Vaughn, Jr., known universally in those days as "Bob" Vaughn. Even his family called him Bob to avoid the obvious "Junior," and to avoid confusion with his father.

Vaughn had come out to the front to fly SE-5s in June and immediately demonstrated that exaggerated dash and flair were not essential to victory in the air. His ability to comprehend situations as they developed, coupled with superb flying and deadly shooting, had moved him up quickly in the RAF squadron. By the time Eckert came calling he was already a deputy flight leader and an

Vaughn was an ace with seven victories when he arrived in the 17th. He is pictured here at RAF 84. Left to right: George A. Vaughn, Lt. Tidler, Capt. Saunders, Lt. Thompson, and Lt. Reid. The SE-5s shown have a Lewis gun on a retractable gun-mount on the upper wing. (George A. Vaugh)

George A. Vaughn photographed the headquarters of RAF 84 Squadron when he flew with that distinguished unit. Notice the nice porch complete with awnings, furniture, and other comforts of home. The 17th was quite a comedown. (George A. Vaughn)

ace. Indeed, during the very week the 17th was so badly mauled, he had shared in the destruction of two German planes and downed an enemy balloon on his own to bring his score to seven.

Although he hated to lose such a man, Douglas yielded to Eckert's need. He dispatched Vaughn to Auxi-le-Chateau within twenty-four hours with a personal note. "He would make a first rate flight commander," wrote Douglas. "He is up for the Distinguished Flying Cross which should come along in a day or two."[4]

Eckert agreed with Douglas's recommendation. Since it was obvious that leadership was Vaughn's forte, he was immediately named B Flight commander—this in spite of the fact that the man had never set foot in a Camel. It was a daring situation and there must have been considerable uneasiness when the new flight leader began to slip off for practice flips.[5]

The man who was soon to be his deputy leader suffered from the same problem; he too had never flown a Camel. But with four kills confirmed in flying SE-5s at the front with RAF 74, Harold Goodman Shoemaker was a logical choice for a top slot.

Shoemaker was one of the first pilots commissioned in the 17th Aero Squadron in Texas—and a hot shot. It was he who had written so casually a year earlier about an instructor and cadet being burned up, then added, "but nothing out of the ordinary has happened." In Canada he had pulled a loop on his own volition (which American cadets were not required to do at that time) and, to the horror of his instructors, he did it in the slack old photography training ship. His explanation was that he felt he might not get another chance to try it right away. While training in England, he had coaxed his plane down with a crumpled wing following a mid-air collision—long after those on the ground had given him up for lost.

So he was hardly a timid pilot. Yet after moving to the 17th and flying the Camel for the first time he told his tent mate, "I can't fly that thing." The more he worked at it the more he became convinced that the Camel would kill him.[6]

But for the moment the problems of B Flight seemed settled. Staff turned next to the needs of C Flight. The man picked to be the new flight leader had been a Camel merchant from his first day at

A typical Curtiss JN-4 photography training plane, perhaps the one Shoemaker looped. Notice how the lower wing has been cut away to provide clearance for the camera's long lens. (Mrs. John McBride)

the front. He was William T. Clements, the Virginia banker who had arrived in Europe by way of Ohio State. In his time abroad Clements had developed into the complete professional. At flight school in England he had soloed after only two hours instruction and was himself instructing after five hours of training. He drove himself to do these worrisome things for duty's sake, and had hassled through the case of bad nerves that resulted by simply toughing them out. Having won, he'd moved to the front and fought well with the 148th.

At first Clements was none too happy about giving up a scheduled leave to come to the 17th, although expressing himself as looking forward to the "prestige and work" of a flight commander's position. Within four days, however, he was confiding to his diary

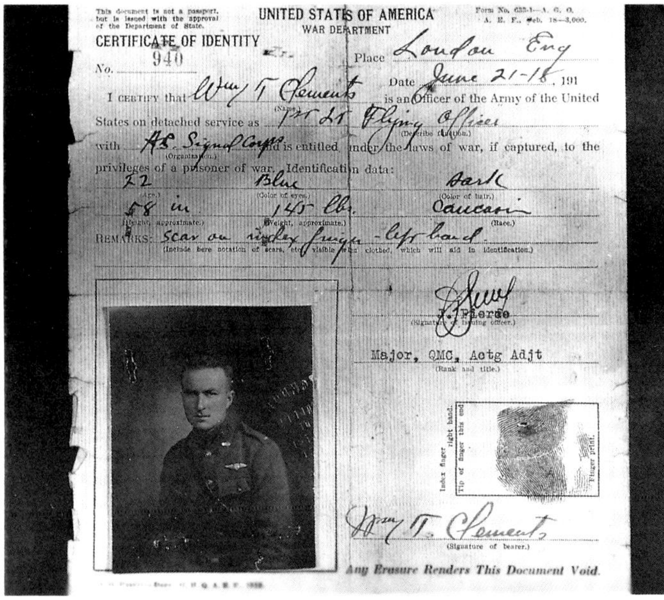

This document is not a passport, but is issued with the approval of the Department of State.

UNITED STATES OF AMERICA
WAR DEPARTMENT

Form No. 633-1—A. G. O. A. E. F., Feb. 18—3,000.

CERTIFICATE OF IDENTITY

No. 940

Place London Eng

Date June 21-18, 191

I CERTIFY that Wm T Clements (Name) is an Officer of the Army of the United States on detached service as 1st Lt Flying Officer (Describe function.) with AS. Signal Corps (Organization.) and is entitled, under the laws of war, if captured, to the privileges of a prisoner of war. Identification data:

22 (Age.) Blue (Color of eyes.) Dark (Color of hair.)

58 in (Height, approximate.) 145 lbs. (Weight, approximate.) Caucasian (Race.)

REMARKS: Scar on index finger - left hand (Include here notation of scars, etc., visible when clothed, which will aid in identification.)

J. Pierce (Signature of issuing officer.)

Major, QMC, Actg Adjt (Rank and title.)

Index finger right hand. Tip of finger this end. Finger print.

Wm T. Clements (Signature of bearer.)

Any Erasure Renders This Document Void.

Command of the rebuilt C Flight was given to William T. Clements. Originally posted to the 148th Aero Squadron, he transferred to the 17th in late August. This is a typical U.S. Air Service, Signal Corps identity certificate. Through some mix-up, Clements was receiving no flight pay which, as a banker, must have stirred his ire. (Mrs. Gordon Kellogg)

Thomas L. Moore. He was transferred from the 148th as part of the rebuilding program after the 17th's debacle in August, but was sent back almost immediately when the 148th also had a very bad day. (Mrs. Gordon Kellogg)

that, "The change, coming when it did, saved my life...yesterday the old flight I was in, with the exception of one man, was completely wiped out. [Elliot White] Springs, the flight commander was the only one to return out of a flight of four. Mandell, Forster, Kenyon were shot down, and I probably would have been also had I remained with 148th three days longer...I came to the 17th just after they had their big loss..."[7] The 148th's losses, coming on September 2, meant that Lt. Thomas Moore, who had been shifted to the 17th to be deputy flight commander under Clements, went back to his old unit after only five days with the 17th.

Through these developments, Eckert now found himself scrounging in competition with the commander of the 148th, Mort Newhall, who had been kind enough to let him have Clements and Moore in the first place. After Moore departed, Eckert talked with Vaughn and heard good things about Irving Corse, another RAF 84 officer with a brace of recent kills to his credit. When Clements heard the talk he noted in his diary, "that is the best news I have had in weeks. He is not only coming to our squadron but is going to be in my flight to replace Moore. There is not a man in France that I would rather have. As a flyer, Corse is very fine, and he is a darn good fellow."[8]

Unfortunately, he would have to be a darn good fellow elsewhere. Corse came in on September 10, limping from a wound in the left thigh, received five days earlier. He was inclined to scoff it

Irving Corse spent his first months flying with RAF 84. He came to the 17th with a leg wound and was sent out immediately by Dr. Ross. (U.S. National Archives H466)

off; after all, he had downed a balloon two days after it happened.[9] But Doc Ross wasn't sure the injury didn't deserve more attention and sent him off to hospital, not to appear again until after the Armistice. At that, Jesse Campbell took over the position of deputy commander.

With his top slots filled, Eckert next drew in Charles France (a former 17th man from the early days) from RAF 60 where he had been flying Camels with varied success. This short, wide-shouldered, good-natured man, had had some wild times with the RAF. Shortly before he returned to the 17th, a Fokker triplane shot him down to crash amidst shell holes in an area just secured by British forces that morning. "I was so scared, I've never grown an inch since," he declared ever afterward.[10]

Satisfied that he could now achieve a reasonable mix of seasoned warriors and neophytes, Eckert turned finally to the pilots pool. Shortly Lts. John A. Myers, Gerald P. Thomas, James A. Ellison, and Martin C. Giesecke came up to fill out the flights.

Almost simultaneously, many of those with experience at the front started getting away for a while—which no doubt hastened the change of character now taking place in the 17th. Showalter, Goodnow, and Dixon went on leave. Alderman went to recuperate elsewhere. Everett went to hospital in England, and the long-suffering Jimmy Bennett, who had led a shadowy existence with the Aeronautical General Supply Depot since squadron reorganization, was finally posted to flight school along with Glenn Hathaway and Herbert Curtiss, two enlisted men who showed promise as pilot material. And, having worked with B Flight for two weeks (and remained convinced that the Camels would kill him), Shoemaker now requested and got his scheduled leave and took off for a vacation in Ireland.[11]

As if again to signal the end of the old days, there came now another sad reminder of those times—perhaps the saddest. Word was received from B Battery, 95th Brigade, that Mert Campbell's aircraft and grave had been found. The Germans had buried the body just behind the smashed plane and marked the burial site with the broken propeller and a cracked bottle into which they inserted a blood-stained envelope addressed to the dead American.[12]

It was a poignant and unique development, for this was the only instance of the 17th learning the location of a dead comrade's grave. A week later, Sgt. Roy Hively went out with a crew to salvage what could be had from the Camel. They passed through war-ravaged territory, heavy with the smell of countless bodies that had been buried hastily in too-shallow graves, and brought back the plane's engine.

Their dismal account of conditions at the crash site inspired the squadron to mark the grave more suitably. As Clapp reported it in his history, "We made a cross of a broken four-bladed 'prop' of fine mahogany that we got from salvage and engraved a nameplate on a copper disk. We took it up past wrecked villages and then more wrecked villages, into the No Man's Land of some of the fiercest battles of the war. At the head of his grave, without ceremony, we set it up. He lies there, one of the stoutest, by a file of tree trunks smashed and stripped and grotesquely rigid against the sun, under a little slope of ground rising toward the east that has been blasted into dust by months of artillery fire."[13]

And now there was a new beginning. The squadron soon saw that many a lesson first encountered at Petite Synthe would return to be seen again as new men learned to deal with the Camel. Dixon had showed them how when he smashed his Camel on the 27th. Knotts (who—along with Burdick—through depletion was catapulted overnight from being a new man to being an experienced veteran) taught the second course when he tore another ship to pieces on the 28th.[14] The plane had been in the squadron only five days.

Accidents suddenly became so common that it seemed the squadron might self-destruct without waiting for the enemy. The most spectacular mishap came on September 3, when John Myers managed to drop his plane on top of Clements'. "Just as I was landing," wrote Clements in his diary, "a dark shadow appeared on my left wing. Well, about the only thing to do in such a case is to close your eyes and sit tight. His [John Myers] undercarriage hit my wing and prop, taking off most of my prop. This threw him down on his nose, to my right, and over he went on his back, completely 'writing off' his machine and getting a few scratches about the face. Part of my prop was gone, and a piece of one wing, but otherwise O.K. I jumped out and helped to get the boy out of his machine—he was practically unhurt. We just did not see each other when landing."[15]

Despite such antics, it was the next day that remained most

John A. Myers in a natty uniform. He was assigned directly to the 17th near the end of August and became a member of A Flight. From Kansas, he said his main ambition was to go home and fly a tractor for wheat. (James F. Myers)

Left to right: Martin C. Giesecke, Harriss P. Alderman at an unknown site. Giesecke arrived at Auxi-le-Chateau in early September and was a member of C Flight. (Mrs. Louise Umstead)

James G. Bennett gave up his chance to complete flight training in the spring to command C Flight ground personnel. At long last he was detached to England, in late August, to resume flight training. (Rodney D. Williams)

vividly in squadron memory; that was the day they managed to do nearly everything badly. Desson started things off that morning by breaking his tail skid off at the fitting upon landing. It then crashed into the plane's lower right longeron and broke that also.

Next, Giesecke came near to getting finished before getting started during aerial target practice. Not having fired on the local range, he walked out before his scheduled run to get the lay of the land. He was poking about familiarizing himself with the set-up when suddenly he became aware of the sound of a plane in the air. This plane was not drowsing about on a routine test; it was making for the range full throttle. Instantly Giesecke went racing, scampering, scrambling away with a hail of lead bouncing about him. Then as the plane heaved off, he glanced up to see a very stylish J painted on the side of the disappearing Camel; it was Eckert, and he had nearly killed a valuable new pilot.[16]

The day wasn't over. Burdick went out in mid-afternoon and conked half an hour later when his engine quit while hedgehopping west of Ameins. He hitchhiked back, rounded up a repair crew, and returned in a lorry to reclaim the ship. He did not get into the air again until 6 p.m., at which time a most bizarre incident was taking place back at Auxi. Engine fitter Albert Beebe described the event in an accident report. "So as to be ready for the (ground) test—and that the engine might start immediately," he wrote, "I climbed into the machine. Noticed the switch off, had turned the petrol on, climbing again to the ground and proceeded to 'suck in'—In doing so I noticed that somewhere a valve was blowing. Now I turned the engine over to find the cause of the improper valve action, with my left hand I was working the propeller. On the downward stroke, the engine fired, turned over several times and in so doing threw me to the ground. By the time I could recover, the machine was out of reach, heading due north." It ran for about 200 feet with a horde of men scrambling after it, turned to the right, then raced another 100 feet before encountering a deep rut. At that the right wing caught the ground and the machine spun about and turned over just as the pursuers came panting up. The switch was found to be short-circuited.[17]

As background music to these events, the overworked enlisted men began to furnish Eckert with other unseemly diversions. Eckert's relationship with the ranks was largely benevolent. An official report from the 17th headed "Discipline—Treatment of Mechanics," stated his policies clearly. "The tendency of discipline is to treat the men primarily as mechanics, rather than 'Guardsmen.' Slack discipline is not tolerated, but less attention is paid to perfect drill and soldierly bearing off duty than to mechanical efficiency. The personnel work very hard and to late hours at night with perfect content and good feeling."[18]

And it was true. The CO treated his troops like people, and they responded by calling Eckert "Major Sam"—out of hearing—and doing their best for him. And they had been doing that strenuously since the food poisoning incident and the ongoing Camel

Samuel B. Eckert's Camel with its distinctive J marking and its tail on a stand. It is likely that the plane is being sighted in for the sort of range work that nearly led to the demise of Martin Giesecke at Eckert's hands.

demolition derby that started with the losses of August 26. As a result Eckert was giving them their head as much as could be allowed decently. But finally, in early September, they went into Auxi-le-Chateau and played too hard.

On this occasion several men had been given leave until midnight and they went straight-away to town to help with the liquor situation. They were just warming well to the task when British MPs showed up, announced it was nine o'clock, and stated that regulations called for everyone to be off the streets by then. The men showed their passes—good until midnight—and opined that the regulations did not apply in the face of Major Sam's permission. The constabulary believed otherwise and ordered them back to camp, which the men took as a piece of sneaking meanness.

Loran Cooper recalled the incident years later. "Thirty of us refused to be run off the streets...With the help of some Canadians, who kept in dark corners, we cleaned up on the MPs.

"Sgt Wellborn, in charge of transportation, came to our rescue with a truck and got us back to the airfield. The next day, General Salmond, chief of RAF and four or five carloads of 'brass' and a bunch of bandaged MPs called on us. Fortunately, we got advanced notice, so those of us skinned or bruised-up hid in the brush... The MPs could not identify anyone so that was that..."[19]

Then the story developed uglier overtones. It seemed also that persons unknown had invaded an Officer's mess in town. One of the invaders had been knocked down and the British were offering in evidence a paybook belonging to a man in the 17th and supposedly lost at the scene. Worse yet, now came reports that a local business had been burglarized during that wild night.[20]

This created a major dilemma for Eckert. He could not indulge himself in the stiff justice demanded by regulations simply because he needed his mechanics. Nor could he ignore the British demands for explanations. So he took it out in investigations. In time he reported that his men weren't involved in the burglary and that he was convinced that his soldier had lost his paybook earlier. With these troublesome points resolved, he informed the British that, except for the business of failing to comply when ordered off the streets, his men were without sin. "The men who were party to the earlier trouble have been confined to camp for a month," he concluded. And that turned out to be longer than the time left at Auxi.[21]

It was a good thing when the 17th finally began to inch back into the war. It rained a portion of almost every day following the first of September, but the squadron put up formations throughout. They alternated between three- and five-ship units and worked to relate the training to what they supposed had happened since last they had ventured near the front.

On September 5 they accepted assignments from Wing that brought them up for balloon patrols along the lines. Aggressive types were much annoyed by such assignments (although aware that they were needed to season new pilots). Clements wrote, "Tom Moore was called back to the 148th and left this morning...I certainly wish they had taken me back as well. I have not gotten quite accustomed to things here yet and although the C.O. is O.K. the spirit of the camp in general is way below the 148th."[22] And well that spirit might be; the losses on the second of September had been the 148th's only serious set back and they had scored at least eight kills since the 17th's calamity of August 26.

But now at least the 17th could see what was going on. And

Samuel B. Eckert in command. His regalia is fairly typical for 17th warriors by late summer: English style blouse and trousers with hacked-off flying boots. Wing was not amused at the mutilation of the footwear. (Frank A. Dixon)

soon Clements could speak more positively about the situation. "On our patrol this morning, we saw plenty activity. Huns were chasing our fellows back about as fast as they would go over the lines. The Huns are on the offensive around here now and we can't exactly make them out. It must be a circus of some kind because they have all kinds of machines mixed up among them. Nearly every squadron on the front now has lost a bunch of men on account of these new Huns coming up here. Our line is steadily advancing beyond Bapaume and toward Cambrai. Here's hoping they soon take Cambrai."[23] This wish would be granted in time. Continuing pressure all along the front had resulted in a general withdrawal toward the Hindenburg Line and the spring offensive was quickly being undone. When the 17th finally got back into action, they found that they were now half an hour's flying time from the front.

By the evening of September 7, the 17th began bending their assignments to venture across the lines a bit. And they paid for this as always. Ellison's ship was badly shot up when Archie struck it almost directly. "It nearly scared him to death," Clements wrote. "Just think of what he has to go through."[24] This was the first of a series of mishaps that would eventually destroy the young pilot's usefulness.

On Tuesday, September 10, the squadron got a specific assignment and began participating in a technical kind of warfare. The exercise was aimed specifically at enemy observation planes, some of which now flew along radioing running reports via a telegraph key and trailing wire antenna. While a primitive radio triangulation system had been developed for locating them, the retiring lines had placed squadron aerodromes so far west that the offending enemy pilots were generally gone before the fighters could come on station.

It was believed the problem could be solved by establishing lightly-manned forward landing areas equipped with radio, which would receive reports from numerous sources and steer attackers to the enemy accordingly. Flights would man the station in rotation and there await a call to action. Also, a small supply of bombs was to be stored onsite for occasional forays against local adversaries.

The site chosen for the 17th was a ruined field three miles north of Bapaume near the remains of Beugnatre, a locale until recently in German possession.[25] A dozen enlisted men went first. They splashed their way there by lorry one long night, amid gusting winds and slashing rain, to arrive at daybreak and behold a sorry sight. Trees around the area were smashed to flinders. The airdrome itself was a mass of interlocking shell holes, the quarters were unrecognizable, and the service roads proved nearly impassable. With sinking hearts they realized that, while pilots would fly home every night, this was to be their lot until the game was called.

Finding no other really suitable shelter, they took refuge (despite a swarm of sleek corpse-fattened rats that already held possession) in the deep dugouts built there by the Germans. Offended at the cold-footed way the rodents had of walking across his face while he was trying to sleep, medic A. V. Haig soon announced that he had no intention of abiding there further. Although it was said that German soldiers still sometimes prowled the area, Haig scrounged up a serviceable German rifle and some ammunition and established his home and clinic in one of the ruined shacks above ground. He made it clear that if he heard anything at night he would challenge first in English, then in French, and then in gunfire—aimed straight through the door of the hut. If nothing else, this kept malingerers from consulting the medic after hours.[26]

The troops were just setting about making the place fit for aircraft when A Flight swooped in, spearheaded by Eckert who came to assess the situation for himself. At 9 a.m. Ralph Snoke led Desson, Donoho, France, and Myers on offensive patrol from there to an area across the lines, the first time they had officially gone into the enemy skies in fifteen days. They managed to chase an enemy two-seater away from Cambrai, then turned for Auxi.[27]

Rain curtailed activities for a bit, which gave the ground crew a chance to better prepare the landing area. And by the fourth day (another Friday the 13th), the triangulation plan was beginning to function well. That afternoon the 17th scored its first victory since

August and Howard Knotts gained the glory.

B Flight had held sway at the landing area all morning, with no luck. About 3 p.m., Eckert led in C Flight for their first visit and the two flights went out and worked the lines together without success. At that, B Flight turned for Auxi and C Flight returned to the outpost to see what might develop. Soon after 6 p.m. the radio began to pick up urgent chatter concerning German planes moving north along the lines directly abreast of them. Shortly Clements, Knotts, Giesecke, Schneider, and Ellison were a mile high in the air and heading northeast with the sun at their backs.

It was an ideal attack position and they soon spied two Fokkers stalking an RE-8 working on the near side of the lines. One of the Fokkers went for the British machine just as the Camels came out of the sun in attack formation; the second pilot spotted them and instantly fled eastward with the five Americans in hot pursuit. Realizing what was happening, the first Fokker pilot broke off his attack on the RE-8 and rushed to his comrade's aid. He swooped across the lines and went at the Camels firing steady bursts intended to distract them from their game. Knotts saw him coming and made a climbing turn that put him behind the brave German, who now fell to raking Ellison's ship fore and aft. This neophyte was startled to find tracers blazing between his wings and bracing wires parting from random bullet strikes. The troubles ended abruptly, however, as Knotts opened from eighty yards and the attacking Fokker

Left to right: Howard Burdick, Howard Knotts, possibly at Auxi-le-Chateau. On September 13 Knotts shot down the squadron's first enemy since the bad day in August. Five days later Burdick achieved his first victory. (Clinton Burdick)

snapped over on its back and spun downward in wide circles to disappear, still inverted, into the gathering mists below. The 148th was flying a low patrol in the area and saw the German machine crash near Inchen-Artois. The other Fokker escaped, although so badly shot up that the 17th pilots figured it was only luck if he made it home.[28]

At that, they returned to Auxi and held a general celebration. The squadron was back in the war, this was Knott's second victory, and there was news that Vaughn, Hamilton, and Mert Campbell had been awarded the Distinguished Flying Cross by the British. Sadly, Hamilton and Campbell were no longer around to receive their honors, and Vaughn's was in recognition of efforts with another squadron, but still the event was inspirational. These were the first decorations to arrive in the squadron.[29]

It was not long before Knotts scored again, racking up one and possibly two kills—and again blasting a Fokker off Ellison's tail. This followed three days of sporadic and fruitless sorties over the lines in response to radio messages. On the fourth day Clements, Campbell, Knotts, Schneider, and Ellison left the advanced landing area around 6:30 p.m. on a line patrol that would end with their returning to Auxi. Just as they were turning for home they had, as Clements wrote, "the good fortune to have about twelve Huns come down on us."[30] Actually there were seventeen Fokkers on the scene, eleven that came down to attack and six that stayed above to pounce on stragglers.

C Flight turned to meet the attack and Ellison almost immediately got into trouble. Again he was being tailed by a German pilot and shot to pieces. His every maneuver to escape ended with his coming once more into a hail of lead from his pursuer. Fortunately Knotts saw. He broke off his attack on another Fokker and fired a single burst that sent the enemy plane spinning off apparently out of control. At that Knotts turned back to the mêlée.

While no longer being attacked, Ellison's situation was not much improved. He found that his aileron controls had been shot away leaving him without lateral control of his ship—a dire situation in a Camel. Fortunately, he was headed for the friendly side of the lines. He chopped the throttle and went along waggling the rudder to ease the machine down without using the stick. Skilled Camel pilots called this "floating" and used it only as a last-ditch measure.[31]

Ellison was at 4,000 feet when hit and for a time it seemed that, being unable to do anything to extend his glide, he was doomed to land in German territory. But finally, he squeaked over through some heavy ground fire sent his way. He smashed down at Berthonval Farm, northeast of Mount St. Eloy with an impact so devastating that only the machine guns and Aldis sight were salvageable. Ellison emerged without a scratch, if one discounted a long jagged scar in his peace of mind.

Behind him, the fight raged on. Clements got a Fokker in his sight and was pounding him from the side when Knotts raced back and began to help from the other side. Caught in this crossfire, the

James A. Ellison came to the 17th in late August and was assigned to C Flight. Shortly thereafter he ventured across the lines to become involved in a series of close calls. He is seen here chopping wood for a fireplace of his own devising. (Lorenz K. Ayers)

George A. Vaughn, Jr. was known universally as "Bob" Vaughn in those days. He was a seasoned warrior when he transferred from RAF 84 to lead B Flight in the 17th. He is shown here in the rear of his home in Brooklyn, New York. (George A. Vaughn)

Jesse Digman. While refueling a Camel one night, Digman was amazed to see flames erupt around a nearby lantern and streak toward the aircraft on which he was working. (Roy Hively)

German pilot had no chance and went down immediately. The pair split the claim.[32]

Intent on raising the score to one apiece, the two then went for a White-tailed Fokker whose pilot Clements nominated, "the best I have run up against in France. Just as soon as we got within range we started shooting. He looped and nearly hit me. When he came out of his loop he did a 'half roll'. I was shooting continually but had small chance of hitting him with such maneuvers."[33] Soon both Clements and Knotts had gun malfunctions, at which they scooted for home. It was again a jubilant evening once Ellison called in and reported himself whole.

The next day, Wednesday, September 18, Wing unexpectedly ordered the 17th to move some 20 miles farther east to an aerodrome called Soncamp, near the town of Sombrin. In response to this sudden development all flights journeyed to the advanced landing field to assist in concluding their business there, for that experiment was also at an end.

Since the squadron had drawn a balloon assignment for the afternoon, the flight leaders decided to merge the two situations; they would expend the available bombs on the balloon assignment instead of hauling them to the rear. The plan was for B Flight to approach and decoy the enemy while A and C Flights swept in from elsewhere and bombed the winch that controlled the balloon. At that, B Flight would turn and go for the bag itself.[34]

But these plans had to wait a bit. Suddenly, while the bombs were being trucked to the planes, the radio began to chatter that two observation craft ripe for the taking were working just across the line. Since B Flight was first on call, Vaughn, Wicks, and Burdick took up the message. They crossed the lines and found a pair of LVGs coasting over Rumilly. The two seaters spotted them and sank into some nearby clouds, but Vaughn kept his command prowling above the cover, certain that the prey would reappear. They did just that, rising gradually through the mist, and the trio was on them immediately. Vaughn and Wicks straddled one and caught it in a cross fire. The gunner responded valiantly but futilely. Eventually, he pitched over dead, and shortly afterward the German craft nosed into a steep dive straight for earth.[35]

Meanwhile, Burdick took the other craft broadside from the left, braving the observer's fire until he was firing from only fifty yards out. The observer suddenly flopped and in a moment the entire plane burst into flames and began falling. Burdick was ecstatic. "I have broken the ice at last," he wrote home the next day. "Yesterday I shot down my first Hun machine. It was a two-seater and burst into flames while I was still firing. He burned all the way to the ground, and although it's a cold-blooded thing to say, I watched him every foot of the way (there being no other Huns about) and I was quite tickled to death."[36]

The jubilant youth and his companions were back at the landing area by 11:10. At that, C Flight departed to scout the intended afternoon target and came back shortly to report it bobbing happily just where expected. The fliers then had an uneasy lunch—balloon strafing was easier as a sudden inspiration than as an assignment—and whiled away time until the appointed hour of 2:45 approached.

The morning's work had been glorious; the afternoon attack did not go quite so well. The basic plan was fine. Fourteen planes went off. Eight carried bombs to use against the ground crew, five were assigned to fly cover for the operation, and one—Vaughn—carried the Buckingham (incendiary) ammunition with which to fire the bag.

They found the target still tugging at its anchor at 3,000 feet.

Howard Burdick's Camel, serial number F2141, with its identification letter L. A big part of this particular Camel's excellence was the man in the cockpit. (Clinton Burdick)

The Camels were stacked down from 8,000 feet and trying to appear disinterested in anything as trivial as a mere balloon. Then suddenly Campbell and Giesecke, carrying the main load of bombs, tucked down and went for the winch mechanism. Others followed closely behind and intense ground fire rose to meet all. Vaughn came last, striving to catch the bobbing sinking bag in his sight. He saw bombs strike the winch area and quickly took up the now more stationary target. Everything looked perfect. The target grew and grew and then he was only a hundred yards above it and firing. There was one good burst, and a second, then both guns went stone dead under his thumbs. He hauled on the stick and simultaneously searched along the left side of the cockpit for the handle on his hydraulic reservoir. It was down and the system was on the fritz. There was nothing to do but turn away. Twelve more bombs went into the area, but the 17th headed home without being positive that anything had been accomplished. Wicks thought he noticed the bag smoking a bit after Vaughn's brief attack, but there had been no sudden flash of extinction.[37]

The rest of the day was spent in closing out the Beugnatre base and getting back to Auxi. Then, after settling in and sharing their balloon misfortune, the fliers were entertained with yet another bit of drama. At about 9 p.m., there came sudden shouting from the tarmac and the sounds of many running feet. A fire had broken out in A Flight's hangar and the officers joined the rush of enlisted men to discover Jesse Digman, Herb Wilson, and Howard Falkenstein battling a blaze that was threatening to devour John Myers' Camel. Extinguishers soon put an end to the matter amid heavy smoke and much coughing.

Digman had been working on the plane by night and since the only available drop light was being used by Wilson on another aircraft, he had resorted to a covered lantern, which he placed on the ground some ten feet away. As he went about the business, Digman was astonished to see flames suddenly erupt from the ground around the lamp and race toward him and the Camel. Of course, heavy gasoline fumes had drifted down the fuselage and wafted across the grass to the lantern.[38]

Despite such thrilling events, the big excitement of that night had to be the pending departure for the unit's third base of the war. Old hands who could remember the ordeals that followed the last move must have gone to bed a bit uneasy the night of September 18.

A better idea of what Burdick's Camel looked like can be had through this museum-grade model made by Mr. John Bell. The markings are based on views of the original machine. Notice how the fabric was cut away in the center section to improve visibility. (George Roland)

This picture was taken on September 21, as the officers were erecting their tent at Soncamp. Left to right: Glen D. Wicks, Gerald P. Thomas, George A. Vaughn, Theose Tillinghast. The next day Thomas was shot down in flames and Tillinghast was captured. Wicks had a little over two weeks to live when this photo was taken. (Lorenz Ayers)

9

The Proof of the Pudding

How well the 17th Aero Squadron had been rebuilt was demonstrated quickly. Within days of arriving at Soncamp, the flights began dealing the enemy the kind of blows the 17th had suffered on August 26. It is probable that, without loss, they shot down seven Fokkers on a single patrol.[1] Their happiness at such heartening developments was, however, somewhat tempered by reflections on the nastiness of their new bivouac.

Soncamp aerodrome was on an ancient farm close by the village of Sombrim, a scattered and nondescript settlement on the road from Grand Rullecourt to Saulty. Nothing about it was very inviting. While the mechanics were quartered in battered Adrian huts erected by some previous occupants now long gone, the officers again had to eke out an existence in tents, not a particularly desirable situation with October coming on. And since the weather had become very rainy, the chief characteristic of the new station was mud.[2]

The ground troops discovered this first. They arrived on September 19 amid a steady rain to find the small roadway leading to the station soundly blocked by two lorries sunk more than axle deep, in which condition the vehicles had obviously been for some time. Next it developed that there were questions about which quarters the squadron was to occupy if ever they did manage to slog their way onto the base. At that, Bingo Wells contacted Eckert to delay the departure of the pilots and planes until things could be sorted out.

Thus eighteen Camels came flying into Soncamp in the mist and rain on Friday, September 20, a day later than so ordered. Eckert had not been able to contact Wing about this problem and immediately sat down to pen a report to Fowler should there be any criticism.[3] Meanwhile, amid much slipping and sliding, the pilots pitched their domiciles and wandered off to meet the Dolphin pilots of RAF 87 with whom they were to share the base and collaborate on missions.

This collaboration was an affair dreamed up by Headquarters. The theory was that the Dolphin, a Sopwith creation specifically designed for service at altitudes around 22,000 feet, could hover overhead during engagements to fend off unexpected threats and deal with planes chased higher by Camels. However, these were notions about which pilots in the two squadrons were not hopeful. Dolphin men looked upon the Camel as a frightful relic of little use and pitied their new-found friends for having to fly it. Camel merchants, in turn, lamented the Dolphin's poor handling qualities at

This panoramic view at Soncamp was created by combining two pictures made from the same spot. To reach the flight line, one went straight ahead and turned right at the end of the lane where the squadron office can be seen. Left: Floyd Showalter with Harriss Alderman resting his arm on Showalter's shoulder. Center: Albert F. Schneider. (Mrs. Gordon Kellogg, Cuthbert Tunstall)

At Soncamp the 17th was in support of RAF 87 Dolphin squadron. Since the Dolphin (seen here) was designed for high altitude service, it was a poor mix. Camel men scorned the Dolphin, saying it had a tendency to shed its wings in tight corners. (Frank A. Dixon)

low altitudes and spoke sorrowfully of its tendency to shed wings when jerked about in combat.[4]

These things being as they might, the squadrons decided to try the idea that very day. Together, A and C Flights went off on September 20 with the Dolphins in mid-afternoon for a long familiarization run that passed as an offensive patrol. They saw a derelict balloon and two enemy aircraft below them when they approached the lines, but judged them not to be worth breaking formation. During this patrol the Camels were flown at 14,000 feet, higher than the squadron had flown in a month, and Howard Knotts was obliged to turn back ill after an hour at altitude. If there were any blessings in the new marriage, they were not discovered.[5]

Saturday was windy and rainy and gave the squadron a chance to better understand the bleakness of their situation. They slogged around in the mud and tinkered with problems. There was a bit of chaffing now to be assuaged in A Flight because Snoke, commanding during Goodnow's leave, had allowed the pilots to contemplate

A moment of silliness at Soncamp. Enjoying what appears to be a champagne breakfast are left to right, seated: Leonard Desson, Howard Burdick, John Donoho (face hidden by bottle), Frank Dixon. The four are under the watchful eye of Dr. Jacob J. Ross. (Frank A. Dixon)

Weston W. Goodnow with his ever present pipe. Seen in the background is George Vaughn. (Samuel B. Eckert)

increased freedom in the pursuit of targets. Goodnow soon nipped this idea in the bud, however, and called for even closer, tighter formations—and, of course, had his way. At that, Snoke took off for French leave (which in those days meant authorized leave spent in France). The passage of time and the changing of technology make it difficult to say which leader's philosophy was right. True, A Flight would never again lose a man. But on the other hand, they never again downed an enemy plane.

However, having the most seasoned pilots did make A Flight the most stable unit in a fairly new organization. Accordingly, just as it had done with C Flight the day before, when the weather cleared enough for an evening patrol on September 21, it accompanied B Flight (sans Dolphins) on that unit's first foray to the front. Although the patrol turned out to be a relatively passive affair, the flights found the sky filled with swarms of German planes. The formation passed under a flight of eight Fokkers as they crossed the lines, tangled briefly with five more north of Cambrai without results, and carefully avoided a trap on the way home. This consisted of a German two-seater wallowing about at 10,000 feet as though helpless while six Fokkers watched from 13,000 feet and another six backed the play from higher up. The most exciting and disturbing observation regarding the patrol was made by Goodnow. By their black-and-white-checked tails, he recognized the five Fokkers engaged near Cambrai as belonging to one of the units (Jasta 26) that had so decimated the 17th a month earlier.[6]

Dixon, who had also seen those Fokkers on that occasion, confirmed this the next day following a deadly struggle over the front.

This is an F2.b two-seat Bristol fighter (Brisfit) the type that participated in the morning battle on September 22. RAF 87's Dolphins were also present at the major scrap. Clements wrote in his diary of the period, "Each day we think we have seen the worst fight." (Clinton Burdick)

Howard Knotts' Camel, D3328. On September 22, the 17th's C Flight jumped two Fokkers of Jasta 26. Flying this plane, Knotts joined Clements in chasing the enemy for nearly a mile before Knotts got in a burst for the squadron's first kill at Soncamp. (Mrs. John B. Dixon)

B and C Flights lifted off at 8 a.m. in the company of the Dolphins to try again this new arrangement. As they crossed the lines at 12,000 feet (with the Dolphins up another thousand) they immediately encountered fifteen Fokkers flying above all. Vaughn and Dixon saw the formation first and quickly called attention to it to Wicks, Tillinghast, and Thomas—the last two being still fairly new at this game. At about the same time the Dolphins spied the enemy and turned to challenge.

Despite these developments the Fokkers seemed only vaguely interested. This was because C Flight, consisting of Clements, Campbell, Knotts, Schneider, and Giesecke (another inexperienced man), had come along behind and below B Flight and flown on into Hunland without recognizing the impending confrontation for what it was. Clements took his unit over Rumilly where they soon discovered two Fokkers with black-and-white-checked tails (Jasta 26) worrying a Bristol Fighter crew and making it plenty hot for them.

C Flight moved to help the embattled Brisfit. Clements and Knotts jumped on the Fokkers and immediately chased them down and westward, away from the harried British pilot. The four planes whirled about firing on each other for nearly a mile. Then, while racing free of Clements, one of the Fokker pilots made the mistake of turning in front of Knotts. Knotts swung on him in an instant and sent a long burst into the plane from twenty yards out. The effect was immediate; the pilot involuntarily threw up his hands as the bullets struck him and the Fokker went spinning away. As Knotts watched the plane came under momentary control, then flopped onto its back and crashed in some woods just across the line. It was the 17th's first kill on the new front.[7]

C Flight's pilots had so concentrated on this fight that they were still unaware of the danger above. But the Fokkers saw C Flight at work and immediately nominated them for extinction. The enemy shifted their attention away from B Flight and the Dolphins and made directly for Clements' crew.

Vaughn saw this evolving and simultaneously spied fifteen more Fokkers moving into the fight higher above. It occurred to him at once that now there were two puzzles working: there was a need to deflect one group of Fokkers from diving on C Flight below; and there was a need to position B Flight to respond to attack from above. Since it seemed to him that C Flight was doomed without intervention, he chose to work that puzzle first. Without hesitation he flung his five Camels directly into the path of the first fifteen descending enemy planes.[8]

An awesome dogfight erupted. Gerald Thomas (nicknamed "Kewpie" for his elfinlike resemblance to the latest souvenir doll) was killed quickly—the last man to die in the 17th as a direct result of enemy action.[9] The more experienced Theose Tillinghast fared some better, but not much. As Vaughn led the flight among the foe, Tilly fastened onto a Fokker piloted by a very skillful flier and tried his best to down him. "I didn't get a shot," he wrote later, "though I rode his tail for probably a minute or perhaps more. As other Fokkers joined the scramble I could see no Camels about and decided I'd better get out. I put my plane in a near vertical dive (80 degrees) and twisted around to watch my tail. When any chap came near shooting position, I rolled 180 degrees. Of this I am certain—from 10,000 feet to 25 feet where I leveled out to zigzag home, I was untouched.

"Three Fokkers followed me down and probably were taking long range shots at me as I took evasive action at 25 to 50 feet altitude. During this, no tracers came anywhere near me. As I was over the trenches, my engine suddenly quit. I have always suspected a bullet from the ground, as that instant I was only about 20 feet and nothing in sight but shell holes and barbed wire. I determined to keep zigzagging and crash rather than land straight ahead with those three Fokkers behind me, but I guess habit was too strong. I did at the last minute straighten out for a crash landing. At that instant, I was surrounded by tracers and my lower wings were riddled. I landed upside down in a large shell hole surrounded by German infantry."[10]

Behind him, Vaughn, torn between his desire to protect C Flight and the realization that he had led his men into terrible danger, was fighting like the ace he was. He dived steeply on a Fokker circling toward two unsuspecting Camels and gave him a good burst. The German pitched upward, then went spinning down through the rest of the milling planes. Dixon saw it burst into flames and drop to the ground southwest of Cambrai.

Vaughn had no time to admire his handiwork—a second Fokker was trying to stick to his tail. Vaughn managed to loop and double back on his pursuer, turning hunter into hunted. He hit the German from above and behind with steady fire and the plane began to drop in a series of sideslips and steep dives. Again the B Flight commander's attention was diverted, for the second wave of Fokkers had arrived on the scene and tracer bullets began to whistle by his face. Dixon saw Vaughn's last opponent spin into the earth.

Now it was time to work the second puzzle. Among the attackers was Lt. Fredrich Noltenius of Jasta 27, the man who had helped Bittinger to his grave on August 26. In his diary he later gave his version of what happened next. "When we arrived in the battle zone, the Sopwith [Vaughn] attacked another Fokker even though I sat immediately behind. I, too, fired at once. Then another Fokker wedged himself between the Sopwith and me and the dogfight continued. Alternately, Mesch, Neuenhofen, and I were behind him. Finally, Neuenhofen got close enough, kept behind him and forced him down for good."[11]

Not quite. The mistaken claim no doubt resulted from the general confusion. Vaughn certainly was driven down by a trio of Fokkers, down to where he could see barbed wire spinning toward him. He pulled out at last, and at that Lt. Neuenhofen struck him with a long burst. Vaughn leaned on the throttle to pull away—and nothing happened. Somewhere earlier in the fight, a bullet had pierced his fuel tank and it was dry. As his attackers broke off to fly home and make a claim, Vaughn switched to his reserve and flew away. He was on the carpet on the wrong side of the lines, but he was alive and limping homeward.

Above and behind him the fight died away. The Dolphins had never gotten near enough to the action to fire a shot. Wicks had been chased below the main fight, but found an enemy plane west of Rumilly and sent him crashing. And the rest of the Americans merely survived.[12]

Some were home making their reports when Vaughn came drifting in. His plane was a flying wreck, but he managed to set it down safely and deliver it to his appalled ground crew. The spar in the right upper plane was shot through, three struts on the right side of the fuselage forward of the cockpit were splintered, and the lower left main plane and aileron were shot through. On the way home, Vaughn realized that his wild maneuvers had drenched him with gasoline from the damaged tank.

A cousin to the much published photo of Vaughn in the field. Vaughn is wearing a ribbon representing the British Distinguished Flying Cross. Behind Vaughn, left to right: John A. Myers, Charles W. France. (Samuel B. Eckert)

Strangely, so successful had been Vaughn's gambit (for which he received the American Distinguished Service Cross) that C Flight scarcely realized that it had been under attack. Geisecke knew; it was almost the last thing he knew. He had been at the back of the formation and concentrating on the earlier action when suddenly tracers began ripping into his fuselage. He would have been doomed had not Vaughn's move turned the attack aside. Thankfully, Giesecke swung for home and managed to get his shot-up Camel across the lines and down at an aerodrome operated by RAF 12.[13]

It had been quite a morning. The four victories were confirmed shortly, making it one of their more productive days. In fact, five victories were confirmed that day for the powers-that-be also erroneously credited Rodney Williams with a kill—and Williams had been flat on his belly in hospital for exactly a month.[14] It was, no doubt, belated confirmation of some earlier victory. This made Williams the squadron's fifth ace. The others were Vaughn, Hamilton, Tipton, and Todd.[15]

The 17th stood down for the rest of the day and cleaned up its mess. Two planes had been badly damaged and two were lost, so there was much to be done. B Flight was again cruelly reduced in numbers and the survivors began turning covetous eyes upon Lt. Edgar White, who had been in the squadron five whole days. White

John F. Donoho was with the 17th about a month before being caught up in a major scrap. He sailed away unscathed. Seen here at Soncamp. (Cuthbert Tunstall)

was yet another Cornell graduate, a slight young man of less than average height who had celebrated his 23rd birthday the day he arrived in France. He was as anxious to get in the game as B Flight was to have him, and, with special handling, would cross the lines two days before he had been on station two weeks. He would be on his way home, wounded, by the end of his third week.

The weather improved enough for C Flight to go on patrol at 5 p.m. But it cost the squadron another man before the formation got out of sight. Immediately after liftoff, Ellison's engine went dead and he had a dicey time making it back to the field. That was his last flight with the 17th. In his brief history with the squadron he had been come back in a plane trashed by Archie, flown down with his controls shot away, survived a major crash resulting from enemy action, and landed dud from low altitude. It seemed that he was nearly killed every time he went into the air, and Doc Ross grounded the badly-shaken man. The squadron was short another pilot.

The weather broke for better flying on Tuesday and the squadron made it memorable. September 24 proved to be a complete

Edgar G. White joined the 17th on September 17, just days after his twenty-third birthday. These documents are his A.E.F. identity card and his Aero Club of America aviator certificate. (Edgar G. White)

disaster for German fliers. The 148th started things off with a 7:30 a.m. patrol to Cambrai. They found the sky filled with enemy planes and soon tangled with a German unit known among local fliers as the Bavarian Blue Tails. Six of the enemy went down in battle without loss to the 148th, which soon headed home to make sure the 17th heard about it.[16]

The 17th arrived on the scene about 10 a.m. They were fourteen strong: Desson, Donoho, France, and Myers were behind Goodnow; Burdick followed Vaughn with Dixon and Wicks; in C Flight, Clements had Campbell, Giesecke, Knotts, and Schneider. This patrol would prove a perfect counterpoint to the one of two days previous—before long C Flight would mount an effort to save B Flight from annihilation.

The Americans saw twenty-nine Fokkers in three formations at about three miles altitude when they crossed the lines, but these showed no interest in them and all passed along peaceably. A few minutes later, however, B Flight, which was in the lead at about

A long shot of Camels on the field at Soncamp. (Clinton Burdick)

The man from the paint shop has apparently finished painting the spinner on Howard Burdick's plane. It cannot be determined if such a spinner was thought to be beneficial or if it just represented individual dash and style. (Cuthbert Tunstall)

William Clements in the field attired in a mixed RAF/U.S. costume. (Mrs. Gordon Kellogg)

This photo was taken in the field during the very heavy aerial combat period of late September. Second from left: Jesse Campbell. Far right: George A. Vaughn. Others unidentified. (Lorenz K. Ayers)

10,000 feet (with the other flights stacked up and back at 2,000 foot intervals) dived to engage two observation planes low over Havrincourt. It was an ineffectual move because both Dixon and Wicks found that their guns had gone dead. The already undermanned flight was now half armed. Still, the flight did chase the foe past a canal south of Cambrai, then climbed back to 6,000 feet—only to find that they had been suckered. Sixteen Fokkers were diving on them.

Fortunately the other flights had retained their altitude and Clements led all ten planes into the fray. As had been the case two days earlier, a wild dogfight broke out when they met. Clements wrote in his diary of the affair, "Each day we think we have seen the worst fight. The climax was reached this morning when the worst yet happened. Some people think the Hun can't scrap. Well, I thought they couldn't either until I ran into the best scrapper this morning I have ever seen, including Allied and Hun...

"It was a darned good crowd and you had to fight. I fought one bird from 6,000 feet to the ground. I used every possible maneuver I have ever learned but he could do them all as well and better than I could. Around and around we went, until I was absolutely on the carpet. I had just gotten a good burst into him when another Hun got on my tail. I don't think my burst went wild that time because when I had a chance to look again, there was a Fokker on his back right beneath me. I claimed him, of course...My machine was all shot to pieces. Explosives had hit all around me, I was darned lucky to get out alive..."[17]

They all were. France and Giesecke soon found that their guns were also out, leaving the fight to ten Camels. Goodnow's policy worked well in keeping the enemy off troubled B Flight. Desson lined up on a Fokker and began chewing the cockpit away, then lost sight of the prey under the attack of others. Donoho, in his first major dogfight, found himself head-on with a Fokker and exchanging fire at fifteen feet before the plane passed under and into Goodnow's sights.

But undermanned and half unarmed, B Flight was having a bad time of it. Vaughn drove a Fokker off the defenseless Wicks with a 200 round burst into the side, which caused it to spin down and out of the fight. Just then he was himself jumped from behind and forced to bank away. A bright yellow and green Fokker attaced itself to Dixon's tail and was following him through a half roll when Burdick came to the rescue. Burdick executed the same maneuver and poured tracers into the enemy from twenty-five yards out. The enemy plane turned on its back and went spinning to the ground northwest of Havrincourt.

But ultimately, the day really belonged to C Flight. Schneider managed his first kill by hopping onto an adversary's tail and peppering him through a long descent. The enemy turned over on its back, righted itself momentarily, then flipped over again and crashed. Schneider missed seeing this because he spotted an SE-5 from another unit under attack from the rear while it was, in turn, attacking another Fokker. Schneider joined the parade but was too late to save the British craft. The enemy got away.

Leonard Desson on laundry day. Remembered by others for highjinks, he looks here as though something has just gone splendidly. (Lorenz K. Ayers)

Jesse Campbell caught his man at 8,000 feet. They had come slipping, twisting, turning downward for nearly a mile before he finally sent a burst directly into the German's cockpit. The Fokker flopped over and dropped.

This morning was a triumph for Howard Knotts. Clements was to write that night, "Knotts shot one Hun off my tail and probably saved my life...[he] got two Huns and celebrated the scrap by going out in the afternoon and blowing up an ammunition dump. He is a priceless fellow and worth his weight in gold to me."[18]

The lanky midwesterner had been riding a enemy's tail when he looked down and saw a red Fokker with a green tail boring in on his flight commander. Clements, preoccupied with downing his own prey, was unaware that he was about to be attacked. Knotts immediately turned for the German, gave him 100 rounds, and watched with satisfaction as the Fokker crashed at Coupez Mill.

At that point he too began to experience gun trouble. As he began climbing west to seek safety among the other Camels, he suddenly heard the stuttering of Spandaus behind him. He immediately banked hard to the right and caught a glimpse of a black-and-white-checkered plane with a white tail after him. Knowing that nothing could turn tighter than a Camel, Knotts held the turn until finally he was behind his attacker. At that he thumbed his machine guns, which fired instantly, much to his surprise. The Fokker burst into flames and went down. It was his fifth kill, but there was no time to celebrate. Four more Fokkers came over to see if something couldn't be done about this. Knotts nosed over and went diving away, rocking from wing tip to wing tip to provide a trickier target.[19]

It worked. Knotts arrived back at camp ten minutes after everybody else. The pilots were black faced, tired, and ecstatic. They believed no less than seven German planes had gone down in the battle (five were officially confirmed), which gave them an impressive total on this new front.

Knotts was now an ace. Most had had enough work for that day, but the young pilot was wired and longing for more action. He found a willing ally in his buddy Burdick, who had also scored that day and was also still thirsting. Finally, they made up their own afternoon patrol. They took Ed White out to show him the front, during which Knotts was to slip across the lines and try to confirm a kill made by Jesse Campbell that morning.

And it worked just that way. Shortly after leaving his companions at the lines, Knotts saw the wreckage where Campbell thought it might be. He was down at 1,000 feet at the time and keeping a wary eye on twenty-nine enemy planes some 7,000 feet above him. Just as he was prepared to turn and run out from under this blanket of Fokkers, he spied a large number of soldiers and two trucks moving along the Bapaume-Cambrai road dead ahead of him. Figuring this chance was too good to pass up, he extended his dive until he was spreading death among the troops and smashing the trucks. Then, as he passed over, he caught sight of a suspicious lump beside the road and guessed that he might have stumbled upon a hidden ammunition dump. He changed his line of fire and immediately proved his hunch. The results, in fact, exceeded expectation. All the real estate visible to him suddenly pulsed up to meet his Camel, then dropped back around him amid boiling smoke and dust. The explosion was reported by troops as far as fifteen miles away.[20]

It dawned dull and rainy on Wednesday, September 25. The squadron had opportunity to sit and savor their victories and to contemplate their latest assignment. They were now to start their missions with a bombing and strafing run, after which they would climb to altitude and engage the host of enemy planes in the area.

Howard Knotts became an ace on September 24 when he downed his fifth enemy plane. The next day he badly bent his plane (seen here inverted). Although he was uninjured, Dr. Ross considered him to be suffering from combat fatigue and sent him off for a rest in the hospital. (Clinton Burdick)

This was not a totally unexpected turn of events. The squadron's move to Soncamp was part of a two-week push by the British First, Second, and Third Armies (and eventually, the Fourth Army) in the area between Cambrai and St. Quentin to the south. Since this was the last and strongest of the German's prepared positions it was believed that victory here would set the stage for the last drive of the war.

But the squadron was hardly eager for an extended assignment. Not counting the losses of August 26, more pilots had been lost in the 17th during ground attacks than through aerial combat. They had only nine armored seats to share among fifteen available pilots. And these few pilots got fewer still at the end of evening patrol. Knotts crashed on landing when the left axle broke on his plane and sent the craft over on its nose. He was unhurt, but the resulting physical showed that he was suffering from nervous fatigue, and probably Spanish influenza. Doctor Ross sent him out for a week's rest at the local hospital. The 17th would have to embark on its dangerous assignment without the man deemed worth his weight in gold.[21]

The dreaded duty came quickly, although Thursday turned out to be almost totally dud and the fliers droned quietly through two uneventful patrols. But then word came that on Friday the British would rise on a thirteen-mile front before Cambrai and attempt to carry the city. All fighter squadrons were expected to harass the enemy east of the lines and see that enemy planes did not do the same to the attackers.

It was all very exciting, if worrisome, and early in the morning Major Fowler flew in to tie up with B Flight and get a look at the show. Shortly all were suiting up, for already the weather was chilly at altitude. This was the tricky part of their new assignment. Plan as they might, pilots would usually find themselves too heavily dressed for low level work, then sweaty when they climbed after the enemy.

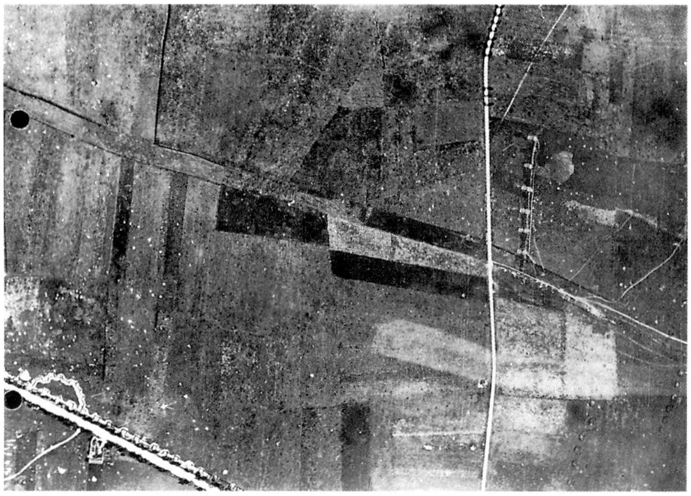

This aerial view shows an artillery battery along the road at the right and a trench system at lower left. Note the pock-marked fields. The 17th and 148th were directed to attack targets of these types in support of forces moving against Bapaume and Cambrai. (Clinton Burdick)

At 10 a.m. the squadron put up seventeen planes, one being flown by Harriss Alderman (who had arrived back the night before declaring himself cured and demanding to become part of the drive) and another transporting Ed White (who was going along to show Alderman the lines). This pair turned off as the others crossed the front. Later Alderman noted coyly in his log that he had been "showing Lt. Alderman the lines."

The morning turned out to be easy. Showalter developed engine trouble at once and had to set down in a field. Schneider could only drop two of his four bombs and had to turn back before the patrol lifted for high altitude work. And Geisecke's engine went bad just after dive bombing Fontaine-Notre Dame and the surrounding Bourlon woods. Still all were home shortly after noon without a scratch or scrape. They had seen nothing to strafe; no pitched battles had developed in the air. Tensions were eased and nerves loosened a notch.[22]

Fowler went away to make a mission with the 148th, but the 17th had no trouble getting up a 4 p.m. patrol. Both Alderman and White announced that they were major warriors and ready—and went along, although neither carried bombs.

The Camels crossed the lines at 4:40 and turned toward a bridge crossing the Canal De L'Essaut at Marcoing. It was carrying heavy traffic as a result of the drive, and Allied command wanted it hit. Although five Fokkers were heading for them from Cambrai, the squadron ignored them, dropped to 2,500 feet, and placed fifty-two bombs among the troops clustered along the approaches to the structure. Apparently none hit the bridge itself.

At that the squadron rose to greet the Fokkers only to find them fleeing east at high speed. They saw no more until they prowled toward Cambrai, at which a large formation of German planes arrived and hovered above them awaiting their opportunity. Shortly the 17th turned for home with the cloud of enemy following. Then as they neared the lines Jesse Campbell noticed a lone Fokker skulking under clouding at 4,000 feet. He cut from formation and dived for the German who saw him coming at the last minute and tried to pull away. Campbell peppered his tail from seventy-five yards, at which the German rolled into a slow, downward spin and was last seen dropping at about a hundred feet. Now the Fokkers overhead began coming down in vengeance, but the squadron scooted across the lines and headed home well satisfied with their day.[23]

Duty pilots in the air weren't the only members of the 17th heading for home well satisfied that day. Theose Tillinghast, having sampled German hospitality for a day or so and found it wanting, was also on his way.

After being hauled from his plane by German infantry the previous Sunday, Tilly had been sent to the rear for questioning. There he met Lt. Hans Schröder, a German aviator turned intelligence officer.[24] Schröder, who had also interrogated Tipton and Todd a month earlier, had developed a modus operandi based on elementary psychology that hardly seems persuasive today. When he heard that a captured airman was down in his area he would arrange to be

Jesse Campbell proved a most staunch and dependable warrior during the fierce fights of September and October. (Mrs. Gordon Kellogg)

driven immediately to the site. There he would stop, as if by chance, and offer his aid to a distressed comrade of the air who just happened to wear a different uniform. The prisoner would thus find himself in friendly hands that wined, dined, and pumped.

In easier times the victim was often moved to relatively comfortable rooms where hidden dictaphones and such paraphernalia would gather tidbits from conversations with other pilots gleaned from the battlefield. But with the start of the present drive, times had ceased to be easy for the Germans and, since Tilly would volunteer nothing, he was summarily sent to a temporary prison at Fresnes. He arrived there in the company of a British airman, Robert A. Anderson, who had also been downed that day.

The prison was a converted farmhouse where the two immediately fell into bad company. They were tossed in with Oscar Mandell (well known by Tillinghast), who had been shot down from the 148th, and Lt. John Donaldson, an American attached to RAF 32 squadron. At the time of Tilly's arrival this pair was abiding in a sort of solitary confinement and feeding on bread and water, for having once escaped and caused their captors much grief.

They were a troublesome pair. They escaped from a prison at Douai on the very day they arrived by simply jumping out of a second-story window. And they managed to stay free five days, despite some near—and often comic—disasters. Once they were sleeping in the woods when a young German soldier unexpectedly came upon them. Mandell, who spoke excellent German and was wrapped in a greatcoat which covered his uniform, managed to persuade this innocent that they were a pair of German pilots who had sneaked into the woods for a nap.

Next they decided that, being near a German aerodrome, they should steal a plane and fly away. They got onto the station at daybreak and spent two hours in removing a craft from its hangar without exciting suspicion. Soon Donaldson was in the cockpit and Mandell was pulling the prop, at which a German mechanic came on the scene. He talked calmly with the two officers quite a while before realizing that they were wearing the wrong uniforms. He then began yelling for help and managed to stab Donaldson in the back before Mandell knocked him cold with a nearby flashlight.

They got away (but not by air) despite Donaldson's injury and then actually made their way through the German lines. But just as they were about to swim a small stream to the British side, they were apprehended by a German wiring party repairing the barbed wire and were marched back for punishment.

Such were the desperadoes into whose care Tillinghast now passed. And they were already planning a second escape. Sick of bread and water, and much worried that he had heedlessly willed his violin to a friend in the event of his death, Mandell wanted very much to get back to his squadron before the beneficiary could lay claim to the property.

As Tillinghast later reported: "Mandell recognized me as I walked through the prison doors and obtained permission for me to visit them. They advised that they had plans to escape that night and invited me to join them." Already, with the help of smuggled equipment provided by the British soldier-prisoner who served their meager meals, Mandell and Donaldson had cut a hole in the roof of the room next to their cell. The three Americans went out that night, together with Anderson and RAF Corporal George Rogers, who was serving a ten-year sentence of solitary confinement for hitting a German officer.

This 1919 view shows a Zeppelin hangar filled with German aircraft slated for destruction. The huge doors of the building, which frustrated escapees in the market for an aircraft, are most obvious. (U.S. Air Force Museum)

Due to a series of canals and deep marshes, they managed to get only a short distance from the prison that first night. But soon they made contact with French and Belgian farmers who savagely resented their German conquerors, and accordingly were only too happy to help the escapees along.

Furnished with civilian clothes, the little group reached the outskirts of Brussels within five days. Here Rogers and Mandell decided that the best thing for all would be for the two of them, as experienced escapees, to go into the city and seek additional help. They did so and were soon discovered, shot at, wounded, and recaptured.

When these comrades failed to return as expected, the other three soon guessed the reason and directed their trek toward the Netherlands by another route. Again and again they were provided with food, clothing, and money by local people. At one point they passed so near a German aerodrome at Berchem that they actually got on a streetcar in their donated finery and rode out to that installation to shop for a plane that they might steal. They had to abandon this when they saw that large zeppelin sheds were being used as hangars and that it would take more manpower to open the doors than they could muster.

The escape of Theose Tillinghast and his companions succeeded because of aid received along the way. Seen here are two such benefactors, who took them in, clothed and fed them, and hid them from sight. Left to right, seated: Jan and Gustaaf Hus of Baelen-sur-Nethe, Belgium. Left to right, standing: John O. Donaldson, Robert Anderson, Theose Tillinghast. After this picture was taken, the film was buried until the war ended. (Harper's Magazine)

As it turned out, one of the greatest problems facing this band of escapees was that of being mistaken for German deserters. By now it was apparent to most on both sides that the war was about over and that Germany was losing. Accordingly, many in the ranks of the Kaiser's forces were taking foot in hand and departing for places where they were less likely to be killed. In one instance Tillinghast's general appearance alone saved the trio from being turned away from safe haven. They had arrived at the farmhouse of a man named Jan Hus near the little town of Roul, Belgium. "We talked to Jan quite a while before we convinced him we were not Germans," Donaldson wrote later. "He finally said he knew a lot of Huns, but he had never seen one with a face like Tilly's, which is long and thin, so we must be Americans."

After that they were embraced and cared for. They stayed there a full week and during that time actually shared their quarters for three days with twenty German soldiers and three officers who came by on a copper collecting errand. Incredibly, these people paid no attention to the trio of strangers who kept so much to their rooms.

Two days after the Germans departed, the trio made it into Holland—completing the 150-mile clandestine journey in twenty-eight days. The final leg was accomplished by using a pair of insulated wire cutters to snip their way through the complex electric fence erected at the border by the Netherlands to keep the warring world away. As Donaldson described it; "As soon as the wires were cut the lights on top of the fence went out, showing the current was broken...We got through and ran on and on across the half-mile neutral land between the countries till a swamp stopped us, two miles away. The German sentinel started yelling when we cut the fence, 'Halt! Halt!' and fired. We did not answer, but ran like hell to Holland."[25]

10

Events in October

The approaching end of September supposedly meant that the 17th's stay with the British would soon terminate. A long-standing agreement called for them to leave the northern front at the end of three months and travel south to take their place among American squadrons serving at Toul. In view of this, Eckert began to dole out leave to his pilots, and to point out to headquarters how really important it was for him to have leave before this critical move occurred.

But these actions proved a bit premature. Each day brought new signs that the Hindenburg Line was collapsing; with it would go the war. Accordingly, RAF Chief of Staff Lt. General H. A. Lawrence soon contacted Fowler to stop the move. Wrote he, "I would be glad if you could obtain permission for these squadrons [the 17th and 148th] to remain with the British Army until active operations cease. Their work has been invaluable, and their removal at this juncture will cause serious inconvenience. Moreover, a move to a strange area would result in these squadrons being out of action for several days."[1] And that was that; the units stayed.

As if to disprove Lawrence's point about their invaluable work, the 17th Aero Squadron often stood down in heavy rain as the end of September approached. However, the storm on September 28 proved to be only a local phenomenon and by late afternoon the squadron had an assignment to bomb and strafe roads and railways leading to Cambrai. Reports indicated that these routes were choked with military traffic of every sort.

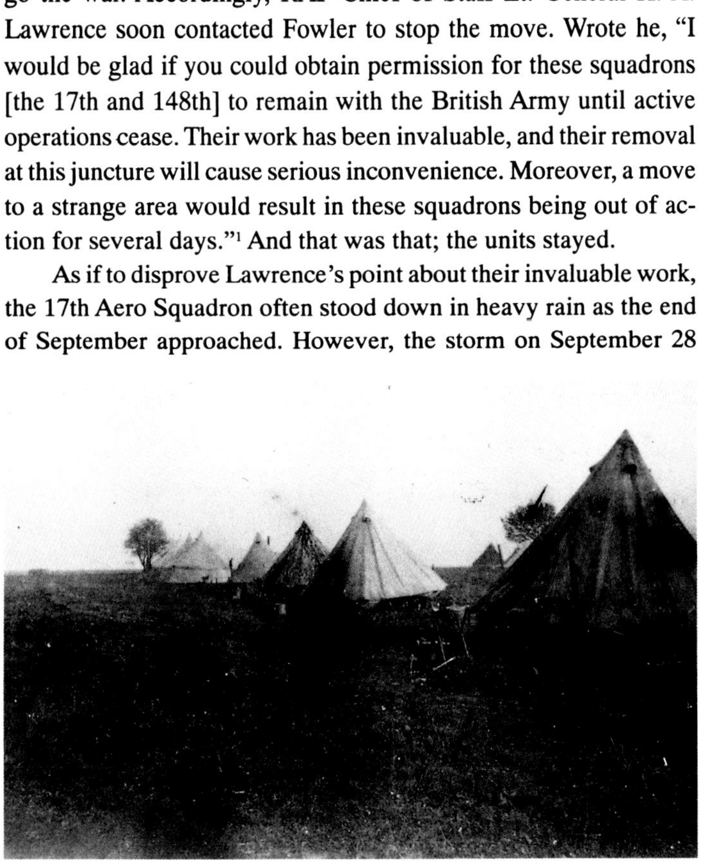

Another view of the ubiquitous British field tents at Soncamp aerodrome. (Lorenz K. Ayers)

The flights went out that day in groups of four at five-minute intervals. They crossed the lines south of the Bapaume-Cambrai road, and soon fanned out to attack the arteries to the south. Flight A was in the lead and Goodnow shortly initiated an attack on a balloon tethered near the road to Marcoing. The flight devoted ten bombs to it and reserved those remaining for the town of Awoingt, dead ahead. C Flight arrived to bomb Awoingt at about the same time and, that done, the two flights pulled up and spread out to machine gun the town from edge to edge.

In the meantime, B Flight was occupied at Marcoing. Vaughn found a heavy concentration of troops and equipment there and led Burdick in a slanting dive to bomb. Dixon and Wicks followed but held their bombs for targets spotted farther along. Then B Flight also split up and attacked targets of opportunity. Burdick repeatedly raked a train standing at a railroad station near Wambaix.

Before long it was time to withdraw and the flights began to form again. But as B Flight came together at 3,000 feet, Vaughn spied an observation plane in the area east of Eswares being protected by Fokkers prowling above it. It seemed to him that the two seater was just a shade too far from its guardians and that with a sudden move he might down the plane and slide out from under the Fokkers. Burdick was of the same opinion and the pair soon lashed out together. Shortly Vaughn was camping on the enemy's tail while Burdick struggled to take the plane head on. Vaughn rode the enemy for half a mile and at last had the dubious satisfaction of seeing it go down, although seemingly under control. But there was no more time for it, then. The Fokkers were coming in.

Vaughn was in position to work his way out from under the attack as planned. The rest, however, had gotten scattered and were easily engaged. Burdick was caught between a pair of Fokkers as he rose from attacking the two seater, managed to roll out of their sights, and turned into one of the pair from only twenty-five yards out. He hit it with one hundred rounds and it burst into flames—his third kill. When he turned his attention to the other plane, he found it fleeing eastward.[2]

In the meantime the remaining planes had struck Dixon and Wicks. Dixon saw the wave coming and dived for safety, firing all the way. He soon joined Vaughn across the lines as did Burdick. But then they saw that Wicks had not been so lucky. He was caught behind at low level and was under attack by three Fokkers. His comrades turned at once to help, but Burdick was closest and went after the Fokkers as if he had them surrounded.

Had Wicks not been a masterful pilot, there would have been little chance of saving him. But he rolled, joggled, and side-slipped until Burdick could make himself part of the equation. This Burdick did by first firing at long range on one German and causing him to break off. By that time a Fokker with a red nose and white tail was machine gunning Wicks very close to the ground, so Burdick half-rolled onto its tail. At that very moment Wicks flew through a copse of trees east of Sancourt and staved in the leading edge of his right lower wing. While the plane wrenched free immediately, Wicks found himself with his hands full of badly damaged aircraft. Burdick eased the situation by firing a burst into the cockpit of the Fokker at which the enemy plane flipped over and crashed.[3] The young pilot from Brooklyn had destroyed his fourth plane in ten days and brought the total downed by the rebuilt 17th Aero Squadron to fourteen for the month of September. The remaining Fokkers departed and the Camels swung west for home.

As it turned out, these thrilling adventures signaled an end to the month. Sunday was rainy and dud, the next two days even more so. And in a way, these successes signaled an end to the colorful days of the war. Not often thereafter would brightly colored planes tangle chivalrously with each other high in the bright blue sky. Now the war had come down to the simple pounding of people into the mud amid filthy weather.[4] It was to be a time of nasty shocks and endless incidents.

October came on cloudy, misty, and chilly. On the first the 17th launched into a nine-day bombardment program based on the current state of things. Since the program called for regular bomb runs morning and afternoon, the squadron had to stretch a bit to meet the schedule. Alderman was allowed back in action now. Myers, Giesecke, White, and Donoho were being shoved across the lines like veterans. And on October 2, Harold Shoemaker came back to take up his problems with the Sopwith Camel.

The morning of Shoemaker's return, B Flight recorded the 17th's first aerial victory of the new month. They were out on a bomb run that resulted in a large explosion thought to be an ammunition dump going up near the rail center at Awoingt, southwest of Cambrai. As Vaughn, Burdick, Wicks, and Dixon rose from their bomb run they spied a second pair of enemy two seaters above and to the east. Vaughn turned for the pair immediately with Burdick following like a shadow. They singled out an orange DFW with camouflaged wings and attacked it head on. It abruptly went into a half dive, half spin and dropped to the ground. Wicks and Dixon saw it smash with no apparent attempt being made to regain control.[5]

The next day there were minor strikes and minor incidents. Jesse Campbell had his fuel pressure pump shot away as the 17th hit six miles farther along the tracks at railcars backed up by the attacks on Awoingt. Campbell (leading in place of Clements who had departed on leave) immediately pulled up and left the formation followed by Ed White, whose engine had suddenly gone funny. When they had crossed to the friendly side of the lines, Campbell was content to land at an advanced area north of Bapaume to await help. White decided, however, that he could get closer to home and flew on in the direction of Soncamp—or so he supposed. But he was flying with a faulty compass and was half out of France before he was forced down by lack of fuel. He was astounded to find himself at Berest, far south and west of where he meant to be.

Undaunted, he refueled, repaired a loose wire on the engine, and started home again. But the engine still ran rough and he had to bring it back for another look. This time he discovered a bearing that had been damaged by a shell splinter, so he was forced to await repairs. So far from home was he that he could not reach Soncamp by phone and was carried as missing until he returned the next afternoon.[6]

By the time he arrived his mates had finished a day almost without incident. The run had gone deeper than ever before into enemy territory, hitting the rail lines at Bertry and Busigny—a good dozen miles south and east of Cambrai. Shoemaker, having finally caught the hang of the Camel, was being acclaimed for a spirited one-man, low-level battle against a vicious machine gun emplacement he uncovered.[7]

The weather continued chancy. On October 5 the morning run slashed at Awoingt again, then prowled on east to Caudry without opposition. The evening patrol was dispatched to the same area to pay particular attention to the roads south of the rail line where trucks were being used to bypass the damaged tracks. C Flight left first and struck Wambaix without incident. B Flight followed twenty-

This is the plane in which Wicks was killed in a mid-air collision with Shoemaker on October 5, 1918. Since parachutes were seldom available to pilots (and never to Camel units), both died. (Cuthbert Tunstall)

five minutes later and suffered the worst calamity that can befall fliers.

Vaughn was leading with Shoemaker trailing up and to the left and Wicks in the same position on the right. Dixon and White were more to the rear and slightly higher still. As they approached the target area they saw Campbell and C Flight coming south and turned in front of them to begin a dive on Esnes.

Reportedly they went down well tucked in despite erratic turbulence in the area. White, who was still a relative neophyte to bombing, was somewhat disconcerted by the maneuver. After peering over the leading edge of his bottom wing to judge his bombing angle, he glanced up to see how the formation was faring. At that instant he saw Shoemaker's plane jump suddenly sideways into Wick's machine. There was a brief wingtip entanglement, then both planes whipped out of formation. From his position in C Flight, Schneider saw the two going down, one in a slow spin, the other spinning rapidly. There was no hope for either. Wicks had lasted almost the whole summer; Shoemaker was lost on his sixth mission with the 17th.

Vaughn wasn't aware of the collision until the Flight returned to Soncamp. His speculation was that one or both might have been struck by anti-aircraft fire. Having good positions to witness the accident, Dixon and White thought it unlikely that Shoemaker had been hit by Archie. White offered another interesting and quite probable theory. He had noticed on previous occasions when flying in that area that he could sometimes glimpse large artillery shells passing from one side of the front to the other. He believed that the pair had been thrown together by the wake of a passing missile.[8]

Once again B Flight had got in a bad way. Dixon now assumed the deputy commander position and the team took on a replacement. He was Lt. William P. House, an energetic insurance man from the west coast who had brought his typewriter into the field and was soon conducting business by mail from "somewhere in France." Since House had only been aloft in the area three times, his usefulness, however, lay in the future.

Eckert began to hold the line and call for replacements. Mercifully, the weather cooperated by remaining generally bad. Pilots stuck to their tents or lounged about the officer's mess, often in fur-lined "teddy bear" suits. This mess comprised two large field tents pitched end to end and was a place of much joy and mirth. Upon being grounded, Jim Ellison had turned his mind to furnishing it with a fireplace and chimney, which he soon constructed of empty fuel cans lined with the local clay.[9] This contraption was fed green wood harvested from the nearby woods or bark covered slabs delivered from a local sawmill by Frenchmen bribed with cigarettes.[10] Not to be outdone in pyromania, Giesecke set about inventing a toaster made from a blow torch paired with a screen.

It happened that among the neighbors was RAF 203, a Camel squadron stationed at Ezil le Hamel. These worthies were much addicted to making music and had formed themselves into a small band. This aroused the Americans to remember that, indeed, they too were musicians of many parts.

The officers had owned a piano since Auxi-le-Chateau. Alderman bought it from the locals with mess funds and was badly stung in the bargain. Clapp was to describe it as an ancient instrument on which, "every other key stayed put when struck and even the *Missis-*

Harold Shoemaker of Bridgeton, New Jersey, rolls a snowball at Camp Hicks, Texas. After the war, Charles France returned Shoemaker's camera to his parents and a roll of film was found in it. This was the only picture on the roll. (Mrs. Lois Shoemaker)

Frederick Mortimer Clapp takes a walkabout at Soncamp. In 1919 Clapp published an account of the 17th's experiences that was probably based on the unit's official war diary. (Lorenz K. Ayers)

Howard Burdick chops wood while armament officer Lorenz K. Ayers supervises. (Lorenz K. Ayers)

sippi Volunteers died away on it after the first ten bars..." This problem had been resolved, however, and when other instruments had been gathered in support, the mess awakened to the sound of unforgettable endeavors in music.

Vaughn, who could play almost any instrument, was installed at the piano. Burdick took on the mandolin, Schneider had a cornet, and whoever was nearby manned the bottle traps and shell casings used to set time. Permeating over-all were the syrupy sounds of Eckert, who played the saxophone; or at least said he played the saxophone. Most were of the opinion only that he had the authority to play it.

Thus was born the "musical mess." Often they tormented away the damp evenings with music of a sort while roasting on one side and freezing on the other. And should an instrument be wanting for one of their numbers, something would be worked out. In a diary entry near the middle of the month Burdick wrote, "Took dinner at 203 RAF with Major [Raymond] Collishaw, Major Gerard, and Capt. Mackay—Eckert, Desson, Dixon, Goodnow. Stole 203's drum."[11] The next evening he noted, "203 came over and stole our cornet and saxophone—eighteen of them to two of us." There is no record indicating that the 17th made any effort to recover the saxophone.[12]

By October 8, word came that Cambrai was falling. Germans were seen streaming east from the city and rumor had it that some Allied troops had already entered. Orders came crackling to bomb and strafe as often as possible with as many planes as possible. Now the weather, which had been considered a haven for days, became a serious hindrance. The squadron was unable to get aloft until 11:35 a.m., but they proceeded with orders giving them lots of latitude; they were to work along any of the three main roads stretching east from the city and strike anything that moved.

Again B and C Flights drew the assignment. Vaughn led Dixon, White, and Leonard Desson of A Flight, who had volunteered to fill in. Jesse Campbell followed immediately with Alderman, Donoho, Giesecke, and Knotts.

They crossed Cambrai and fanned out, with C Flight drifting south and B Flight going north. Knotts had been back from hospital for four days and was chafing for action. As might be expected, it was he who struck first. He spotted an odd motor-driven vehicle moving along the railroad tracks near Awoingt and sent two bombs toward it. These overshot the mark and hit the tracks instead, but to Knotts' great joy, he saw the vehicle dive into the crater and flip onto its side. He came around and descended.

As he had anticipated, the car was filled with German soldiers who were now scrambling to get away from the area. He opened fire and felled many of the hurrying figures. He next gunned an artillery piece being pulled by a four horse team, shot at straggling troops that he came upon, drove masses of soldiers into the ditches, and made a general nuisance of himself. Finally, completely out of ammunition he turned for Awoingt and home. On the way he lofted his two remaining bombs at the railway. One missed. The other was a direct hit that started a serious fire.

Jesse Campbell, in the meantime, had spotted two lorries and shot them up to little effect. He then unloaded all four of his bombs on them in exasperation. They stopped. Giesecke dropped his bombs amid scampering figures in Awoingt, then turned his machine guns on a local factory that seemed to be infested with the enemy. Donoho hit the railroad, then followed Campbell in lorry hunting.

Alderman somehow got completely off from C Flight during all this and attacked Villers en Cauchies a good eight miles northeast of Cambrai. He strung his bombs along a convoy heading into town and swung down to pound troops. He then turned onto another convoy that was, strangely, heading back into Cambrai; moving counter to all other German troops.

So well north was Alderman by now that he was more properly a part of B Flight. Desson, in turn, soon became more nearly a part of C Flight to the south. Vaughn had led his quintet north in formation to bomb four lorries on the road between Cagnocles and Naves. Following the strike, Desson had somehow lost his place and arose alone to be fired on by three Fokkers coming from the

This is the "Musical Mess" that became the center of social life among the officers at Soncamp. It was created by pitching two field tents end to end. (Cuthbert Tunstall)

The interior of the mess tent. Alderman's prized piano is at right, and Ellison's fireplace made of mud-filled gasoline tins rests at center. Here the 17th often hosted RAF 209. (Mrs. Gordon Kellogg)

Edgar White was following George Vaughn on a low level patrol when he (White) was shot through the nape of the neck. He flew back to Soncamp despite his wound and was sent out of the war. He was the first 17th pilot to return to the U.S. (Clinton Burdick)

Jacob J. Ross, M.D., stands before his tent at Soncamp. Ross not only tended to the 17th, but often rushed to the front to assist with the wounded. (Rodney D. Williams)

Howard Knotts was shot down by ground fire on October 14 and, although wounded on foot, nearly escaped through the lines. He was finally captured after a hand-to-hand struggle with a German soldier who accidentally killed himself. (Cuthbert Tunstall)

direction of Cambrai. He banked away and the German planes disappeared to the east before he could come about and fire. With that Desson lost all track of B Flight. He could see C Flight working the area around Awoingt, however, so he wheeled in that direction and began systematically gunning his way along the trucks and troops he found moving south between Estormel and Cattenieres.[13]

Back north Vaughn was engaged in strafing two horse drawn guns on the road from Cambrai to Naves and was unaware that he was short not one, but two men. The second missing member was Ed White, who had begun a dangerous ordeal just after the bomb drop on the trucks. As he was swinging away in a climbing right turn, something suddenly knocked him face down in the cockpit. "I thought nothing about it," he reported later, "supposing I had flown through the wake of a passing shell. As I continued on I began to notice a wetness developing around my collar and, on investigating, found that I was bleeding profusely. My first thought was that I might pass out and crash, so I headed for the advanced landing ground north of Bapaume.

"After I had gone along for several minutes and had more chance to take stock of the situation, I decided that I wasn't going to faint or I would have already done so. It further occurred to me that I was walking wounded and would be sent back to England so bed space could be saved for those more seriously wounded...That being the case, I decided that I would...go on to Soncamp where I could get my walking out clothes. If I were going to England, I had no intention of arriving there with my oil and blood stained clothing to support my social life."

So off to Soncamp he went where he made, before he collapsed in a swoon, what Doc Ross termed in a letter to White's family, "the nicest landing I ever saw made." Ross' letter detailed the wound that he found when he examined the young pilot from Syracuse: "He was struck in the back of the neck in line with the ears. From the point of entrance to exit was about two inches, the exit was about an inch...You have reason to be proud of a son that has the nerve to fly forty miles being wounded as he was..."[14] What Ross did not tell the family was that if the bullet had gone just slightly forward it would have severed White's spine; had it gone slightly aft it would have cut his neck muscles. Either would have been fatal while flying.

Ross also feared infection, fears which were substantiated when White arrived in England. A severe abscess developed in a jaw tooth on the left side, no doubt related to the wound, which spread poisons throughout the young pilot's system. Eventually he became so crippled with rheumatism that he could not get about without a cane. He would fully recover, eventually, after being shipped to the U. S. in December, the first member of the 17th to return home. While crippling his way about England on convalescent leave, however, he found that he was "quite a hero in bars where the tale had preceded me. I hadn't thought much about it," said he. "Nor had anyone else in the squadron. Camel pilots were used to the unusual."[15]

About the time that White was being wheeled away from the 17th, the squadron was rising on their second attack of that day, another turn in which Knotts would again spread himself about grandly. Coming up abreast of Cambrai, he found the roads teeming with targets and swung along a likely looking avenue to put all four of his bombs among some moving troops. He followed his payload down before the dust had settled and leveled off at fifty feet to gun the survivors down like tenpins. Lifting a bit for better visibility, he sprayed a gun battery. Lifting again he spied a pair of automobiles and went for them. His laconic report on the matter says simply, "Chased a closed car on the road through the village of Naves. Car turned over. Two occupants rolled out. One started to get up and I fired on him. The other did not move. My height was 200 feet."[16] A more dramatic picture of the event was painted by Martin Giesecke later in a letter supporting a recommendation for the Distinguished Service Cross. Said he, "Lt. Knotts chased and destroyed a German general staff car out of which two general staff officers emerged to be shot down." He then added, "On this occasion Lt. Knotts flew below the level of the trees and was forced to land. He recovered the use of his engine before it became necessary for him to come to a full stop and very coolly proceeded to take off again."[17]

On October 9, squadrons all along the Allied front struck in a concerted effort. The 17th unleashed half a ton of bombs on Cambrai in two sorties. South and east, American bombers unloaded thirty-two tons of bombs on Verdun in what was considered to be the greatest raid in aviation history until World War II. But dismal weather soon brought these operations to a halt and thereby probably extended the war by a month.

The 17th now stood down for four rainy days. Again they rested, kicked up their heels, and visited. Wrote Burdick during this period, "Dud all day. Slept till lunch. Played crap after dinner with Major Collishaw—RAF, Major Fowler, Capt. Mackay, and Eckert. Lost every damn franc I had (200)."[18] The winners had taken nearly thirty-three dollars from him.

There were some occasional breaks in the weather throughout, and the squadron used them to push House along in his familiarization and training. Consequently, when the weather abated a bit on Monday, October 14, the 17th was able to order out a strike force of fifteen Camels. Two soon dropped out with engine trouble following the early morning take off, but the remaining planes made their way far beyond their old targets to find that the enemy was now entrenched fifteen miles east of Cambrai. They soon located the target and dropped on Bazel. As B Flight rose, it encountered two enemy observation planes, a Halberstadt and an LVG, dead ahead. Vaughn and Burdick caught the Halberstadt between them and sent it crashing out of control. The LVG got away.[19]

Things did not go as well that afternoon. It became a blue Monday for Knotts. The same pilots were back in the air at 1:00 p.m. to strike from Monchaux to Veudegies along the Escaillon River. The view was generally more unsettled than that found on the morning run. There were major dogfights going on overhead and troops scurrying everywhere on the ground.

Goodnow led A Flight in bombing transport about Veudegies. Then the flight dropped to machine gun targets of opportunity. On this occasion, Goodnow descended very low and engaged a pompom gun emplacement that was vigorously working the sky. Vaughn led B Flight in an orderly assault on the many vehicles in that same area. C Flight was north in the area of Monchaux and Querenaing, here they crossed to rip at a mass of soldiers manning a sunken road.[20]

It was following this that Knotts got in trouble. As he later wrote, "I saw quite a number of Germans digging in...and it looked suspicious. I flew low to determine that they were building a regular machine-gun nest with six machines [sic]. I meant to fly down and shoot at them enough to harass them and prevent their making the nest, for it meant death to our men to advance in the face of such fire." [21] His intentions were good, but his luck was not. As he started to turn for the attack, ground fire raked his Camel and he felt jagged metal slice into his right foot.

His engine stopped. He was too low to make the friendly side of the lines, so he pressed on south, prudently trying to get as far away as possible. He also sought to put the Camel down in an area being shelled by the British so it would be destroyed. He made an excellent landing and was observed by Burdick who recognized that his buddy was in trouble. Burdick saw him climb out of his machine and, "start running down a nearby road to beat hell."

Knotts was down near the village of Solesmes. Burdick followed his travels with a half-formed notion that he might land and pick him up. He was rid of his bombs, after all, and it was a conceivable thing for a daring pair to pull off. But Burdick never got a chance to try. Suddenly, from nowhere—and for some unknown reason, a Fokker came spinning down almost into the midst of B Flight. It flattened out in front of Vaughn who gave it a short burst. It then tipped over to Myers who gave it more of the same. At this, it went again into a spin and came out in front of Burdick. Burdick hit the hapless craft with fifty rounds and it went down and landed safely below.

Burdick had lost sight of Knotts during the encounter and was now unable to find him. He went into a cold fury over the interference by the enemy. "He...landed all right," he wrote to his brother later, "but he made me so mad when he interrupted me in trying to see what would happen to Howard, that when he got out of his machine, I chased him around the field and finally killed him. Then I spent the next ten minutes trying to set his machine on fire with no results except using up all my ammunition, so I had to go home."[22]

Knotts, on the other hand, never lost track of Burdick. He could identify his buddy immediately by his letter L and a shiny metal spinner on his propeller hub. And Knotts, being in a shell hole on the very field where the German landed, was much too close for comfort when Burdick came down in ire. "The Hun pilot in evident despair quickly landed," Knotts reported, "abandoning his plane and running out across the field almost in my direction. Lt. Burdick, flying to the ground, pursued him with a vengeance and after a couple of hundred yards the Hun was bowled over by accurate fire. By this time...it seemed to me every enemy machine gun in that vicinity was trained on Burdick. The red spurts of their tracers and incendiaries were much easier for me to observe from the ground than they would have been from the air. Apparently unmoved by this terrific counter-fire, Burdick then turned his attention to the abandoned Fokker. Scarcely higher than the tree tops, he dove time after time on it, but was unable to set it afire...I don't yet see why he was not brought down..."

Most were equally mystified when Burdick arrived at Soncamp. So thoroughly riddled was the plane that as Burdick walked off to the squadron office, his mechanics came running to ask if he was certain he wasn't wounded. They had found where a bullet had passed through the cockpit at leg level and, sure enough, on examination the young pilot's flying suit was found to be bullet creased and scorched on both legs. He showed absolutely no concern.[23]

Because of the events that had occurred before him, Knotts decided that he ought to leave the area as the Camels pulled away. Now he headed for the lines in hopes of crossing into no man's land and thence to safety. His decision to descend amid shell fire now worked against him seriously. "Shells bursting on all sides," he reported, "and great pieces bounding along the ground like stones skipping over water." He dashed from shell hole to shell hole despite his injured foot.

As he recounted later, "I finally got out into a low road on both sides of which were Germans. I had succeeded in getting outside their lines at one place and hoped that I could get back to our lines now...I came to a place where there were two dugouts in the side of the road, just shelter places meant for refuge in case of shell fire. They were low, about four feet high and as many deep. They were not meant to communicate, but the partition between them had given way so there was a hole next to the back big enough to crawl from one to another.

"I crawled into one of these, my hopes being to find shelter for the night and then try to reach our lines...Just after I had crawled in and drawn in my long legs, I saw the face of a German peering in at me. I flung myself through the hole into the next dugout and came right out and threw myself at him. Then we went for each other, just like a couple of beasts, biting and doing anything to finish each other. He had an automatic. I got my left arm around his neck and my right hand tight on his wrist as he had the gun in his right hand. I was trying all the time to keep him from turning the gun on me. Once...I felt the muzzle of the gun against my face, but I managed to push his hand back and after that I kept dodging my face from side to side out of range of the gun.

"Then, all of a sudden, without any warning or reason, there was a deafening roar. One cannot imagine what an awful noise it was there in that small place. It came with so much force and so suddenly that I just relaxed—and so did he. But in an instant I was alert again, and felt of him, over his shoulders and then his face, and found it covered with blood. He had killed himself by accident."

Knotts then took the dead man's gun and burst out of the dugout. "I was so unstrung I did not stop to reason," he reported, "and when I crawled out there were five Germans walking along the road. I flattened myself against the embankment and began shooting at them as they did at me. I used all the shots...I was desperate. And then it seemed that all the earth just tumbled down on me as part of the embankment gave way, and the next thing I knew they were on top of me..." Knotts was a prisoner, the fifth member of the 17th Aero Squadron to fall into enemy hands.

Following his capture, Knotts was marched for seven hours to St. Waast, near Bavia. His antics—and those of Burdick—did not endear him much to his captors and while they did not mistreat him, neither did they give him succor. His wounded foot bled through the entire march and the only food he received was given to him by a little boy along the road. He went foodless and without medical attention for the two days he was imprisoned at St. Waast, then was marched into Bavia with five Australian prisoners who had recently been recaptured after escaping.

The little group was put on a train bound for Mons that night where, being obviously painfully crippled, Knotts was largely ignored by the guards. The aviator took this as a challenge and, late that evening, worked into an adjoining car to see what it might offer. To his surprise it contained three German aircraft being transported to another front. Inspired as ever, he hobbled from plane to plane and, using his good foot for leverage, managed to break the main bracing struts in the bottom of each, thereby putting the aircraft out of commission.[24]

At Mons, Knotts met Lt. Walter Avery of the 148th, who had gone down in Hunland in the first week of October. And on the fifth day of imprisonment, October 19, he was interrogated by the ubiquitous Lt. Schröder, from whom he learned the location of the graves of both Lloyd Hamilton and Gerald Thomas. He liked and trusted Schröder (never suspecting that he was an intelligence officer) partly because he found that what the German said confirmed his own knowledge of Thomas's death.

Despite this growing trust, and a painful and unattended wound, Knotts escaped four days later. He was free for only a few hours before being taken again when he stumbled directly into the arms of a German noncom. That was to be his last taste of freedom for a while; he spent ten more days under careful watch at Mons, then was moved to the prison camp at Soignies for the duration of the war.

Back at the squadron, people were again struggling with the discontinuity caused by frequent loss and replacement. Early in the month Harry Traxler had returned (weeks after being poisoned on the way to Auxi-le-Chateau) to note in his diary, "most of the old pilots gone west that I knew."[25] More recently, Clements had re-

William T. Clements, flight commander of C Flight, pens a message in his quarters. (Mrs. Gordon Kellogg)

turned from two weeks leave to note, "...found when I got back that three of our boys had gone west...One landed safely enough but was taken prisoner...Both 148 and 17 are going to pieces now and will take a lot of rebuilding."[26]

But truthfully, Knotts was downed just as the war was beginning to fade to its end. Already players were taking their places for the final scene and the curtain call. Eckert put Goodnow in command of the unit and went on leave in anticipation of the departure south. Soon Albert Everett returned to be, by virtue of coming into the field twice, one of the few members of the unit who knew the first players as well as the last. And now there were five new pilots: Edward Lubbers was from Brooklyn and had much in common with Burdick and Vaughn. Ernest Mason was a cowboy from Arizona who wore spurs while flying. William Fredrich Schadt of Texas arrived after having been delayed enroute by a Camel crash that hospitalized him for two months. William H. Spindle took the field ill and went out immediately unassigned. Finally, along came Cuthbert Tunstall, one of the first to arrive in England early in the year and just now making his way into the field. A medical student turned pilot, Tunstall was a favorite among acquaintances because he could speak entertainingly on nearly any subject and sang beautifully when properly stoked.[27] Near the end of the month, Army Armstrong returned, pale and wan, and worn out by a thirteen-day search for the squadron.

As it turned out, there was little for the refurbished 17th to do. The few patrols following the day Knotts was lost proved virtually impossible because of generally foul and unrelenting weather. Campbell's report of seeing a huge explosion at Landrecies while patrolling on October 19 showed precisely what was happening. The enemy was now sixty miles from Soncamp and still retiring.[28] A patrol on October 22nd groped through heavy weather to report barges burning in the Canal De La Sambre and a fire at Prisches, four miles further east.[29] In the squadron office it was seen that the war was quickly moving off the large map on the wall.

On October 24, all three flights put up planes on a proposed bombing mission, but it was a futile try. Only Clements, Schneider, and Alderman were able to strike. They put four bombs apiece on the Landrecies-Maroilles road by the Forest De Momal in clouding so heavy that they weren't sure they were not bombing allied troops. Giesecke got detached and managed to straggle back to Soncamp with his bombs unlaunched. Eight Camels had to land at an Australian aerodrome without bombing.[30]

Twelve tried it again the next day. Snoke commented in the official report by noting simply, "Vis. impossible." They had flown as low as they dared in what was thought to be the target area, then gave it up and climbed in search of open sky. Breaking out, they came across enemy planes—three flights of six each stacked up at 8,000, 11,000, and 14,000 feet. So unpromising were the conditions (out-numbered, generally lost, and far from home) that even the aggressive Clements wanted no part of it.

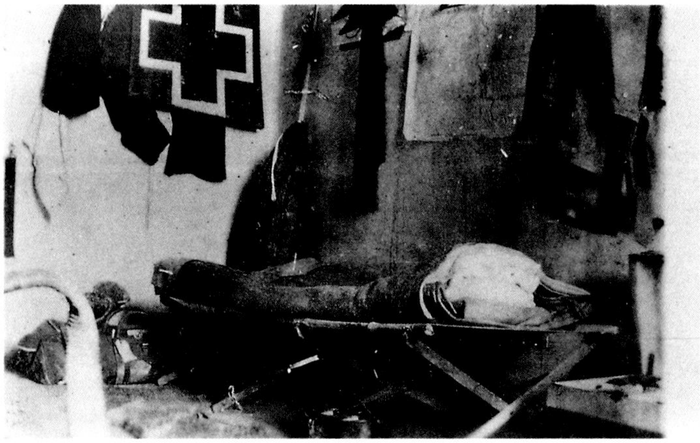

A view of Clements' digs at a place unknown. Note the German Latin cross insignia on the wall. This was probably a personal souvenir from an early combat. (Mrs. Gordon Kellogg)

The 17th suited up for patrol during the last week of October. Left to right, standing: Weston W. Goodnow, Floyd M. Showalter, Ralph W. Snoke, Edward S. Lubbers, Albert J. Schneider, David T. Wells, John F. Donoho, Jacob J. Ross, Cuthbert Tunstall, Harriss P. Alderman, William F. Schadt, William T. Clements. Left to right, seated: Howard Burdick, Ernest S. Mason, William R. House. (Clinton Burdick)

William Henry Spindle. Spindle came into the field ill and departed the 17th without being assigned. (Mrs. Frank Maxian)

The last of the lot to arrive in the 17th. Left to right: William R. House, Ernest S. Mason, Cuthbert Tunstall, William F. Schadt.

Albert F. Everett on returning to the field in mid-October. By coming into the field twice, Everett became one of only a few to know all the pilots who flew with in the 17th. (Lorenz K. Ayers.)

Then Burdick decided that he could drop one of the Germans from the lowest flight. While most watched and wondered what was happening, he tipped out of the formation and pounced on a silver Fokker decorated with forest green crosses. He wrote later, "I left formation at 10:50 AM and attacked leading EA of a formation of five Fokker biplanes at 7,000 feet that was going NW...I fired about forty rounds at seventy-five yards, diving on him from the front and immediately pulling up in a climbing turn and went to rejoin my formation."[31] It was over just that quickly. The Fokker dropped out of control, went into a spin, and burst into flames a thousand feet farther down. The ease of it all led Burdick to note in his diary that evening that, "If we had worked together in the flights, we could have gotten six or seven."[32]

By now the unit had been ordered to move to an aerodrome near Esnes (where Wicks and Shoemaker had collided) because the lines had moved so far east that the Camels could barely reach and return. From Esnes the unit was to use an advanced landing ground at Estormel, two miles east of Awoingt.

The staff went scouting for the new sites and what they saw made them shudder: litter, ruin, damaged barbed wire, bandoleers, tin cans, blackened and torn structures, unburied dead decomposing amid rusting weapons. And everywhere there were holes—large holes, tiny holes, enormous holes, smooth holes, jagged holes, and holes filled with reeking water.[33]

These were things with which fliers chose to remain unfamiliar and no one wanted to go forward. And they did not. Soon there was word that the American units were going to be relieved of duty with the British.[34] The Americans were executing an option put in place when the British were granted an extension in early October. They gave a week's notice, then summoned the Camel pilots to the fold.

Flying was nearly over. The squadron went out the evening of the 26th to be jumped by two Fokkers and five silver planes of an unrecognized type, but the attack was of little significance. The Germans came down on the lowest flight, then fled east as the other flights came down on them.[35]

On Monday, October 28, the 17th flew its last mission. The foray took the pilots over Mormal Forest where they spotted a two seater in the company of twenty-four scouts. The highest element of the 17th was at 14,000 feet with most of the enemy above that, so the Camel pilots contented themselves with watching. Only Goodnow saw anything even approaching action. Noticing a Camel

The Red Cross visits the 17th at Soncamp. From the car: unidentified Red Cross representative, Harriss P. Alderman (back to camera with scarf and cap), Ralph W. Snoke, William F. Schadt (back to camera, hands in pockets), Frank A. Dixon, Cuthbert Tunstall, Albert Everett (back to camera), Leonard J. Desson, Weston W. Goodnow, Ernest S. Mason. (Clinton Burdick)

The crowd grows. Left to right: Weston W. Goodnow, Martin C. Giesecke, Ralph W. Snoke, William F. Schadt, Cuthbert Tunstall, Leonard J. Desson, Dr. Jacob J. Ross, Harriss P. Alderman, Frank A. Dixon, Albert J. Schneider, Albert F. Everett, Ernest S. Mason, Howard Burdick, David T. Wells, William R. House, Red Cross representative, William T. Clements. (Clinton Burdick)

from another squadron going for a retreating enemy plane below, he suddenly swung out of formation and joined the chase for several hundred feet. Then, seeing that the enemy was bound to escape, and perhaps feeling a bit sheepish at having violated his own rules concerning formation flying, he zoomed back into place.[36]

And then it was over. Soon throughout the 17th Aero Squadron things British began being rendered to the British. There were some problems; the cut down flying boots for example. And questions: Who had sawed up petrol cans to make a chimney?[37] And where, exactly, did it say that pilots could cut away the fabric from the center section of an upper wing to improve visibility? And...

The planes were returned to British No. 2 air depot on October 30. Nineteen strong they rose nearly as one and the mechanics watched them fade into the distance to disappear forever. Most found

The pilots play a rough house game called "roly-poly" in front of their tents at Soncamp. There are few details regarding the game, but it had something to do with being dumped face-down in the mud. Left to right: Martin C. Giesecke (back to camera), Harriss P. Alderman (with distinctive knee socks), John F. Donoho, Charles W. France, Albert F. Schneider, John A. Myers, Jesse Campbell, George A. Vaughn. (Samuel B. Eckert)

Again, the crowd grows. It is probable that roly-poly was more fun to watch than to play. (Lorenz K. Ayers)

at the end that they had grown fond of the little ships. Wrote Burdick, "Took my dear old Camel to #2 ASD. Whoever gets it will have some bus..."[38]

Now there were only odds and ends of aircraft about—spare fabric, an extra engine, bits of cable, some support tools. Wanting no part of the crude ring and bead sights used in other air services, George Vaughn kept his Aldis sight for use on enemies to the south.[39]

Visitors dropped by, among them RAF General Longcroft who was delivering a message from the commander of the 3rd British Army expressing "sincere appreciation of their excellent and valuable work." Clapp was to write later that Longcroft "added simply but briefly, but very feelingly, his own appreciation of our work and his thanks."[40]

Other visitors, part of a growing breed of experts, arrived to inquire into views and attitudes. One, styled a commissioner, so outraged Burdick that the young pilot was still steaming when he tackled his diary that night. "They think they know everything, which they don't by a damn sight," wrote he, "...thinks the 300 Dolphin better than the 300 SE-5—the damned fool—a Camel can whip a Dolphin."[41]

By October 31, the area was stripped of nearly everything but that required for subsistence and shelter. Even the piano was gone, the officers having matched RAF 87 squadron for it double or nothing and won. As night drew on, the squadron held bottles at the ready and set off on an enormous binge. It was Halloween and the 17th was determined to indoctrinate their British comrades concerning the noble holiday. Tomfoolery ran high, and in time the pilots climbed aboard the remaining transport and went careening off across the face of France to entice RAF 203 into the celebration. Between them they managed to destroy the mess wherein the 17th had spent so many harmonious evenings at the British camp. Then, not to be outdone in hospitality, the Americans transported

This informal picture of the 17th was taken in the field at Soncamp sometime after October 22. Left to right, standing: Floyd M. Showalter, Jacob J. Ross, John A. Myers, Charles W. France, Albert J. Schneider, Weston W. Goodnow, Frederick M. Clapp, John F. Donoho, Harriss P. Alderman, Samuel B. Eckert. Left to right, seated: Howard Burdick, Jesse Campbell, Frank A. Dixon, Martin C. Giesecke, Cuthbert Tunstall, Edward S. Lubbers. (Frank A. Dixon)

Evidently Dr. Ross has left the ongoing champagne breakfast mentioned earlier in dismay. The black things dangling from the heads of the celebrants are women's silk stockings. They were often pulled over the face to combat frostbite. Left to right: Leonard J. Desson, Howard Burdick, John F. Donoho, and Frank A. Dixon. (Lorenz K. Ayers)

the British airmen back to Soncamp where, together, they destroyed the musical mess.[42]

It was a wild evening. Clements later confessed, "I have never seen such."[43] Even the prudent Goodnow was fallen. His comrades carried him into his tent like a side of beef, tucked him into his sleeping bag, puffed out his candle, and were moving quietly away when he roused the least bit. "Thank you," he breathed, always the soul of politeness, "but you forgot to wind my watch." [44]

11

Armistice and After

One hundred and thirty-five days after reuniting at Petite Synthe, the 17th Aero Squadron was on its way south to serve on the American front. The eight-car troop train that transported the unit was "not the fastest thing I have ever seen by any means," Clements noted.[1] The journey took four days, with the train leaving the station from Saulty near Soncamp and arcing through Paris before arriving at Toul on November 4.[2]

Burdick described the trip in a letter home. "Two boxcars about half as big as freight cars (US) were assigned to the officers, which meant that eleven of us had to sleep in each car. In our car we hung bunks to the ceiling with rails and barbed wire which left seven of us to sleep on the floor...It might have been worse. We had two lamps in the car, two oil stoves, a couple of chairs and a folding table. The rations consisted of beans, bully beef, and coffee three times a day, but any time the train stopped for any length of time, we all got off, went to the nearest town and got food..."

Such stops occurred several times a day and lasted from two to three hours while the feeble French engine cooled. Since the train moved at only about five miles an hour, daily progress was minimal. No one begrudged the stops, however, "We were pretty comfortable when the train was standing still, " Burdick added in his letter, "but oh! When we were moving! One of our wheels was square, I'll swear; the track was about as straight as a dog's hind leg and an inch between the rails...On top of that, there were tin ventilators, four in number, which rattled every inch of the way until I thought I'd go crazy..."[3]

If things were uncomfortable in the officers' four cars, they were torture in the six allotted to the enlisted men. There men were packed in thirty to a cubicle and took turns standing, lying down, freezing at the doors, and smothering in the corners. And when they grew jaded with these amusements, they clung to the sides of the cars, or clamored out to ride on top. Eckert knew of the conditions in these "40 and 8" cars and risked, and eventually received, a reprimand for allowing such conduct. It was only when his mechanics got unruly enough to endanger themselves that he felt obliged to order them back inside.

So the 17th rattled along. When the train stopped, they swarmed out to shave in hot water fresh from the engine and to make a quick survey of the local countryside. Everyone kept a sharp eye on Dixon, since with his knowledge of French, he soon proved to be the best food scrounger among them. Any little movement on his part was likely to start a parade in that direction.

Once they hit a jackpot of sorts. "We were sidetracked alongside a French train with wine tank cars and box cars full of bottled goods," Loran Cooper recalled. "Everyone got drunk, or at least feeling good. About that time we were fed up with the war, the English, the French, and everything in general." While the spontaneous celebration was building, Eckert was conferring with the station master about their seeming lack of progress. At last satisfied that they would someday reach their destination, he came back to find his squadron stumbling and whooping about the rail yard. Outraged, he sought out the first sergeant and ordered him to call roll and get the troops back aboard. "Yezzir," said the top kick with

OPPOSITE: Harold G. Shoemaker's wings with the soil of France still upon them. These were cut from the body and sent to his parents when he was first reburied. Like Merton Campbell, he was destined to have three graves. Mrs. Lois Shoemaker, Mrs. Ester Phares, (George Roland)

The "voitures des chemin de fers" railway carriages. The 17th suffered on these conveyances for days on end to take up duty on the American front. (Lorenz K. Ayers)

A group of photos showing the 17th's flight line and hangars at Toul. While the 17th moved rapidly to become operational, the Armistice overtook them. (Clinton Burdick, Mrs. Gordon Kellogg, George A. Vaughn)

a suspicious slur in his speech. "You too?" bellowed Eckert in solid astonishment.[4]

From then on, Eckert kept a tighter grip on things when the train wasn't moving. Near the midpoint of their journey Clements recorded, "No kick can be made about events today. Our lovely train stopped for two hours in Paris. I had time to walk out on the street and look around a bit..."[5] Only one enlisted man was able to elude Eckert's vigilance and promenade in Paris. He was grabbed up by the local MPs and clapped in durance vile. Unknowingly, the squadron went on without him.[6]

As they drove on toward their destination, spirits began to climb. Eckert relaxed a bit and so did the troops. Burdick felt inspired to go forward and ride on the engine one afternoon and got so dirty it took him hours to clean up. But it didn't matter at this point. There was a feeling of coming home. Soon they would be among Americans, fliers like themselves who had undoubtedly heard of their exploits on the western front and were starving for a chance to congratulate them. They were justly proud of themselves, for surely everyone had heard of Vaughn and his thirteen kills, and little Willie Tipton, the courageous Mert Campbell, Todd, Knotts, and Burdick, and the poker-faced Williams—aces all. And of Lloyd Hamilton—it hardly seemed likely that there could be a spot on the globe that had not heard of the preacher's dashing son who had cut such a swath in the northwest. Surely not.

They were in for serious disappointment. Toul was the headquarters for the U. S. 2nd Army and one of the major aerodromes for the American Expeditionary Forces. Located two miles west of the city from which it took its name, it housed a conglomeration of pursuit, bomber, and observation squadrons and served as the final training area for members of the U. S. Air Service. With its wide mixture of experienced men and students, it was used to odd birds. But it hardly seemed ready for those claiming to be the 17th Aero Squadron now assigned to the Fourth Pursuit Group under Major Charles J. Biddle.

Men of the 17th were suspect at once by the base at large. As the locals saw it, here came some vociferous ragamuffins. They paraded about in curious uniforms half American, half British, and claimed to have spent the summer fighting in the north. Their Adjutant, a skinny older man, was wearing a uniform of his own design; American in color, British in cut—with a bit of French styling thrown in.[7] Worse yet, these people exhibited a suspicious lack of rank for a unit claiming to be combat warriors with the blood of dozens on their hands. Why, they all seemed to be lieutenants! The commander—whose mail came addressed as lieutenant although he claimed to be a captain—was referred to by the men under him as "Major Sam," which didn't exactly help local perception.

Of course these very things were the proof of the story, but sober people at Toul would have none of it; they saw the 17th (and the 148th when it arrived) as seedy, quarrelsome young men who had somewhere learned to name the parts of an airplane wrong and call for "petrol" when they wanted gasoline.

At this, pilots of the 17th became determined to fly their way out of the situation. They reckoned that a few flips about the base would show just who had arrived. But it wasn't that easy. They ordered up their planes, fully expecting the excellent SE-5s, and received instead a consignment of Spads in varying stages of decay. One was so spavined as to be rejected immediately. The rest were obviously steeds that had been rejected by everyone else. Burdick reviled the lot. He found he could not grow accustomed to aircraft with gaping holes where instruments should have been. The ring and bead gun sight drew scorn from a man used to seeing his enemy through the excellent Aldis instrument. Soon after the initial

This is the laundry facility at Toul Air Base. Basic and functional, it seemed fine to men who had been roughing it in the field for months. (Lorenz. K. Ayers)

One of the less-than-new Spads issued to the 17th at Toul. (Lorenz K. Ayers)

run-ups, the pilots came away swearing that the throttles worked backward[8]; and they did to a seasoned Camel driver.

But the mechanics went to work on these hulks and set about restoring and repairing. And as they doped the canvas, they took time to paint on a swooping Great Snow Owl insignia designed by Sergeant Hayden Kellum and authorized by headquarters. At Soncamp Clements had noted in his diary that "from reports, people down there (at Toul) are rather dumb as far as aviation is concerned. In the first place, the Huns have air supremacy, so it is going to be a glorious time for us—provided we get decent machines."[9] Burdick settled that proposition after a little experience. "These people down here know S[hit] F[rom] A[pple butter] about fighting and flying—the Hun comes over our lines as often as he pleases and does what he pleases," he wrote. "We'll have a hell of a lot of fun learning to fly new strange machines, with new motors, equipped with new guns and no instruments—but we'll learn and then show these people down here..."[10]

It never happened. Time was running out on the 17th Aero Squadron and the only action it saw under the Great Snow Owl was observed from the ground. It happened on a sunny Sunday shortly after their arrival and was one of those improbable events people remember for the rest of their lives. That day a little German Rumpler C-IV came buzzing about the sky over Toul with impunity. Operating at its ceiling of 21,000 feet, the craft sailed along declining evasive action since the French anti-aircraft fire was bursting a good mile or so too low. Hundreds of airmen poured out of the noon mess and gathered on the aerodrome to watch the show.

Then something amazing happened that drew a collective gasp of astonishment from the ground. A burst of Archie struck home and the German craft went into a sudden, violent spin. It soon fell a mile twisting and turning, obviously out of control. Suddenly the observer shot from the rear seat and began to plummet down separately, a dark speck against the cloudless sky. Then his parachute jerked open and he commenced drifting to the ground. One feeble attempt was made to right the Rumpler at 10,000 feet, then it pitched down in a straight dive, not even spinning; falling, falling, falling. The sound of the crash was heard from three miles away.

It was a strange event; stranger still to the pilots of the 17th, few of whom had ever seen a parachute used from an airplane. No less strange was the observer's story. Somehow fragments from one of the exploding shells had been hurled upward several thousand feet and struck the plane. One piece slashed into the observer's

A Spad bearing the Great Snow Owl. The original squadron never used this emblem in combat. In World War II, the first kill was scored by the 17th Pursuit Squadron using a variation of this insignia. (Lorenz K. Ayers)

Irving P. Corse with a Spad at Toul. Having been sent from the squadron in September with a leg wound, he apparently rejoined at Toul. (Lorenz K. Ayers)

Enlisted men of the 17th pose wearing the spoils of war at Toul. They would be ordered away shortly. (Lorenz K. Ayers)

William T. Clements addresses a Spad at Toul with a swagger stick. Canes were common among British officers, which probably suggested this mode to members of the 17th. (Lorenz K. Ayers)

leg; another neatly slit the pilot's throat.[11] It was a freakish death made poignant by the fact that the unfortunate pilot lost his life on the last full day of the war. The date was November 10, 1918, and the Armistice would be signed in a matter of hours.

So it was the end of the war that finally ended the antipathy toward the Camel drivers. Talk of peace had been in the air since the Hindenburg Line cracked. Some kept an ear expectant while others scoffed that peace might be as much as a year away. One who believed in staying posted was medic Alfred Vernon Haig, who made a point of establishing friendly relations with the local telegraph operators wherever he went. Thus he was among the first who heard, late on the evening of the 10th, that the war would end on the eleventh hour, of the eleventh day, of the eleventh month, 1918. Knowing full well what would happen when this news was announced, Haig spread the word generously to everyone he met, then promptly went AWOL before a lid could be clamped down on celebrations.[12]

Haig did his work well. Even Eckert first got word of the final hour from a friend of a friend, etc. Of course he rushed off to confirm it, then spent some time in colorful discourse concerning a unit where the very kitchen police habitually found out such news before it could reach the commander.

In the euphoria of November 11, all mattered little. "Today marked one of the great events in the world's history," wrote Clements that Monday evening. "There is rejoicing everywhere. The guns stopped firing at 11:45 AM. Everything is in a high state of confusion. France is wild. Celebrations are going on everywhere tonight."[13]

A week after the signing, Burdick was able to wax philosophic in a letter to his mother, "It is a great deal of satisfaction to know that I won't have to fight any more Huns. Fighting in the air is the greatest sport in the world, but it is also the most dangerous and life is awfully sweet—especially when you stand a good chance of losing it. But that's all over now and as old 'Bill' Shakespeare says—'all's well that ends well' and this has ended."[14] And Clements acknowledged what few of them would have said while the fighting continued, "I never expected to live to see the end, but I guess I have now."[15]

Shortly, Toul erupted in an orgy of picture taking. Gunny sacks were spread across the mud of encroaching winter and group by group, officers of various units were marched into position and recorded for posterity by the Signal Corps. As the shutter clicked there was likely but one thought extant among the subjects. They would go home. Why, they might go at once! Or so it seemed standing amid the muddy sacks and being photographed as conquering heroes. A month later any of them would have laughed at the idea.

Some were soon ordered away based on the length of time spent in France. It seemed likely that those would be home by Christmas. But they weren't. Generally they got no farther than a replacement depot, often Issoudun for the pilots, and there they stayed until Uncle Sam figured out how to get 2,000,000 men home as fast as he had gotten them over. Burdick said it for them all when he wrote a series of letters to his family that ranged from anticipation to despair.

"I haven't the faintest idea when I'll get home," he wrote on November 14, "maybe before Christmas and maybe not until Easter."[16] Four days later he wrote, "I think it fair to say that I ought to be home for my Birthday (February 18)—perhaps before, probably not after."[17] He felt the same on December 5, "I have sort of a hunch that I will get home just about my birthday."[18] "I'm on my way home but how long it will take to get there I can't say,"[19] he admitted on December 29, and on January 8, 1919, he felt that "with a little luck I ought to be home for Easter."[20] He wrote one more time, on February 18, the birthday he'd expected to spend with the family, announcing that he was "darned mad and disgusted" about the entire demobilization process. "Don't count too much on my being with you this summer. I've given up all hope of getting home be-

The staff and flying officers pose together. Left to right: Frank A. Dixon, pilot; Ernest S. Mason, pilot; Floyd M. Showalter, Pilot, Frederick M. Clapp, adjutant; Edward S. Lubbers, pilot; David T. Wells, supply; William F. Schadt, pilot; Paul B. Myers, engineering; George A. Vaughn, B Flight commander; Jesse Campbell, pilot; Lorenz K. Ayers, armament; Weston W. Goodnow, A Flight commander; Samuel B. Eckert, squadron commander; Howard Burdick, pilot; Leonard J. Desson, pilot; Jacob J. Ross, M.D. medical; John A. Myers, pilot; William R. House, pilot; Ralph W. Snoke, pilot; William J. Armstrong, engineering; Albert F. Everett, pilot; John F. Donoho, pilot; Martin C. Giesecke, pilot; Cuthbert Tunstall, pilot; William T. Clements, C Flight commander. Note that Ayers wears the distinctive wings of an observer. (Samuel B. Eckert)

This picture, taken after the Armistice, shows the 17th and 148th staff officers and pilots together. The 17th is left of the propeller hub, the 148th to the right. Commanding officers Samuel B. Eckert and Morton Newhall are at the center. (U.S. National Archives SC39372)

This group of disgruntled officers are the previous month's heroes sent off to Issoudon supposedly for immediate deployment home. They stagnated there for weeks. Walter Knox, left; and Henry Starkey, fourth from right; were from the 148th. Frank Dixon, second from left; was from the 17th. (Frank A. Dixon)

fore Easter. When is Easter, anyway? Before the fourth of July, isn't it?"[21]

It was a sad situation, even considering the enormity of the task. Practically nothing worked right after the Armistice. Replacement camps became places where young pilots were sent to lose their spirit. They lounged around in rebellion, refusing duty and partaking casually of whatever France had to offer for their money. One officer, late of the 17th, got away to Paris for a lark and caught syphilis in a famous fleshpot.

Perhaps those not ordered out so early were luckiest. Albert Everett was held at Toul and put on duty ferrying Spads to Issoudun for scrapping. He reported later, "I don't see why they didn't have a riot at Issoudun. The place was so crowded that when I brought a plane in I had to sleep on the floor somewhere, huddled back to back with other pilots under two loaned blankets which were invariably issued full of lice. Every time I left I would tell the supply sergeant about the lice and he would look at me in shocked sympathy and say 'is that so?' The sergeant never lost his sympathy—or the lice."[22]

Things could have been worse. There were many prisoners who would have welcomed these inconveniences gladly compared to those found among the Germans. Still, the squadron's POWs had an easier time of it than many. Tillinghast had, of course, made his way to freedom before the war ended. He arrived in England on November 1, just as the 17th was embarking for Toul. Tipton, Todd, and Wise were released to the Red Cross from Villingen prison on November 29.[23] Although all were in good health, none ever rejoined the 17th.

Knotts did rejoin, despite suffering the most of the five unfortunates. The prison camp at Soignies to which he had been sent on November 2 was a "reprisal" camp, one to which the Germans sent Australian and Canadian enlisted men whom they suspected of killing German soldiers who were trying to surrender. It contained 1,500 men, had deplorable sanitation, and offered no medical services. Knotts was there until the Armistice.

With the acknowledgment of defeat, the German army went into complete disarray. Knotts and several other prisoners were taken on a forced march from Maransart to Boucet, purportedly for eventual release to the Red Cross. Finally, though, Knotts realized that he was not so much being taken as simply going along. With that, he and five British officers finally stopped, on November 14, at a chateau near Boucet where he was nursed back to health by the family that owned the chateau.[24]

On November 29, he was able to post a letter to Eckert; "If this gets to you within three or four days of this date, please advise me what to do. On the 14th of this month I was abandoned by the Germans just in front of the chateau where I am at present. Even now I am only able to walk a little bit so that I can't get anywhere and

Left to right: John Myers, Frank A. Dixon. As they pose in front of a 17th Spad XIII at Toul, they seem happier than they probably were. (Cuthbert Tunstall)

there are no trains to take. Besides, the people who have taken me in want me to stay with them until I am well and it is such a wonderful place, I want to too.

"I am at Boucet, with Monsieur Stanislas Seny, a little village near a somewhat larger place called Hannut, which is about halfway between the two large towns of Tirlemont and Huy. If you get anywhere near here, please come and see me or fly over and bring Burdick along. There is an old Hun aerodrome right up against Hannut and the canvas hangars are still there so it would be easy to see.

"There are so many things I want to know. Where my clothes are, if they still are, and what I want most of all is to get back with the squadron. I would like to have a little leave first, but I would willingly forego that to get back to you people and in a week or ten days I will be fit as a fiddle. I'm just crazy to see everybody again. If I dared be so unmilitary, I'd ask Major Fowler to help me out too.

"Tell Burdick I've simply got to see him. I hope to goodness this reaches you tho' only the Lord knows how I'm going to send it. Best to everybody, especially Bingo."[25]

Of course, no one ever came for him for the letter was addressed to Soncamp and by the time it was received at Toul, he'd rejoined the unit. He came in on December 18, just one day before the 17th ceased all flying and turned in their aircraft to depart.[26]

The squadron arrived as a unit at Colombey-les-Belles for "demobilization and transportation to the United States," on January 12, 1919. Just after Christmas, the enlisted men were shipped out to Aigrefuille for six weeks to continue the training for which they no longer saw any use. Loran Cooper recalled that, "One day, we

This set of photographs show the enlisted men of the 17th soldering like infantry at Aigrefuille, France. One man died of pneumonia there. Another was killed on the boat coming home. (Lorenz K. Ayers, Clinton Burdick)

In 1919, Edward, Prince of Wales (later Edward VIII and Duke of Windsor) visited the U.S. and presented decorations. Here, Howard Knotts gets the British Distinguished Flying Cross. The affair was so crowded that some family members did not get in. (Mrs. John B. Dixon)

Knotts with his British decoration. Later he received a Distinguished Service Cross from the hand of General William "Billy" Mitchell. (Mrs. John B. Dixon)

double-timed nine kilos to be inspected by General Pershing, near Dijon, and then stood in the drizzle for four or five hours to have him show up to look at us. However, it wasn't too bad as he did stop long enough to congratulate the CO on the appearance of the men."[27] There was a strange twist in this since it had been Pershing's official policy throughout the war that Americans units would never be asked to serve under foreign command.

In time, this official policy overrode fact. Clapp recognized that this was happening when he fell in briefly with an officer he knew from Texas and remembered as one who did much to disrupt the orderly formation of the Air Service. The man hitched a ride with Clapp from Colombey-les-Belles to Chaumont, then—remembering that Clapp was both a writer and historian—enticed him to see a Colonel Gorrell at Air Service headquarters at Chaumont. Gorrell, according to Clapp's notes, "sat at a large desk with his back to a window in a room in which there were many desks and maps and charts with pins stuck in them or made up of odd circles or rectangles in quaint and inexplicable juxtaposition. The uninterested might have thought that these objects bore some relationship to the front, but having been at the front, we understood better."

Clapp listened in amazement as Gorrell addressed his companion: "Your business will be to visit all English aerodromes and units where American flyers have served—laying especial emphasis on organization, hours of service, victories, with careful comparison with British victories obtained under the same circumstances, etc. What we want to show is the superiority of American material." Clapp was even more astonished when Gorrell turned to him and said, "Lt. Clapp, you will assist the Major [Clapp's companion] in this work as much as possible."

Clapp finally pieced the matter together. As he understood it, there was to be a history written, written from a preconceived point of view that would boost the American Air Service record through downgrading the work of the RAF. He saw at once that this would entail minimizing the 17th's accomplishments; their exploits would be diminished with those of the host's. Clapp believed that to participate in the project would require him to engage in wholesale distortions against a noble ally. Affronted by the very idea of such disloyalty, he declined on the grounds of imminent business on the continent and, after much wrangling, managed to escape back to the squadron. Shortly thereafter, he arranged a local discharge and went away to Italy with Maud.[28]

There remained two last tragic and ironic bits of drama to be played out before the 17th again set foot on American soil. The squadron, which had lost no enlisted men during its days of active service, lost two men after the Armistice was signed. Benjamin E. Fisher died on February 9, 1919, of bronchial pneumonia as a complication of an attack of mumps. George R. Herbsleb was killed in a freak accident aboard ship on the journey home. As Loran Cooper recalled, "I believe the steel railroad ballast shifted so that the ship's crew had to get into the hold, leaving a manhole open. The young seaman guarding the open hole got interested in a crap game going on nearby and forgot his watch. I had returned a book to whoever loaned it to me and Herbsleb thought he would like to read it and so crossed the deck and started to return to his bunk while opening the book and examining it. He stepped into the open hole and broke his neck on the ballast below."

Herbsleb was one of the few married men within the ranks and earlier that day he had managed to persuade the ship's radio operator to send a message to his wife to meet him in New York. Fortunately, some quick minds remembered and managed to stop the message from being sent.[29]

After this last bit of tragedy, the 17th came home led by Eckert, now officially the Major he should have been ten months before. The squadron arrived in New York two weeks after sailing from St. Nazaire on March 7.[30] Within a month, most had mustered out and disappeared into peacetime America.

> We love you for coming over
> And always the best to you.
> Do as an English girl asks
> And remain loyal and true.

Masie Lea
of the Palace Theatre
and Case Bar.[31]

Undoubtedly the saddest picture in this book is this view of Mrs. Charles Campbell surrounded by mementos of the departed son, Merton L. Campbell. The propeller by her side is the grave marker fashioned by the men of the 17th and erected at his grave on the battlefield. (George Campbell)

Epilogue

The surviving members of the 17th Aero Squadron went away to distinctive achievements in many endeavors. However, through a combination of ignorance and indifference, their successes as members of a distinctive military unit remained obscure. In a sense, their service ended as it began. Born in confusion and disappointment, the unit never recovered, in terms of recognition, from that bad start.

Still, fate was not entirely unkind. As a low numbered unit, the 17th was one of the few fighter squadrons to survive the long military drought that followed The Great War. Reorganized and re-equipped, it was stationed throughout the 1920s and 1930s at Selfridge Field, Michigan, where S. B. Eckert had long before flown out the first plane. When the clouds of another war gathered, the unit migrated to Clark Field in the Philippines. And when battle again erupted, Lt. Boyd D. "Buzz" Wagner, commanding officer of the 17th U.S. Pursuit Squadron, became the first American ace of World War II.

Wagner was a worthy successor to those half-wild boys of a generation earlier. He initiated a spectacular five-day strike at the enemy on December 13, 1941, when he downed four zeros in combat on a single reconnaissance flight and destroyed three to five enemy aircraft on the ground at the Japanese base at Aparri. Three days later, on December 16, he destroyed several more in a bombing and strafing attack at Vigan Field, like an echo of the famous day when the 17th Aero Squadron struck so soundly at Varssenaere. Finally, on December 18, with the U.S. having been in the war only ten days, Wagner became an ace when he sent a fifth Japanese Zero flaming from the sky into the Pacific Ocean.[1] Painted on his triumphant P-40 was the Great Snow Owl created by Hayden Kellum.

The Sopwith Camel, for which that emblem had been intended, was of course but a memory in 1941. Even the mighty Sopwith Company itself, after a disastrous attempt to survive by building motorbikes, had gone into voluntary receivership in September 1920—and reappeared as Hawker Aircraft.

Frederick Mortimer Clapp 1879-1969. (George Roland)

Appendix A: Field Assignments—Spring of 1918

One of the reasons that 17th Aero Squadron mechanics were sent into the field in the spring of 1918 was because in teaching Americans, the British got terribly behind in training their own. Accordingly they took the men of the 17th and applied to them job titles known to British troops in the field. Here we see them identified by R.F.C. trades on a list located by Michael Dickinson in London. While this roster of enlisted men does not exactly match that published in Clapp's history, we have left things as the British saw them. Note the odd idea of alphabetizing by job title.

R.F.C. stands for Royal Flying Corps—then one of two branches of British military flying. The other was the R.N.A.S.: the Royal Naval Air Service. On April 1, 1918, the two services were combined into the Royal Air Force.

H.Q. Flight

Rank	Name	R.F.C. Trade
Private	Morin, F. P.	Acetylene welder
Corporal	Mitchell, David S.	Aerial Gunner
Private	Cox, R. M.	Aerial Gunner
Private	Routt, W.	Aerial Gunner
Private	Price, S.	Aerial Gunner
Private	Wessels, Clarence	Aerial Gunner
Private	Oldfield, C. S.	Armourer
Private	Pickett, S. G.	Armourer
Private	Tero, H. D.	Armourer
Private	Stephens, H. W.	Armourer
Corporal	McCarthy, N.	Carpenter
Private	Lastovica, F. R.	Carpenter
Private	Ellis, W. A.	Carpenter
Sergeant	Brown, Ned L.	Clerk (gen)
Corporal	Digman, Jesse A.	Clerk
Private	Koop, Lamonte P.	Clerk
Corporal	Wallace, Clyde B.	Clerk
Corporal	Gardner, Earl W.	Clerk
Corporal	Hathaway, G. S.	Clerk
A/Sergt.	Bower, Bishop F.	Cook
Private	Williams, Clarence L.	Cook
Private	Miller, Virgil L.	Cook
Sergeant	Johnson, Alvin M.	Coppersmith
Private	Parker, Edward L.	Coppersmith
Private	Wilcavage, John	Cyclist (motor)
Private	Winchester, Harry M.	Cyclist
Sergeant	Lehr, Louis A.	Driver (mit.)
Sergeant	Fellay, Dean R.	Driver
Corporal	Burns, Forest L.	Driver
Private	Urquhart, Davis L.	Driver
Private	Hill, Reginald E.	Driver
Private	Booth, Claud L.	Driver
Private	Spurling, Ernest E.	Driver
Private	Cavan, James H.	Driver
Sergeant	Miller, Hays B.	Fitter (gen)
Private	Wray, H. L.	Fitter (mach)
Private	Tyrell, H. J.	Fitter
Sergeant	Baur, Edward L.	Fitter (M. T.)
Corporal	Buchanan, Robert B.	Fitter
Private	Smith, J. G.	Instrument rep.
Private	Kolb, John K.	Photographer
Private	O'Keefe, J. J.	Sailmaker
Sergeant	Bauman, C. A.	Medical orderly
Sergeant	Baslow, Max	Medical orderly

"A" Flight

Rank	Name	R.F.C. Trade
Private	Attwood, A.	Armourer
Private	Herbsleb, Geo. R.	Carpenter
Private	Cooper, L. J.	Carpenter
Private	McBride, Ralph C.	Carpenter

Private	Johns, L. H.	Clerk (gen)
Private	Bardot, H. E.	Clerk
Private	VanHousen, C. E.	Cook
Private	Toms, Cedric D.	Coppersmith
Private	Gabel, Wm. J.	Coppersmith
Private	Malloy, L. J.	Cyclist (motor)
Private	Rose, B. H.	Driver (M. T.)
Private	Cottner, E. R.	Driver
Private	Chapman, G. B.	Driver
Private	Johnson, Edwin L.	Driver
Private	Booth, Clifton W.	Driver
Private	Brown, Ney S.	Driver
Private	King, Clark H.	Driver
Private	Decker, Geo.	Electrician
Sergeant	Gipner, Lomas	Fitter (eng)
Corporal	Hivley, Elden E.	Fitter
Corporal	Galloway, Edward E.	Fitter
Corporal	Boomer, Chas. E.	Fitter
Private	Hively, Roy H.	Fitter
Private	Conklin, Orrin	Fitter
Private	Traxler, Harry D.	Fitter
Private	Johnson, Archie	Fitter
Private	Wilson, H. D.	Fitter
Private	Reilly, James F.	Fitter
Private	Horst, Frank H.	Fitter (turner)
Private	Bunyan, John A.	Fitter
Private	Pendleton, Phillip W.	Instrument rep.
Private	D'Olic, Edward	Operator (wireless)
Private	Martel, Clarence A.	Operator
A/Sergeant	Capron, David B.	Rigger
Corporal	Leonard, Lial W.	Rigger
Corporal	Sandford, Jay F.	Rigger
Private	Curtis, Herbert F.	Rigger
Private	Bailey, Paul	Rigger
Private	Devol, Lloyd E.	Rigger
Private	Leary, Carrol E.	Rigger
Private	Lemons, Lonnie	Rigger
Private	Apel, Virdon J.	Rigger
Private	Lature, O.P.	Rigger
Private	Seney, Leroy W.	Rigger
Private	Cobb, J. B.	Rigger
Private	Floystaed, C.	Rigger
Private	Love, Virgil L.	Sailmaker

"B" Flight

Rank	Name	R.F.C. trade
Private	Laughery, Wm. A.	Armourer
Private	Miller, Arthur F.	Carpenter
Private	Heim, Anthony J.	Carpenter
Corporal	Douglas, Cecil N.	Clerk (gen)
Private	Slevin, James J.	Clerk
Private	Laughlin, Edward J.	Coppersmith
Private	Knous, Alfred L.	Coppersmith
Private	Long, W. B.	Cook
Private	Strickland, Nelson J.	Cyclist (motor)
Corporal	Garrett, Robert H.	Driver (M. T.)
Private	Masters, Wm. H.	Driver
Private	McPherson, Wm. F.	Driver
Private	Trezise, R. W.	Driver
Private	Young, H. E.	Driver
Private	Leppine, N.	Driver
Private	Hollis, E. R.	Driver
Private	Feigh, G. H.	Electrician (Mag rep)
Sergeant	Guhm, Louis	Fitter (eng)
Sergeant	Douglas, John B.	Fitter
Private	Miller, Beryl O.	Fitter
Private	Zoubeck, Frank J.	Fitter
Private	Alexander, Jasper R.	Fitter
Private	Holton, Judson N.	Fitter
Private	Stickney, Brune T.	Fitter
Private	Gosney, Howard M.	Fitter
Private	Ratzsch, Emerson R.	Fitter
Private	Blunt, M. A.	Fitter
Private	Karl, F. J.	Fitter
Private	Johnson, A. B.	Fitter
Private	Frater, J. K.	Instrument (rep)
Corporal	Jordan, Geo. R.	Operator (wireless)
Private	Anthony, Earl H.	Operator
Private	Aten, Merrit C.	Operator
Sergeant	Barr, Robert J.	Rigger
Corporal	Johnston, Logan T.	Rigger
Private	Huntington, Lester H.	Rigger
Private	Thompson, Blair M.	Rigger
Private	Ross, Jess	Rigger
Private	Rose, Halla E.	Rigger

Private	Fischer, Ben E.	Rigger
Private	Ransdell, Clarence T.	Rigger
Private	Kenney, John J.	Rigger
Private	Sloan, De Villo	Rigger
Private	Fleahman, Wm. R.	Rigger
Private	Whiteaker, Wm C.	Rigger
Private	Ellerkamp, Harry M.	Rigger
Private	Beers, Lloyd S.	Rigger
Private	Richman, Willie	Sailmaker

"C" Flight

Rank	Name	R.F.C. Trade
Private	Miller, Henry T.	Armourer
Private	Thole, John T.	Carpenter
Private	Berntsen, Carl	Carpenter
Private	Thurman, Geo. J.	Carpenter
Private	Gnagy, John G.	Clerk (gen)
Private	Davis, S. D.	Clerk
Private	Ferris, Huber C.	Cook
Private	Randolph, Frank B.	Coppersmith
Private	Cox, Tom W.S*	Cyclist (motor)
Sergeant	Wellborn, Clay A.	Driver (M.T.)
Sergeant	Wilson, Walter M.	Driver
Private	Baudet, Alfred L.	Driver
Private	Doty, Donald F.	Driver
Corporal	Speth, Roy H.	Driver
Corporal	Brooks, Bernard R.	Driver
Corporal	Oyster, Byron M.	Driver
Private	Irwin, M. A.	Electrician
Sergeant	Kellum, Hayden C.	Fitter (eng)
Corporal	Foster, R. B.	Fitter
Corporal	Falkenstein, Howard W.	Fitter
Private	Brown, Benjamin A.	Fitter
Private	Nelson, Harold W.	Fitter
Private	Beebe, Albert J.	Fitter
Private	Beebe, Claude R.	Fitter
Private	Slover, Geo. W.	Fitter
Private	Buck, Selby H. J.	Fitter
Private	Jensen, Edwin R.	Fitter
Private	Muller, Lewis E.	Fitter (turner)
Private	Passerine, Emil E.	Fitter
Sergeant	Holmes, Walter W.	Instrument (rep.)
Private	Gillman, E. H.	Operator wireless
Private	Thurman, E. G.	Operator wireless
Sergeant	Smith, Cameron	Rigger
Corporal	Fellay, Geo. R.	Rigger
Private	Erdman, Geo. B. E.	Rigger
Private	Allen, Roy J.	Rigger
Private	Strain, Fred	Rigger
Private	Wood, Lawrence L.	Rigger
Private	Portugal, Harold W.	Rigger
Private	Ley, Arthur M.	Rigger
Private	Meek, James W., Jr.	Rigger
Private	Rader, Geo. A.	Rigger
Private	Minehart, Arthur L.	Rigger
Private	Wiley, Samuel C.	Rigger
Private	Haley, R. E.	Rigger
Private	Day, Harry	Sailmaker

** Clapp lists instead: Cox, Daniel J.*

Appendix B: More About Fowler*

Although largely anonymous among American warriors, Harold Fowler (1886-1957) was hardly an inconspicuous man. He was solid, about six feet, blond, blue-eyed, and so well proportioned that August Rodin, who admired the officer's back, once used him as a model. It is said his almost boyish face belied his years throughout his life.

Son of a prominent English couple (Emily Arthur and Anderson Fowler) who emigrated to the United States and became naturalized citizens, son Harold was nevertheless born in Liverpool on a family visit; the seventh of fourteen children. He was both well educated and well traveled; while others went off for a brief tour of Europe after college, upon completing Columbia University, he left for a trip around the world. He is said to have hunted big game in Africa and tiger in Indo-China while still in his twenties.

Fowler was sworn into the secret service by Theodore Roosevelt soon after the turn of the century and was ever after active in such employment. Not surprisingly, he was in London when The Great War broke out, serving as secretary to Walter Hines Page, Woodrow Wilson's ambassador to the court of St. James. Undoubtedly he was functioning to a degree as some sort of agent even then, and he quickly got caught up in the ongoing European games. Somerset Maugham, a British agent of the times and long-time Fowler family friend, wrote of Fowler after his death as, "...a character out of our times today. He was like one of those great adventurers of the reign of Queen Elizabeth I. If he had been alive then, he would have been a buddy of Drake and Walter Raleigh, and they would have accepted him as one of them. He had, of course, the courage of the devil."

The literary references were apt. Other literary friends, Sir Osbert and Dame Edith Sitwell, often said that Fowler belonged in an earlier age and always referred to him in conversation as "The Tudor Character." It is unlikely that such a man could remain obscure without trying, and there is evidence that he did try. The why has not been explored in depth, but his acquaintance with Maugham, who was a special agent in The Great War, suggests that Fowler was not merely dabbling in minor military command.

After a decent interval, Fowler abandoned his activities (of whatever nature) at the American Embassy and took a commission in the Royal Artillery where he served with much distinction. He won the Distinguished Service Order for creeping out across no-man's-land and single-handedly silencing a German battery that was doing great damage to the British forces. A few months later he won the Mons Star at the battle of Mons.

Eventually, he was paralyzed from the waist down by a shrapnel sliver, which several operations failed to remove. Finally, at his own suggestion, an electromagnet was used to drag it out. He was soon back on his feet with a limp that rendered him unfit for ground service.

Within a few months, he wrangled a transfer to the Royal Flying Corps—he'd learned to fly soon after the Wright brothers opened the aviation era—and fought on in the air war. And that's where he was when the U. S. entered the war in 1917. Of course with his Anglo-American connections, he was a natural to become involved in liaison activities between the two nations. Following the declaration of war, President Wilson dispatched a commission under the command of Major Raynal C. Bolling to Europe to find out just how America could best assist in the air war. Fowler gravitated naturally to this discussion group, assisted in the studies, and, when they were done, hand carried the report back to Washington.

This led to his entering the American service. Among the papers Fowler carried back was an agreement whereby the British would undertake the training of a minimum of ten U. S. squadrons in Canada in return for the use of American bases in Texas for training during winter months. The arrangement was advantageous to both sides: the Americans would solve their need for trained personnel to instruct raw recruits—and the British would gain off-season training camps and additional manpower.

Such a scheme just had to have Fowler in it, and while the final negotiations were going on, he changed uniforms and picked up orders for duty in Washington. This proved too sedentary and soon, chafing for action, he managed an assignment to return to England

and take command of one of the initial U. S. squadrons when it arrived there on the way to the front.

He came close to not making the trip, however. At the last minute he learned of a change of plans that would send him to Fort Knox as a flight instructor, instead of to England. Since he was already aboard ship when this knowledge came upon him, he evaded receipt of the orders by locking himself in his washroom until the ship was underway.

Thus he was there to take command when so many others arrived. There is little to show just how he managed to establish two American units (the 17th and 148th) at the front under British command. Doing that was about as conspicuous as he ever got. A story is told that he once went to Buckingham Palace after the war and stood in the background while various distinguished soldiers received military decorations from King George V.

"And what are you doing here, young man?" he was finally asked in a patronizing manner by one of the palace guards.

"I am here for the Distinguished Service Order, the Military Cross and the Order of a Commander of St. Michael and St. George," Fowler replied mildly. At that, he was quickly shown to the King.

He remained largely and deliberately obscure for the rest of his years. Researchers find little to seize upon. He was First Deputy Police Commissioner in New York City from January 1934 to December 1937. He served as a Colonel in intelligence throughout World War II and is believed to have been active in the intelligence community for the rest of his life.

**See Thyrza B. Fowler, Harold Fowler, 1886-1957: a remembrance, [NY] Privately published [at the Spiral Press], 1960.*

Appendix C: More About the Camel*

The Camel first appeared on the fighting front in July of 1917 and gave the British a weapon to match the German Albatross D-III and D-5 aircraft that had been littering European landscapes with the wreckage of earlier British planes since the beginning of that year. The official name of the fighter was the Sopwith Biplane F-1, but it soon became known to pilots as the Camel because of the hump in front of the cockpit, which housed the twin Vickers machine guns. The Camel was the first British single-seater fighting plane with dual guns synchronized to fire through the propeller.

This Sopwith creation was an impressive addition to the arsenal and became, at least statistically, the champion single seat fighter plane of the war. Camels downed 1,600 enemy aircraft. This is to be explained in part by the fact that there were so many of them in service—5,490 units by war's end. Cheap and easy to produce, the aircraft stayed in production and use far beyond its time.

There are many reasons and ways, however, to curse the Camel. Very maneuverable and responsive, it was an excellent fighting machine, but often a treacherous flying machine. Only pilots who mastered it survived. Experienced pilots knew that a moment's relaxation or the slightest inattention could be fatal.

The problem was considerably complex. Camels were powered by one of several rotary engines available at the time, engines that varied in power from 110 hp to 150 hp. These engines operated on a principle that seems quite peculiar today; very simply, the crankshaft stood still while the entire engine—pistons, cylinders, and all the other elements—whirled about it like a ponderous wheel. The propeller was fastened to the rotating mass.

Incredible as it seems, this rotary principle was a major force in the early days of aircraft engine design since it produced the most horsepower per pound of engine weight. Many of the famous World War I planes were equipped with rotary engines, including Nieuports, some versions of the Fokker, and some varieties of Pfalz. In each of these, gyroscopic precession was a force with which to reckon. Only in the Camel, however, did the mating of engine and airframe produce a craft so ruthlessly unforgiving of pilot error or ignorance.

The gyroscopic effect of the spinning engine could cause the Camel to go into a sharp stall or spin if improperly handled. A steep turn to the left caused the nose to rise, producing a stall. A sudden bank to the right tucked the nose under and threw the aircraft into a vigorous spin. On course these dire consequences could be avoided by proper control techniques, but even the proper control for these situations was novel. When entering a steep left turn, the pilot had to apply full left rudder immediately to keep the nose from rising. In a steep turn to the right, one did exactly the same thing, which kept the nose from dropping.

Turns to the right were accelerated by the precession and a Camel could turn three times in that direction while other planes of the times were turning twice. Such maneuverability got Camel pilots out of many a tight spot in combat—and into many a tight spot whenever inattention or faulty technique were present.

While gyroscopic problems were close to the heart of the problems with the Camel, they were only part of the puzzle. The craft was slightly more than eighteen feet in length, with the engine, guns, oil tank, undercarriage, wings, cockpit, and fuel tank all contained within the first seven feet of the fuselage. Yet a regulation-rigged Camel flew as if it were tail heavy, so much so that it had to be flown with a decided forward pressure on the stick. When a pilot had some task that required the use of both hands, he had to chock the stick in place with his knees in order to maintain level flight. And if he lost his hold, the plane immediately started into a climb.

On top of all this, it was generally understood that any Camel could be flown through the same exercise fifteen times with identical results, then display some unaccountable aberration on the sixteenth try.

No matter that the ship was stout and maneuverable, its day had come and gone. The optimum combat altitude for the Camel was about 12,000 feet; in 1918 the war was being fought at 17,000 feet and higher. The Camel was already near its limits in trying to combat the deadly Fokker triplane. Introduction of the vastly superior D-VII in April meant that the little Sopwith could hardly be considered a viable pursuit ship any longer. The worst way to attack in combat is from below, yet that was all that the Camel could be expected to do against the newer and better German aircraft.

** Information concerning the Camel is drawn in part from Great Aircraft, Norman Macmillan, Copyright line, St. Martin's Press, Inc., New York, NY. Copyright © 1960 by Norman Macmillan.*

Appendix D: Flight Assignments

Dates shown in the following assignments are as determined by squadron records, flight logs, diaries, letters, biographies, etc. No claim of perfection can be made, however, since even the squadron records are sometimes in error. For instance, dates shown here do not always agree with Appendix, Part I *Casualties and Changes in Officers of the 17th Squadron During Overseas Service* in Clapp's book. This may reflect a difference in definition as to when service began.

While the pressures of duty sometimes changed flight composition, generally speaking assignments were as follows:

Name	Assigned	Remarks
Flight A		
Howard Bittinger	8/15	Killed 8/26.
Merton L. Campbell	6/20	1st Deputy. Killed 8/23.
Lyman E. Case	6/23	Killed 8/14.
Leonard J. Desson	6/25	
John F. Donoho	8/14	
Charles W. France	8/31	
George P. Glenn	6/23	Killed 7/20.
Weston W. Goodnow	6/20	Flight Commander.
John A. Myers	8/28	
William F. Schadt	10/21	Also served in 148th.
Floyd M. Showalter	6/23	
Ralph W. Snoke	6/25	Injured in crash 7/12. 2nd Deputy.
George T. Wise	7/21	Captured 8/25.
Flight B		
Howard Burdick	8/15	
Frank Dixon	6/25	3rd Deputy.
Ralph D. Gracie	6/25	1st Deputy. Killed 8/12.
William R. House	10/5	
Harry J. Jackson	8/12	Killed 8/26.
Ernest Mason	10/21	
William H. Shearmam	6/29	Killed 8/14.
Harold G. Shoemaker	8/28	2nd Deputy. Killed in collision 10/5.
Murray K. Spidle	6/23	Killed 8/3.
Gerald P. Thomas	9/29	Killed 9/22.
Theose E. Tillinghast	6/30	Captured 9/22.
William D. Tipton	6/20	1st Flight Commander. Captured 8/26.
Robert M. Todd	6/23	Captured 8/26.
George A. Vaughn	8/28	2nd Flight Commander.
Edgar G. White	9/17	Wounded 10/8.
Glenn D. Wicks	8/1	Killed in collision 10/5.
Rodney D. Williams	6/20	Wounded 8/23.
Flight C		
Harriss P. Alderman	6/23	Wounded 8/12.
William J. Armstrong	6/26	Wounded 8/12.
Jesse F. Campbell	8/1	2nd Deputy.
William T. Clements	8/28	2nd Flight Commander.
James A. Ellison	8/29	Grounded 9/22.
Albert Everett	8/14	Out ill one month.
Henry B. Frost	6/20	1st Deputy. Killed 8/26.
Martin C. Giesecke	8/31	
Lloyd A. Hamilton	6/20	1st Flight Commander. Killed 8/24.
Howard C. Knotts	8/15	Captured 10/14.
Bradley C. Lawton	6/27	Injured in crash 7/27.
Edward S. Lubbers	10/21	
Thomas L. Moore	8/28	Returned to 148th sqdn. 9/5.
Laurence Roberts	6/23	Out ill one month. Killed 8/26.
Albert J. Schneider	7/22	
Cuthbert Tunstall	10/22	

Unassigned:
Irving P. Corse, William H. Spindle.

Notes

Readers who wish to examine the history of the 17th Aero Squadron in its earliest form must see the official history and souvenir publication *History of the 17th Aero Squadron* by Dr. Frederick Mortimer Clapp, 1920. It is a thoroughly enjoyable work by a professional author and art scholar and is currently available in reprint.

Many events recounted in the early chapters of this work are drawn from unpublished notes, letters, and diary entries made available to us by Dr. Clapp when we visited him in New York City in 1967 and 1968. They are quoted here by permission of the Yale Collection of American Literature, Beinecke Rare Book and Manuscript Library, Yale University.

While not often cited in this work, another interesting book about Camel drivers is *War Birds, The Diary of an Unknown Aviator*, now generally conceded to have been written by Elliot White Springs from personal experiences and references to several diaries. First privately printed, and then broadly published in the now long defunct Liberty magazine, it is an engrossing look at the life of these young men (including many 17th pilots) as supposedly recorded in a diary by one John MacGavock Grider. It is not exactly a diary, however, and undoubtedly the author projects an overstated air of unruliness among the young pilots. Still, these problems in no way diminish what is possibly the best book about World War I flying.

Robert Todd, mentioned often in this work as a pilot of supreme skill and daring, was also a writer of considerable merit. We recognized this early and were happy to see Mr. Todd publish, in 1978, an account of his experiences as a *Sopwith Camel Fighter Ace*. We recommend this book highly. Copies are available from Mrs. Dorothy Todd in San Diego, California, who graciously permitted quotation from that work here.

Letters by Mr. Todd not included in his autobiography are quoted here by permission of his son, Mr. Miles Todd, who provided copies.

This work makes repeated use of the above sources along with numerous diaries. Recreation of combat action is largely based on study of the official combat reports and the dawn and dusk patrol reports as expanded by diaries, letters, and published sources. To save space, frequently cited sources are identified as follows:

FMC = *History of the 17th Aero Squadron*, Frederick Mortimer Clapp.
UPN = Unpublished notes, Frederick Mortimer Clapp—typed copy.
RT = *Sopwith Camel Fighter Ace*, Robert Todd.
OCR = Official combat reports
OBR = Official bombing reports
DDPR = Daily dawn and dusk patrol reports. These often contain details not included in the combat and bombing reports.
HB = Diary of Howard Burdick
MC = Diary of Merton L. Campbell
WC = Diary of William T. Clements
LR = Diary of Laurence Roberts
HT = Diary of Harry D. Traxler
FN = Diary, "*Jadgflieger Friedrich Noltenius,*" edited by A. E. Fenko, Cross and Cockade 7, no. 4 (1966)
AAHS = American Aviation Historical Society Journal
C&C = Cross and Cockade Journal

CHAPTER 1

1. FMC, 3.

2. FMC, 3. The brothers were: Albert and Claude Beebe, MI; Claude and Clifton Booth, OR; Cecil and John Douglas, OH; Dean and George Fellay, IL; Eldon and Roy Hively, IN; and probably Ney and Ned Brown of Canada. Among aliens were: Edwin Berntsen, Norwegian; Maurice Baker and Harvey Day, Russian (despite their names); Edwin R. Jensen, Dane; and Edward D'Olic, Austrian.

3. The Bolling Commission was one of the first instances of Anglo-American cooperation. It concerned itself primarily with the problems of how best to bring wartime America up to speed in ways that would match the existing situation in Europe. For information concerning its effect on the air services, see *The Measure of America's World War Aeronautical Effort* by Edgar S. Gorrell.

4. FMC, 5.

5. FMC, 5. In later years, Robert Oldys changed his name to Olds. Olds retired as a Major General.

6. FMC, 3. Clapp cites earlier writing on the subject by David T. Wells.

7. The 17th's enlisted men trained primarily at Camp Leaside just outside Toronto. Pilots trained at many fields around Toronto.

8. Forming fours is amusingly discussed in Ian Hay's *The First Hundred Thousand*, Grosset & Dunlap, New York, NY: 3-5.

9. FMC, 6.

10. Loran J. Cooper to O. Reed, undated, mid-1968.

11. George Vaughn and Frank Dixon, interview by authors, St. Regis Hotel, New York City, NY, Jan. 1968.

12. Albert Everett, interviews by O. Reed, Weston, WV, 1965-1966. RT, 20. Todd says that during the summer of 1917, most were housed in the armory.

13. Albert Everett, interviews by O. Reed, Weston WV, 1965-1966.

14. Harriss Alderman to "Folks," dated Saturday. Since Alderman was an orphan, the folks were undoubtedly his aunt, Miss L. J. Agostini, and other friends and relatives around Wilmington, NC.

15. First mentioned to the writers by Lorenz Ayers, Alderman's success with women was still a source of wonder and pride with those of the 17th fifty years later. Fiftieth reunion, interviews by authors, Dayton, OH, June 19-21, 1968.

16. Vernon Castle (real name, Blythe) and his wife Irene were famous performers and dance innovators of the period. He was killed in a crash at Fort Worth, Texas, on Feb. 15, 1918. He died because he chose to ride the forward seat in the JN4 training planes while instructing. This was the more dangerous position in that tandem cockpit aircraft and he wanted to give students a better chance.

17. Harold Shoemaker to Robert Elmer Shoemaker (father), Camp Borden, Ontario, Sept. 26, 1917.

18. FMC, 6. Expanded by discussion: 50th reunion, interviews by authors, Dayton, OH, June 19-21, 1968.

19. Fiftieth reunion, interviews by authors, Dayton, OH, June 19-21, 1968.

20. UPN, 71-83.

21. Months later, Laurence "Bobby" Roberts started a letter home (Laurence Roberts to "Folks," June 26, 1918) by saying, "Somewhere in France at last, and attached to the outfit I swore I would never join..."

22. The Frederick Mortimer Clapp biography is drawn from Who's Who, his official business biography, his unpublished memoirs, and interviews by the authors, New York, NY, Nov. 1967 and Mar. 1968. Dr. Clapp was considered long dead by members of the squadron before these authors found him living comfortably on the upper east side of New York City. He retired as director of the Frick Museum. He died in 1969.

23. The David Terro Wells biography is based on information provided by family sources, discussion with comrades, the writings of Frederick M. Clapp, and newspaper clippings.

24. UPN, 80. While it is probable that the things reported here did happen, it must be remembered that the facts are as presented by a hostile witness; Clapp just didn't like Bonnell. Others, however, found Bonnell to be most energetic and efficient. See Harold E. Hartney, *Up & At 'Em*, Ace books, A Division of Charter Communications Inc., New York, NY (1971): 96.

25. UPN, 71. Clapp's account of Bonnell being arrested over an automobile differs somewhat. The account given here draws upon that as further defined by reunion conversations.

26. Martin F. Scanlon, interview by O. Reed, Philadelphia, PA, 13 Oct., 1968. Scanlon also served in World War II and retired as a Brigadier General.

27. Records in the National Archives report the VD inspection on Christmas Eve. A subsequent report dated Dec. 31, 1917, gave the unit a clean bill of health.

28. While there were already many Americans in Europe and even some bomber and fighter squadrons, the 17th seems to have been first to arrive fully staffed with pilots. Despite his problems, Bonnell succeeded well in this effort. Special order 88 issued at Garden City, NY, on Jan. 8, 1918, reads as follows: "The following 1st Lts. S.R.C.A.S. are assigned to the 17th Aero Sqdn: Ackerman, James H.; Baker, John M.; Bennett, James G.; Carpenter, Jay I.; Cassard, Daniel W. (sometimes seen as Cazzard); Critzman, George M.; Connely, Francis J.; Hughuenin, Stanley; Jenkinson, Harry, Jr.; Moffett, John M.; Pedler, Russell H.; Squires, George; Starkey, Henry Clay; Wheatley, Eugene R.; Williams, Charles S.; Williams, Rodney D." Still a second order seems to be a list of officers who shipped with the 17th and includes, in addition to the above: Regulars—Scanlon, Martin F.; Reserve Officers—Long, Rose D.; Bangs, Henry McC.; Wells, David T.; Lapsley, Arthur B.; Gracie, Ralph D.; Johnson, Oliver P.; Ralston, Orville A.; Creech, Jesse O.; Shoemaker, Harold G.; Snoke, Ralph W.; France, Charles W.; Tunstall, Cuthbert; Wade, Leigh; Cadets—Reese, Robert H.; Keating, James A.; Harris, Don R.; Ellis, Robert H.

29. The Oxford cadets arrived in England on an earlier voyage of the Carmania. Elliot White Springs, who was to be heir to a cotton fortune (Springmaid Cotton Mills), was made a sergeant of cadets at Oxford. See Eliot White Springs, *War Birds*, Temple Press Books, London (1966): 10. Also aboard the Carmania was famed violinist, Albert

Spaulding, who went on to Italy as a language instructor under the command of Fiorello H. LaGuardia.

30. See Thomas G. Miller, Jr., *USAS Fliers with the RFC/RAF, 1917-1918*, C&C 7, no. 1 (Spring 1966): 29, for numerous confirmed victories. While not the final word, it lists many people often overlooked. At the 50th reunion, Keating discussed in detail his being shot down. He reported that he had just downed one Fokker (confirmed) and was so busy watching it crash that the other came upon him easily. "In the excitement, I forgot everything I knew," he explained. Although the wound was through the elbow, he had no residual effects.

31. Anonymous to O. Reed, May 30, 1967. The miscreant in the case was still so sensitive about this matter half a century later that he wrote of it in longhand to keep his secretary from learning the story. We will honor his sensitivity and say only that he later served in the 17th.

32. Loran Cooper to O. Reed, undated, mid-1968.

33. FMC, 9.

34. HT, unnumbered pages 20-24.

CHAPTER 2

1. It was common during both World Wars for parents to hang in a window a banner showing one star for each son in service. The stars were ordinarily blue. A gold star meant that a son had been killed. The title of this chapter is based on that custom and the lines come from a silly tune composed and sung by World War I aviators. It goes:

Oh, Mother, put out your gold star,
Your son's gone up in a Sop. [Sopwith]
The wings are weak, the ship's a freak,
She's got a rickety prop.
The motor's junk, your son is drunk,
He's sure to take a flop.
Oh, Mother, put out your gold star,
Your son's gone up in a Sop.

In *Nocturne Militaire* (Elliot White Springs, Grossett & Dunlap, 257), the author prefers "golden star" to gold star.

2. FMC, 12.

3. Thyrza B. Fowler, *Harold Fowler, 1886—1957: a remembrance*, [NY] Privately printed [at the Spiral Press], 1960. See also the expanded biography in Appendix B.

4. There seems to be no doubt that the 20-horsepower engine difference between the Camels flown by the 17th and those flown by the 148th was frequently a matter of life and death to the pilots. Although the 17th and 148th pilots all trained together, were assigned from a common pool, and were essentially the same sorts of fliers, the 148th achieved more victories and suffered far fewer losses. Springs wrote (Elliot White Springs, *War Birds*, Temple Press Books [1966]: 129,130) regarding the 17th, "They've got Le Rhone Camels and may the Lord make His face to smile upon them..." See also Appendix C.

5. FMC, 30. By secret order signed by H. Breen, Adj. 51st Wing, June 15, 1918.

6. S. B. Eckert, interview by O. Reed, Philadelphia, PA, 1966. There was much confusion on who would really command the 17th. On May 25, the Commander of the RAF 5th brigade recommended Eckert or Morton L. Newhall. On May 28, BG Harts, U. S. N. S., recommended Fowler. On June 14, Lt. Col. Joseph C. Morrows advised that Capt. C. J. Biddle had been given the position and suggested that perhaps Eckert might take the 148th. On 15 June, in special order no. 230, Lt. Col. Van Horn, O.C. Aleshire says that Capt. David McK. Peterson of the 95th Aero Squadron will command. After all that, it seems that Mort Newhall was a flight commander in the 17th for three or four days before moving on to the 148th, at which point Eckert was firmly in the saddle as Fowler had planned. Fowler became liaison between RAF and American headquarters.

7. By Eckert's account (interview by O. Reed, Philadelphia, PA, 1966), he flew the first plane to lift from Selfridge. The field had been formed partly by draining a pond and he took off over numerous dead and rotting fish.

8. The Eckert biography is based on *Who's Who* entries, his official business biography, examination of his service record, and personal conversations. During the war Eckert was credited with shooting a green Albatross down out of control on May 28, 1918, and driving a two seater down under control on Aug. 24, 1918. Eckert died in 1973.

9. The incident with the blouse was reported in a memorial column written by Romeyn Berry, *Now in my Time!*, published in Cornell Alumni News, Fall, 1942. Cazenovia is a rural suburb of Syracuse, NY. Berry also states that when the Great Depression came upon America, "Bingo" Wells, who had made a million dollars, reported that he lost a million dollars and thirty five cents. Concerning the brow injury, George Vaughn came across Wells where he was running a private club afterward and observed the disfigurement.

10. Fiftieth reunion, interviews by authors, Dayton, OH, June 19-21, 1968. Clapp had been serving at Petite Synthe with a contingent of the 22nd Aero Squadron since early spring. His unpublished diary of the period deals splendidly with life in a British Squadron in early 1918.

11. The Lorenz K. Ayers biography is based on his official business biography and numerous personal interviews. Ayers made it his business to have those on leave bring him film and is responsible for the many photographs of the 17th. Ayers was replacing Lt. Arthur Lapsley who was on his way to hospital.

12. Surprisingly, most pilots could no longer remember which flight they served with in the 17th when quizzed fifty years later. Service has been determined by cross referencing information supplied by those few who could recall, dawn and dusk reports, combat reports, diaries, letters, etc. In some cases the assignment decided upon for this work is tentative because pilots sometimes transferred from one flight to another, or simply left little trail to be followed.

13. S. B. Eckert to 65th Wing RAF, BEF, July 8, 1918. This establishes the claims for Tipton, Hamilton, and Gracie, and lists Armstrong as being credited with "one driven down—probably crashed."

14. The Lloyd Hamilton biography is based on the numerous pieces written about him and interviews with those who knew him. Popularly known as "Ham," Hamilton's was a complex personality and his premonitions of death were established even before he shipped to Europe. This is cited by Alan W. Burke to "Miss [Grace] Myrick" (daughter of Hamilton's former fiancee, Ruth McKernon, who married following Hamilton's death), Feb. 27, 1968. Burke says that on his last stateside leave, Hamilton startled his friends at home by singing the last line of *Over There* as:

"...and we won't be back,
we'll be buried over there."

15. The William Tipton biography is based on comments by Mrs. Louise T. Muller (sister), interview by O. Reed, Jan. 1968, and conversations with those who served with him. Tipton also changed his middle name from Dolly to Duncan when he entered service. He signed his letters, "Willie." Tipton was a colonel in World War II and crashed to his death in 1945 when he was overcome by carbon monoxide that seeped into the cockpit of the P-47 he was flying over Ohio.

16. The Weston W. Goodnow biography is based on information supplied by the family and interviews with those who served with him.

17. Serial numbers were first assigned to enlisted men beginning in Feb. 1918. Officers had no serial numbers until the 1920s.

18. C.O. 17 to Chief of Supply, Transportation Division, Sept. 23, 1918.

19. The Great Snow Owl insignia designed by Sgt. 1st class Hayden C. Kellum was put on 17th Spads at Toul, but it was never used by the unit in combat. When, in time, the 17th Aero Squadron became the 17th Pursuit Squadron, the planes carried a variation of Kellum's insignia. Kellum is said to have drawn the illustrations for Clapp's book on the 17th.

20. MC, 42.

21. HT, 62 of unnumbered pages, probable date, July 5, 1918.

22. FMC, 21.

23. FMC, 18.

24. Supposedly an airman nearly killed by antiaircraft fire once yelled out instinctively, "Archibald, Certainly Not!," which was the title of a specialty song popularly performed by music hall's Sir George Robey. The story raced about the front, and the term, "archie," became universal. The song has five verses and starts like this:

VERSE
It's no use me denying facts—
I'm henpeck'd you can see!
"Twas on our wedding morn
My wife commenc'd to peck at me.
The wedding breakfast over,
I said, "We'll start off today
Upon our honeymoon!" then she yelled,
"What! waste time that way?"
CHORUS
"Arch-i-bald—certainly not!
Get back to work at once, sir, like a shot!
When single, you could waste time spooning,
But lose work now for honey-mooning!
Arch-i-bald—certainly not!"

The copy reviewed by the authors was provided by the late Arthur Treacher and bears the following information: Copyright 1909 by Francis Day and Hunter, Ltd. F.&.D. Ltd. Written by John L. St. John. Composed by Alfred Glover.

25. Frederick Mortimer Clapp, interview by authors, New York, NY, Nov. 1967 and Mar., 1968.

26. The Dr. Jacob J. Ross biography is based on information supplied by the family and conversations with comrades who knew him. Ross died in 1929.

27. Lorenz K. Ayers, interviews by authors, numerous dates.

28. C. O. 17th Aero Squadron to C. O. American Air Service Units with B.E.F., Sept. 28, 1918.

CHAPTER 3

1. DDPR, July 7, 1918. A hand written "Combats in the Air" form exists but seems to have never been acted upon.

2. Theose E. "Tilly" Tillinghast had served with Eckert at Selfridge Field and when he heard that Eckert was to have a squadron, wrote to be included. Tillinghast had just recovered from pneumonia. The Murray Spidle biography is from the *Massillon Evening Independent*, Massillon, OH, Aug. 17, 1918.

3. George Vaughn to O. Reed, Jan. 17, 1967. Vaughn outlines common formation practices.

4. DDPR, July 7, 1918.

5. James J. Sloan, *148th American*, AAHS 4, no. 4 (Winter 1959): 253.

6. Hugh Shearman to C. P. Shearman (father), July 2, 1918.

7. Laurence Roberts to Ada Roberts (mother), July 2, 1918. These low flying larks brought much official correspondence saying, in effect, stop buzzing. Ref...65/G/96, R. A. Cunningham, Lt. Col. Commanding 65 Wing RAF, July 2, 1918 says, "This practice will cease forth with, and any culprit will be dealt severely with." Roberts was a blithe spirit so prone to motorcycle accidents that when Clapp was adjutant and Roberts a cadet in the 22nd Aero Squadron, Clapp ordered him to sell his machine.

8. Aviators had much trouble with wind burn and frost-bitten skin during the days of open cockpit flying. The best protection was to cover the face with a silk scarf or a ladies silk stocking. Next best was to coat the face with whale oil. A last resort was Vaseline. Vaseline had to be put on in a heavy coat and not rubbed in since that softened the skin and aggravated the problem.

9. RT, 56.

10. Bradley Lawton to O. Reed, May 28, 1969. In this letter, Lawton does not say he hit the guns when he crashed, but since those were the most prominent objects positioned before the pilots' seat, it is doubtful that he did not.

11. FMC, 25.

12. Postcard, F. A. Dixon to O. Reed, April 14, 1967. Dixon cites a bullet through his gas tank. Dixon enjoyed a long reputation among friends as a man who liked to have a good time. Originally from Pittsburgh, Pennsylvania, he attended Princeton with Vaughn.
13. RT, 62.
14. Harriss Alderman to "Folks," July 11, 1918.
15. DDPR, July 17, 1918.
16. The propeller hub struck in this foray was presented by Mr. Williams to the Air Force Museum in 1968.
17. WC, 71.
18. The loss of Glenn was most mysterious and the subject of an illustrated letter, Eckert to C.O., 65th wing RAF, July 21, 1918.
19. FMC, 55. OCR 1. DDPR, July 20, 1918.
20. Rodney Williams to O. Reed, Dec. 1, 1968.
21. Influenza, which in 1919 killed more Americans than died in The Great War, seemed to be relatively gentle with servicemen who caught it in Europe in 1918. In diaries and letters one reads that pilots who got it often did not even leave off flying. Perhaps it was a matter of age group.
22. Brig. Gen. Air Staff, July 23, 1918. Letter refuses permission. Undated letter, 10 Bgde. RAF, urges permission.
23. Murray Spidle to Father and Mother (L. C. and ___ Spidle), July 24, 1918.
24. DDPR, July 30, 1918.
25. RT, 73.
26. Murray Spidle to Father and Mother (L. C. and ___ Spidle), dated July 24, 1918.
27. HT, 68 of unnumbered pages.
28. FMC, 56,57. OCRs 2-5. Letter, Murray Spidle to Father and Mother (L. C. and ___ Spidle), dated August 2, 1918.
29. DDPR, Aug. 1, 1918.
30. Samuel B. Eckert, interview by O. Reed, Philadelphia, PA, 1966.
31. WC, 73, July 29 entry; 74, July 30 entry; 75, August 2 entry. See also Elliot White Springs, *War Birds*, Temple Press Books, London (1966): 101,117,128.
32. The Glenn Wicks biography is based on conversations with squadron members. Wicks was extremely popular among the officers and men of the 17th.
33. MC. 45, July 26, 1918.
34. George Fellay, interview with authors, 50th reunion, Dayton, Ohio, June 19-21, 1968.

CHAPTER 4

1. The title is from another silly tune sung by World War I aviators. It goes:

> The bells of hell go ting-aling-aling
> For you, but not for me.
> For me the angels sing-aling-aling
> They've got the goods [as opposed to the bads] for me.
> O, death, where is thy sting-aling-aling?
> O, grave, thy victory?
> The bells of hell go ting-aling-aling
> For you, but not for me.

2. DDPR, August 1, 1918.
3. Murray Spidle to Father and Mother (L. C. and ___ Spidle), Aug. 2, 1918.
4. FMC, 58. OCRs. 6,7. DDPR, Aug. 3, 1918.
5. Leonard Desson to Father and Mother (L.C. and ___ Spidle), Aug. 6, 1918.
6. Lewis C. Spidell [sic] to O. Reed, Feb. 28, 1968. Mrs. Spidle accompanied the Gold Star Mother's tour of France mounted in 1928.
7. Circumstances presented in clippings from *Massillon Evening Independent*, Massillon, OH, Aug. 17, 1918, and others undated.
8. DDPR, Aug. 4, 1918.
9. The Varssenaere rehearsal plan was set forth in Secret RAF 5th Group Operations Order No. 3 dated 1 August 1918 signed simply C.O.C. 5th Group. These were uncovered by Mr. Michael Dickinson who, as stated earlier, did much research for us in London on the 17th Aero Squadron.
10. The 148th was ordered to take up station at Allonsville on Aug. 11, 1918. Subsequently they moved to Remaisnil (near Doullons) on Sept. 8, 1918; Baizieux (near Albert) on Sept. 20, 1918; Bapaum on an unknown date; and Toul on Nov. 4, 1918.
11. FMC, 59-61. OCRs 8-10. DDPR, Aug. 7, 1918. Accident report, Aug. 7, 1918.
12. FMC, 61, 62. OCR 11. DDPR, Aug. 8, 1918.
13. FMC, 29. Wilcavage was Eckert's favorite driver when he chose to travel by motorcycle. Said Eckert during one interview, "Oh, he could get the sidecar wheel clear off the ground and just sail along."
14. FMC, 30.
15. FMC, 62,62. OCR 12. DDPR, Aug. 9, 1918.
16. The need to vary the formation is reported in Ref. 1459 10, O.C. No. 210 Sqdn., Aug., 1918. Additional correspondence cites lack of simultaneous delivery and flying too low for bombing.
17. DDPR, Aug. 11, 1918. Strangely there seems to be no OCR or OBR of this affair. Merton Campbell's diary confirms the action and states that he, Hamilton, and Goodnow downed a two seater on the afternoon show discussed subsequently. No confirmation found.
18. The raid was ordered for the next day by Secret RAF 5th Group OP Order No. 4, Aug. 11, 1918; then it was postponed.
19. Rodney Williams to O. Reed, Dec. 1, 1968. Williams reported being severely scolded for violating this neutral air space.
20. William R. Puglisi to G. Roland, Aug. 19, 1968.
21. Ralph Snoke to O. Reed, Mar. 29, 1967.
22. Ibid.
23. FMC, 33,63. OCR 13. DDPR, Aug. 12, 1918. Rodney Williams to O. Reed, Dec. 1, 1968. Strangely, this major conflict provided a single claim among the Americans.
24. FMC, 34. See also Robert Todd to Miles Todd (father), Aug., 1918. Todd, Alderman, and "Casey" Case were best buddies.
25. FMC, 33. Harriss Alderman to "Folks," Aug. 22, 1918.
26. Albert Everett, interviews with O. Reed, 1965-1966. Everett tented

with Jackson and said Jackson was very uneasy about formation flying. He once nudged Everett's wingtip during formation practice at Auxi.

27. Lorenz K. Ayers, interviews with authors, 1967.

CHAPTER 5

1. Moon set and sunrise as determined by Michael Dickinson.
2. Samuel B. Eckert, interview with O. Reed, 1966.
3. British details of the raid drawn from official correspondence. C.O. Major. W. L. Welsh (Tompy) 61st Wing H.Q., RAF. to G.O.C.; 5th Group, from Capt. A. J. B. Jonks 5th Group OPS Order No. 4; from L.C.R.R. Hickey, 204 squadron; Lt. T. W. Nash, 204 Squadron; C. P. Brown, capacity unknown, handwritten account, August 13, 1918.
4. Ibid.
5. Ibid.
6. FMC, 31.
7. Frank Dixon to O. Reed, Nov. 19, 1967. These revelations are not to imply that Dixon was not a daring and intrepid aviator. Once directed to fly a Bentley Camel as high as he could, he pushed it through 21,000 feet before lapsing into unconsciousness. When he came to, he was whirling about upside down. In his struggles to right the aircraft, his Sutton harness broke, whereupon he was actually thrown out of the cockpit and then, fortunately, slammed back in to regain control calmly and fly home safely.
8. FMC, 97. See also MC, 48.
9. Per Michael Dickinson, a note on the 218th bombing report says, "Original objective V.[arssenaere] aerodrome abandoned owing to EA activity."
10. FMC, 32.
11. The Germans returned these favors by raiding Petite Synthe some days later. By then, the 17th had moved to Auxi-le-Chateau.
12. H. A. Jones, *The War in the Air*, six volumes, Oxford University Press, Oxford, England (1931): chapter XIII, The Battle of Bapaume, Pages 469-470. By permission of the Oxford University Press.
13. William R. Puglisi to G. Roland, Aug. 19, 1968.
14. Ibid.
15. FMC, 64,65. OCR 14,15. DDPR, Aug. 14, 1918. MC, page 49. Case was buried in grave 729 at Bruges Cemetery.
16. DDPR, Aug. 15, 1918. RT, 73. Again, oddly, Clapp does not include this although a copy of the claim in the British archives indicates it was confirmed. The confirmation says (although marked out for some reason), "The destruction of this E.A. was seen by Lt. Harris of the 211 Sqdn and his observer who was in the D. H. 9. Lt. Harris saw the pilot hanging over the edge of the fuselage apparently killed and his observer saw the E. A. crash."
17. MC, 49.
18. C. P. Shearman to S. B. Eckert, November 11, 1918.
19. Undated clipping from Chicago Daily Tribune. Postwar.
20. DDPR, Aug. 14, 1918.
21. RT, 82,84.
22. FMC, 65,66. OCR 16. DDPR, Aug. 15, 1918.
23. DDPR, Aug. 15, 1918.
24. Brief biography based on review of Bittinger's service record.
25. The biography of Howard Burdick is based on interviews with comrades, newspaper accounts, and information furnished by the family. He signed his letters both as "Howard" and "Dick." Burdick had attended Adelphi Academy in Brooklyn with another famous aviator, George Vaughn, who later joined the squadron. Burdick was very aggressive in the air and Vaughn said later that he was quite surprised to see him survive the war.
26. The biography of Howard Knotts is based on interviews with comrades, newspaper accounts, and information furnished by the family. Knotts and Burdick were together at Harvard before volunteering.
27. Harriss Alderman to "Folks," Aug. 22, 1918.
28. The move was in response to secret order, Cunningham to Eckert, Aug. 16, 1918. The order was still in the National Archives files when the material was reviewed in 1966. Being still classified, it was pulled at once.
29. MC, 49.
30. Add to the slang that these Americans were adept at avoiding "woofits"—a dread condition caused by overeating and under drinking. Cutting boots down was a long standing problem. As late as Oct. 23, 1918, the 13th Wing was still ordering Eckert to put a stop to the practice.
31. FMC, 37.
32. HT, 75 of unnumbered pages.
33. FN, 323. Arch Whitehouse, *Heroes of the Sunlit Sky*, Doubleday & Company, Inc., Garden City, New York (1967): 335, says Goering was appointed to command July 8, 1919.

CHAPTER 6

1. Quentin Reynolds, *They Fought for the Skies; The Dramatic Story of the First War in the Air*, Rinehart & Company, Inc., New York, NY (1957): 169, cites the spotty history of the RE-8. So bad was its record that Lord Cowdray, President of the Air Board, initiated a series of trials to address the problems. See also William Barrett, *The First War Planes*, Fawcett Publications Inc., Greenwich, CN, (1960): 56.
2. Alfred V. Haig, interview by the authors, Philadelphia, PA, 1971.
3. FMC, 66-69. OCRs 17-21. DDPR, Aug. 21, 1918.
4. FM, 69,70. OCRs 22,23. DDPR, Aug. 21, 1918. Knotts told this story when speaking at a postwar lecture in Middlebury, Connecticut, where he had been invited by Dr. Ross. Undated account. See also Howard Burdick to Clinton Burdick (father), France, Nov. 24, 1918.
5. Rodney Williams, interview with authors, 1971.
6. FMC, 71-73. OCRs 24-27. DDPR, Aug. 22, 1918. Aircraft damage report Aug. 22, 1918.
7. LR, 76.
8. The authors have caught Dr. Clapp in a lapse of scholarship. The second bomb run that day was erroneously labeled as 1. The first, on which Mert Campbell was killed, was subsequently submitted and numbered

0. Apparently when he compiled his book, Clapp could think of no way to handle this and simply left out the report with the odd zero number. And how was Mert Campbell killed? Letters to his home do not rule out a hit by ground fire. However, L. K. Ayers, who was a good friend of Campbell's, said that the pilot was downed by a fighter as stated here. OBR 0. DDPR, August 23, 1918.

9. FMC, pages 98-100. OBRs 1,2. DDPR, Aug. 23, 1918.

10. FMC, pages 100,101. OBR 3. DDPR, Aug. 23, 1918.

11. Rodney Williams to Frederick M. Clapp, England, Sept. 6, 1918.

12. FMC, 101,102. OBR 4. DDPR, Aug. 23, 1918.

CHAPTER 7

1. George Fellay, interview by authors, 50th reunion, Dayton, OH, June 19-21, 1968.

2. DDPR dated Aug. 24, 1918. See also James J. Sloan, *148th American* AAHS 4, no. 4 (Winter 1959): 264.

3. George Fellay, interview by authors, 50th reunion, Dayton, OH, June 19-21, 1968.

4. FMC, 73. OCR 28. DDPR, Aug. 24, 1918.

5. Ralph Snoke to O. Reed, no date.

6. Repatriation interview with Wise on return from POW camp. Undated notes by Lt. L. N. Thayer.

7. FMC, 102-106. OBRs 5-10. DDPR, Aug. 24, 1918.

8. James J. Sloan, *148th American*, AAHS 4, no. 4 (Winter 1959): 263. Curtis was later reported a prisoner.

9. FMC, 40.

10. DDPR, Aug. 25, 1918. Eckert was credited with one driven down.

11. RT, 88. This is one of the first instances in which a pilot originally in one flight appears in a command position of another. Todd's *mea culpa* regarding the action of Aug. 26 ("Tipton and I were leading...") confirms that he was deputy flight leader after Gracie's death. DDPR, Aug. 26, 1918.

12. FMC, 74. OCR 29. DDPR, Aug. 25, 1918.

13. Howard Burdick to Clinton D. Burdick (father), Aug. 25, 1918. Despite the devil-may-care attitude Burdick projected to those about him, his diary shows him practicing considerable self-discipline to increase his chances of fighting and surviving.

14. FMC, 40.

15. Frederick Mortimer Clapp, Interviews by authors, Nov. 1967 and Mar. 1968.

16. Theose Tillinghast to O. Reed, May 29, 1967.

17. WC, 84.

18. FN, entry dated August 24, 1918, 326. See also H. J. Nowarra and Kimbrough S. Brown, *Von Richthofen and the Flying Circus*, Harleford Publications, Letchworth, Herts, England, and Aero, Los Angeles, CA (1964): 130, 131.

19. FMC, 74-77. OCR 30-33. DDPR, Aug. 26, 1918. See also James J. Sloan, *148th American*, AAHS 4, no. 4 (Winter 1959): 326.

20. William R. Puglisi to G. Roland, Aug. 19, 1968.

21. Robert Todd to Lilles H. Todd (mother), Nov. 26, 1918.

22. FN, diary entry dated Aug. 26, 1918, 326.

23. Robert Todd to Lilles H. Todd (mother), Nov. 26, 1918. See also Tipton repatriation interview, undated notes by Lt. L. H. Thayer.

24. Robert Todd to Lilles H. Todd (mother), Nov. 26, 1918.

25. Ibid. Some sources indicate that Frost died at a British casualty clearing station. While Todd's letter seems to refute that, it is possible that the British overran the crash site subsequently. Such a development might explain also why the enemy was so intent on removing Tipton's Camel—they did not want it to be recaptured.

26. Ralph Snoke to O. Reed, Mar. 29, 1967.

27. DDPR, Aug. 26, 1918.

CHAPTER 8

1. P. H. L. Playfair to S. B. Eckert, Aug. 26, 1918.

2. Ralph Snoke to O. Reed, Nov. 2, 1968.

3. Frank Dixon to O. Reed, Apr. 17, 1967.

4. Sholto Douglas to S. B. Eckert, Aug. 28, 1918. Vaughn biography based on many published accounts and personal interviews. Vaughn seems to have had the capacity to reduce warfare to abstractions in thought. In one instance he told the authors of firing at a plane and hitting the pilot whereupon his enemy involuntarily threw up both arms. Said Vaughn to us, "I thought, why, there's a man in there!"

5. George Vaughn to O. Reed, Jan. 22, 1969. Vaughn confirms that he had never flown the Camel.

6. The Harold Shoemaker biography is based on letters, information provided by the family, and discussions with his comrades. Charles France, interview by authors, 50th reunion, Dayton, OH, June 19-21, 1968. France stated that he was Shoemakers' tent mate and spoke of Shoemaker's troubles with the Camel. The incident of landing the aircraft with the collapsed wing is from a letter, Harold Shoemaker to Mary Shoemaker (mother), July 3, 1918.

7. WC, 86. See also James J. Sloan, *148th American*, AAHS 4, no. 4 (Winter 1959): 257.

8. WC, 90.

9. Major Caldwell to S. B. Eckert, France, Aug. 28, 1918. Recommends Corse. When Corse was sent out by Ross it was supposed he would return shortly. On Sept. 14, though, Corse wrote that he was to be sent farther back. He comments on how badly some of those at the hospital are shot up.

10. Charles France, interview by authors, 50th reunion, Dayton, OH, June 19-21, 1968. Like Alderman, France was an orphan.

11. There was a flurry of orders covering the events that sent seasoned hands away and allowed the squadron to assume its new character. The one involving Alderman is interesting because not long after arriving in hospital, he departed without permission. Said to be a misunderstanding.

12. Lt. Charles Miles, RFA, B Battery, 95th Brigade to O.C. 5th Corps—redirected to Eckert, Aug. 27, 1918.

13. FMC, 39. During one of these visits, Ayers went along in command and salvaged the Vickers machine guns from the wreck. He sent one

home as a souvenir. After the war, Campbell's body was returned to Ohio and buried in the family plot. In the late 1960s, the family still had the old propeller that had decked Campbell's grave in France.

14. Accident report, Aug. 28, 1918, cites engine problem.
15. WC, 88.
16. Albert Everett, interviews with O. Reed, 1965-1966.
17. Albert Beebe, accident report, Sept. 4, 1918. This is an interesting account written in longhand by the mechanic.
18. The source of this obviously direct quote is now misplaced. However, at the 50th reunion the troops generally agreed that it was true.
19. Provost Marshall, II Corps A. E. F. to C.O. 17th Aero Squadron, September 8, 1918. Loran Cooper to O. Reed, undated, mid-1967.
20. S. B. Eckert to Provost Marshall, II Corps A.E.F., Sept. 14, 1918.
21. Ibid.
22. WC, 88.
23. Ibid., 88,89.
24. Ibid., 89.
25. FMC, 43.
26. Alfred Haig, interview by authors, Philadelphia, PA, 1971.
27. DDPR, Sept. 12, 1918.
28. FMC, 77. WC, 91. OCR 34. DDPR, Sept. 13, 1918.
29. By the end of the war Burdick, Knotts, and Tipton had also earned the DFC.
30. WC, 91.
31. Ibid, 77. On Aug. 6, 1918, seasoned pilot William Clements discusses floating and speaks of it as a "new stunt."
32. FMC, 78. OCR 35. DDPR, Sept. 17, 1918. WC, 92.
33. WC, 92.
34. George Vaughn, interview by authors, Staten Island, NY, November 16, 1968.
35. FMC, 79,80. OCR 37. DDPR, Sept. 18, 1918.
36. FMC, 79, OCR 36. DDPR, Sept. 18, 1918. Howard Burdick to Clinton Burdick (father), Sept. 19, 1918.
37. DDPR, Sept. 18, 1918.
38. Undated, typed account bearing number C-885.

CHAPTER 9

1. It is difficult to account for the better success enjoyed by the second set of Camel drivers. They went to the same schools, flew the same planes, and faced the same enemy as their predecessors. One would expect roughly the same results. Here are some suggestions as to why it didn't happen:

   A. They got luckier. Had the war gone on longer the odds might have reasserted themselves.

   B. Their enemy got weaker. Certainly many famous German aviators died in 1918. One would expect, however, that the large numbers of enemy squadrons present in the area would have compensated in quantity for a decline in quality.

   C. The new leaders did a better job. This is possible. Tipton and Hamilton had both been out at the front since early spring and may have been what we call burned out. Despite leave, both fell into a funk at about the same time and were soon finished. Hamilton's father, in a letter to Mr. Tipton dated Nov. 30, 1918, wrote that his son's last letter stated, "Oh Dad, Dad, Dad, I shall be so glad to get home again to my wonderful Mother and Father."

   A modern flight surgeon might have seen something in their mental state that Doctor Ross didn't.

   In a diary entry (WC, 92), William Clements offers the opinion that the C. O. was handling the squadron badly—but this was just before the successes of late September.

2. FMC, 45.
3. O. C. 17th Aero Squadron to O. C. American Air Units, undated.
4. See William E. Barrett, *The First War Planes*, Fawcett Publications Inc., Greenwich, CN (1960): 137, for Dolphin design and engine problems.
5. DDPR, Sept. 20, 1918.
6. DDPR, Sept. 21.
7. FMC, 82,83. OCRs 41,42. DDPR, Sept. 22, 1918.
8. Action as described in Vaughn's recommendation for the Medal of Honor. He subsequently received the Distinguished Service Cross.
9. FMC, 47. HB, 172 of unnumbered pages. Burdick erroneously lists Thomas's death as being Sept. 21. Thomas was from Flushing, NY. What little biography exists is based on conversations with comrades. While only twenty-two, his hair was already snow white.
10. Theose Tillinghast to O. Reed, Jan. 17, 1968.
11. FN, diary entry dated Sept. 22, 1918, page 334. The authors of this work noticed early in this endeavor that Noltenius' discussion of the combat that day is a mirror image of Vaughn's account, except that the first named claims that the enemy was downed. We brought this to Vaughn's attention and he tended to agree with us that he had fought Noltenius on that occasion.
12. FMC, 80. OCR 38. DDPR, Sept. 22, 1918.
13. So skillfully did "Gesooks" Giesecke land his plane that all damage was done by bullets. The plane was struck off squadron strength. Giesecke survived only because Knotts saw him being attacked by seven enemy planes and went quickly to his aid.
14. Williams never returned to the squadron. Perhaps this is recognition for the one he shot off Tipton's tail in July.
15. British aviators had to down ten enemy contraptions to be considered an ace. Americans are considered to be an ace after five. Ace is an unofficial position not formally recognized by the military.
16. FMC, 49,50. James J. Sloan, *148th American*, AAHS 4, no. 4 (Winter 1959): 258. There is no doubt the 148th jumped the Bavarian Blue Tails (Jasta 4 of Geschwader I) that morning. There is, however, little to suggest the 17th also encountered them as implied by Clapp. Knotts got a red, green-tailed aircraft (thought then to be a Sargent Major Thom) and a black, diamond-checkered aircraft with a white tail. Burdick got a bright-yellow and green Fokker.
17. WC, 93,94.
18. WC, 94.
19. FMC, 83-88. OCRs 43-51. DDPR, Sept. 24, 1918.

20. FMC, 106. OBR 10. It was not a bombing, but where else would one list it?

21. Howard Burdick to Bob (sic) Burdick (brother), Sept. 30, 1918, states that Knotts was suffering from battle fatigue.

22. DDPR, Sept. 26, 1918.

23. FMC, page 89,106,107. OCR 52. OBRs 11,12. DDPR, Sept. 27, 1918.

24. Hans Schröder played the game now generally known as good cop/bad cop. He was, of course, the good cop who took his fellow aviators under his wing for protection. See Schröder's *An Airman Remembers* (Translated by Claud W. Sykes), The Aviation Book Club, London.

25. See *My Capture and Escape* by John O. Donaldson; copyright © 1919 by Harper's Magazine. See also Lt. John C. Donaldson to BG H. N. Sargent, Nov. 11, 1918.

CHAPTER 10

1. Lt. General H. A. Lawrence to American Mission GHQ (secret), Oct. 7, 1918.

2. FMC, 90,91,112,113. OCRs 54,55. OBR 14. DDPR, Sept. 28, 1918.

3. FMC 89,90,112,113. OCR 53. OBR 14. DDPR, Sept. 28, 1918. See also statements by Dixon, Eckert, and Knotts endorsing Burdick for the DSC.

4. See FMC, 111,114-116, and OBRs 13,15,16 for bombing action on Sept. 29, 1918. Clapp erroneously identifies part of OBR 15 as OBR 13—perhaps to correct his numbering.

5. FMC, 92,123. OCR 56. OBR 19. DDPR, Oct. 2, 1918.

6. Edgar White, interview by authors, May, 26, 1967. So efficient had the squadron paperwork system become that when White failed to return, the plane was immediately struck off strength. When he then came wandering back the next day, there developed a literary brouhaha over the matter. On Oct. 9, Vaughn flew this plane and also got lost. Apparently no one had swung the compass.

7. FM. 129-131. OBRs 23,24. See DDPR, Oct. 4, 1918 for Shoemaker's action.

8. Edgar White, interview by authors, May 26, 1967. WC, 40, reports seeing, from the air, artillery shells passing north of Villers Brettoneux. World War I was particularly hard on the Shoemaker family. They lost the second of three sons when brother Ralph (a captain of infantry in the 29th Division) was killed on October 11, 1918, during the battle of Argonne Forest. Harold Shoemaker was originally buried near a wind mill at Esnes. After being interred in one military cemetery, he was later moved to the side of his brother at the American Somme Cemetery near St. Quenton, France.
Wicks and his plane burned and for a time there was a mystery concerning the identity of the corpse. Finally the body was identified by the numbers of the engine and guns. This was further confirmed by the finding of the word "Thompson" penciled onto the remaining wreckage in the area just forward of the cockpit. It was the signature of rigger Blair McKay Thompson who liked Wicks very much and probably signed the plane off in this manner to assure and amuse the young pilot.

9. FMC, 46.

10. Lorenz. K. Ayers, interviews by authors, various dates.

11. HB, 195,196 of unnumbered pages.

12. HB, 197 of unnumbered pages. While Eckert was on leave, his tent burned. Not knowing that RAF 203 had stolen the saxophone, he stated in later interviews that his fellow officers had burned his tent to be rid of the instrument and his bad playing.

13. FMC, 136-138. OBR 28. DDPR, Oct. 8, 1918.

14. Dr. Ross to Edgar A. White (father), Oct. 8, 1918. Why Ross wrote to the father rather than the mother is a mystery since White listed his mother as next of kin.

15. Edgar White, interview by authors, May 26, 1967.

16. FMC, 138. OBR 29.

17. Endorsement of recommendation by Martin Giesecke to Capt. Lawrence W. Bisler dated Apr. 27, 1920.

18. HB, 194 of unnumbered pages.

19. FMC, 93,142,143. OCR 57. OBR 32. DDPR, Oct. 14, 1918.

20. FMC, 93,94,144,145. OCR 58. OBR 34. DDPR Oct. 14, 1918.

21. The entire account of Knotts capture that follows is from a newspaper clipping (date and source unknown) by Nellie Brown Duff. It appears to be an "as told to" account.

22. H. Burdick to Bob (sic) (brother), Oct. 20, 1918. The killing of the downed enemy pilot is a shocking story not often related. Burdick may have done this to shore up his combat report (the kill was confirmed despite regulations that said that an enemy plane landing safely in enemy territory could not be claimed). About this time German pilots were using parachutes and were sometimes shot during descent.

23. Fiftieth reunion, numerous interviews by authors, Dayton, OH, June 19-21, 1968.

24. Report, Lt. Samuel R. T. Very to Captain F. W. Zinn, Treatment of 2nd Lieut. Howard C. Knotts while a prisoner in the hands of the Germans from October 14th to November 15., certified by Howard Knotts, National Archives. Over the years there have been wild claims that Knotts destroyed the railroad station where he was held captive, or that he set fire to a train while being transported and destroyed numerous enemy aircraft. Note that Knotts made no such claims in this certified statement.

25. HT, 89 of unnumbered pages.

26. WC, 97.

27. In an amusing letter to O. Reed, Tunstall relates how Dixon took him out on a check and told him later that he would not last long if he kept making flat turns.

28. DDPR, Oct. 19, 1918.

29. DDPR, Oct. 22, 1918.

30. DDPR, Oct. 24, 1918.

31. FMC, 94,95. OCR 59. DDPR, Oct. 25, 1918.

32. HB, 207 of unnumbered pages.

33. FMC, 51.

34. HARBORD to RAF GHC, Oct. 25, 1918.

35. DDPR, Oct. 26, 1918.

36. DDPR, Oct. 28, 1918.

37. 4th Army Routine Order No. 1987, Apr. 15, 1918, decried the wasting of petrol tins.

38. HB, 211 of unnumbered pages.

39. Vaughn brought the sight home and kept it for many years. He donated it to the Air Force Museum in 1968.

40. FMC, 52,53.

41. HB, 208 of unnumbered pages. Since the air arm was new to warfare, many experts soon began gathering information and opinions to see what it all meant. When first examined in the National Archives, 17th material contained reports that were the work of early psychologists apparently seeking to profile pilots. These were quickly removed when discovered. One report styled Vaughn as too aggressive for his own good—hardly a valid comment considering the man's lifelong success and popularity. A second sought to understand why Goodnow was able to lead a flight successfully, and yet never achieved a confirmed victory. The decision was that he was simply a poor shot—which is probably correct.

42. HB, 212 of unnumbered pages. At this point, Burdick's diary seems to be one day off.

43. WC, 98.

44. S. B. Eckert, interview by O. Reed, Philadelphia, PA, 1966. While the tale could not be absolutely confirmed as belonging to the final night, it is included as being typical of Goody Goodnow.

CHAPTER 11

1. WC, 99.

2. FMC, 53. During this move the motor vehicles were driven overland by twelve men detailed under the command of Wells. These land rovers were bringing along a machine gun (probably from Mert Campbell's plane) that Eckert was keeping as a souvenir. According to conversations at the reunion, either A. V. Haig or Elroy Hively finally kicked it off the tailgate in order to be rid of the bother of guarding and protecting it.

3. Howard Burdick to Clinton Burdick (father), Nov. 7, 1918.

4. Loran Cooper to O. Reed, undated, mid-1968.

5. WC, 99.

6. Roy Speth was left in "Hard-Boiled" Smith's holding pen in Paris.

7. When the army flying service ceased to be a part of the Signal Corps in the spring of 1918, there was much discussion regarding proper uniform. Being in need of clothing and having no real information, Clapp designed his own. It wasn't far from British cut and wasn't that odd; but it was different.

8. HB, 220 of unnumbered pages.

9. WC, 110.

10. HB, 219-220 of unnumbered pages.

11. Composite account based on WC, 101; HB, 224 of unnumbered pages; and Charles J. Biddle to O. Reed, Oct. 6, 1918. The last reaffirms the account of this incident published in *The Way of the Eagle*, Charles Scribner's Sons, New York (1919), which differs from the other accounts.

12. A. V. Haig, interview by authors, Philadelphia, PA 1971.

13. WC, 102.

14. Howard Burdick to Elizabeth (mother), Nov. 18, 1918.

15. WC, 102.

16. Howard Burdick to Bob (sic) (brother), Nov. 14, 1918.

17. Howard Burdick to Elizabeth (mother), Nov. 18, 1918.

18. Howard Burdick to Elizabeth (mother), Dec. 5, 1918.

19. Howard Burdick to Clinton (father), Dec. 29, 1918.

20. Howard Burdick to Clinton (father), Jan. 8, 1918.

21. Howard Burdick to Elizabeth (mother), Feb. 18, 1918.

22. Albert Everett, interviews by O. Reed, 1965-1966.

23. RT, 104.

24. Report, Lt., Samuel R. T. Very to Captain F. W. Zinn, *Treatment of 2nd Lieut. Howard C. Knotts while a prisoner in the hands of the Germans from October 14th to November 15*, certified by Howard Knotts, National Archives.

25. Howard Knotts to S. B. Eckert, Nov. 26, 1918.

26. After returning to the squadron briefly, Knotts went to hospital in England.

27. L. Cooper to O. Reed, undated, mid-1968.

28. UPN, 74,75 of typed copy.

29. L. Cooper to O. Reed, undated, mid-1968.

30. WC, 103. FZ, 116 of unnumbered pages.

31. Hand-written poem on the back of a souvenir card (Elysee Restaurant) found among the mementos of Harry K. Spindle.

Epilogue

1. Martin Caidin, *The Ragged, Rugged Warriors*, New York: E. P. Dutton & Co. Inc. (1966): 201,202.

Bibliography

1) Barrett, William E. *The First War Planes*. Greenwich, CN: Fawcett Publications Inc, 1960.
2) Biddle, Major Charles J. *The Way of the Eagle*. New York: Charles Scribner's Sons, 1919.
3) Bishop, Major William A. *Winged Warfare*. New York: George H. Doran Company, 1918.
4) Burdick, Howard. Untitled diary of 1918, unpublished handwritten copy.
5) Caidin, Martin. *The Ragged, Rugged Warriors*. New York: E. P. Dutton & Co., Inc., 1966.
6) Campbell, Merton Llwellyn. Untitled diary of 1917-1918, unpublished typed copy.
7) Clapp, Frederick M. *History of the 17th Aero Squadron*. Garden City, NY: Country Life Press, December 1920.
8) ___. Unpublished diary, notes, and letters. Yale Collection of American Literature, Beinecke Rare Book and Manuscript Library, Yale University.
9) Clements, William Thomas. War Diary of W. T. Clements, West Point, VA, 1917-1918. Unpublished typed copy.
10) Donaldson, John O. W. *My Capture and Escape*. Copyright © 1919 by Harper's Magazine.
11) Fowler, Thyrza B. *Harold Fowler, 1886—1957: A Remembrance*. [NY] Privately printed [at the Spiral Press], 1960.
12) Gibbons, Floyd. *The Red Knight of Germany*. Garden City, New York: Garden City Publishing Co., Inc., 1927.
13) Gorrell, Edgar S. *The Measure of America's World War Aeronautical Effort*. Norwich University, Northfield, Vermont, Burlington, VT: The Lane Press Inc., 1940.
14) Hall, James Norman, and Nordhoff, Charles Bernard, editors. *The Lafayette Flying Corps, Volumes I and II*. Boston, MA, and New York: Houghton Mifflin Company, 1920.
15) Hartley, Harold E. *Up & At 'Em*. New York: Ace Books, A Division of Charter Communications Inc., 1940, 1971.
16) Hay, Ian. *The First Hundred Thousand*. New York: Grosset & Dunlap.
17) Jones, H. A. *The War in the Air, six volumes*. Oxford, England: Oxford University Press, 1931.
18) Macmillan, Norman. *Great Aircraft*. New York: St. Martin's Press, 1960.
19) McCudden, James Thomas Byford. *Five Years in the Royal Flying Corps*. London, England: The "Aeroplane" & General Publishing Co., Ltd.
20) Miller, Thomas G., Jr. "*USAS Fliers With the RFC/RAF, 1917-1918.*" Cross and Cockade Journal, 7, no. 1, 1966.
21) Noltenius, Friedrich. "*Jadgfliger Friedrich Noltenius*" (Edited by A. E. Femnko), Cross and Cockade Journal, 7, no. 4, 1966.
22) Nowarra, H. J. and Brown, Kimbrough S. *Von Richthofen and the Flying Circus*. Letchworth, Herts, England, and Aero, Los Angeles, CA: Harleyford Publications, 1964.
23) Reynolds, Quentin. *They Fought for the Sky; The Dramatic Story of the First War in the Air*. New York: Rinehart & Company, Inc., 1957.
24) Richthofen, Captain Manfred Freiherr Von. Autobiography. (Translated by T. Ellis Barker), New York: Robert M. McBride and Co., 1918.
25) Rickenbacker, Edward V. *Fighting the Flying Circus*. New York: Doubleday & Company, 1965.
26) Roberts, Laurence. Untitled diary of 1918, unpublished handwritten copy.
27) Robertson, Bruce. *Air Aces of the 1914-1918 War*. Letchworth, Herts, England, and Aero, Los Angeles, CA: Harleyford Publications, Ltd., 1959.

28)Schröder, Hans. *An Airman Remembers* (translated by Claud W. Sykes). London, England: The Aviation Book Club.

29)Sims, Edward H. *American Aces*. Harper & Brothers, 1958.

30)Sloan, James J. "*148th American*." American Historical Society Journal, 4, no.4, 1959.

31) Sloan, James J. *Wings of Honor*. Atglen, PA: Schiffer Publishing Co., 1994.

32)Spalding, Albert. *Rise to Follow—an Autobiography*. New York, NY: Henry Holt and Company.

33)Springs, Elliot White. *Nocturne Militaire*, Grossett & Dunlap.

34)___, *War Birds, Diary of an Unknown Aviator*. London, England: Temple Press Book, 1966.

35)St. John, John L., Glover, Alfred. *Archibald, Certainly Not!* London, England: Francis Day and Hunter, Ltd. F&D Ltd., 1909.

36)Sweetser, Arthur. *The American Air Service, a Record of its Problems, its Difficulties, its Failures, and its Final Achievements*. New York-London: D. Appleton and Company, 1919.

37)Toliver and Constable. *Fighter Aces*. The Macmillan Company, 1965.

38)Todd, Robert. *Sopwith Camel Fighter Ace*. Falls Church, Virginia: AJAY Enterprises, 1978.

39)Traxler, Harry, D. Untitled diary of 1918-1919, unpublished hand-written copy.

40)Whitehouse, Arch. *Heroes of the Sunlit Sky*. Garden City, New York: Doubleday & Company, Inc., 1967.

Index

Also from the publisher

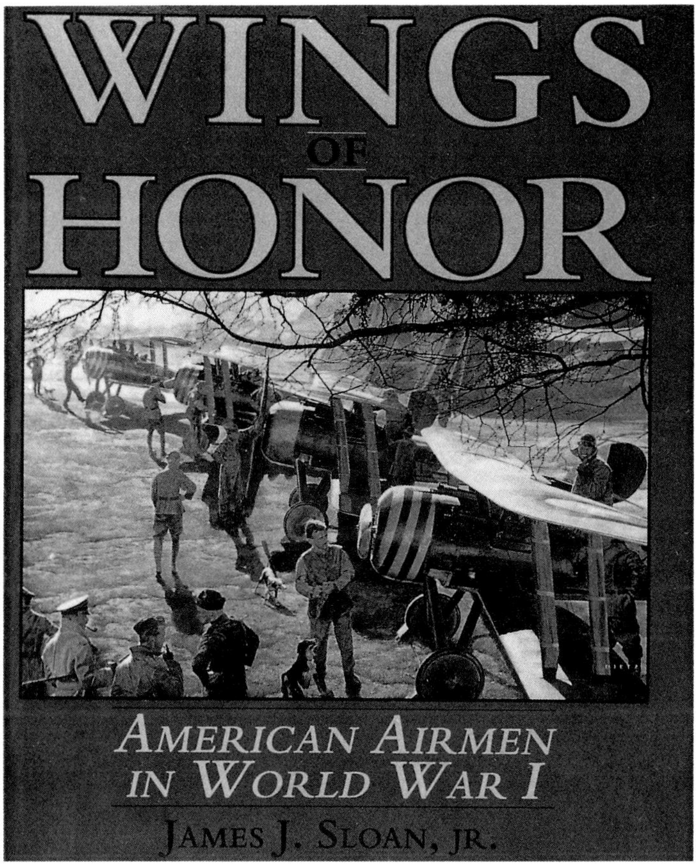

WINGS OF HONOR: American Airmen in WW I

James J. Sloan, Jr.

A compilation of all United States pilots, observers, gunners and mechanics who flew against the enemy in World War I. Covered are Americans who flew with French and British air ser vices, and all other units in which Americans flew.
Size: 8 1/2" x 11"
over 350 b/w photos, appendices, index
460 pages, hard cover
ISBN: 0-88740-577-0 $45.00

THE ZEPPELIN IN COMBAT • A History of the German Naval Airship Division

Douglas H. Robinson

The standard reference now revised and expanded. Dr. Robinson has opened up his vast photo archives to enhance this new edition of his classic work. Much of the new photographic material is published here for the first time.
Size: 8 1/2" x 11" 400 pages hard cover
over 350 b/w photographs, line drawings, charts
ISBN: 0-88740-510-X $49.95

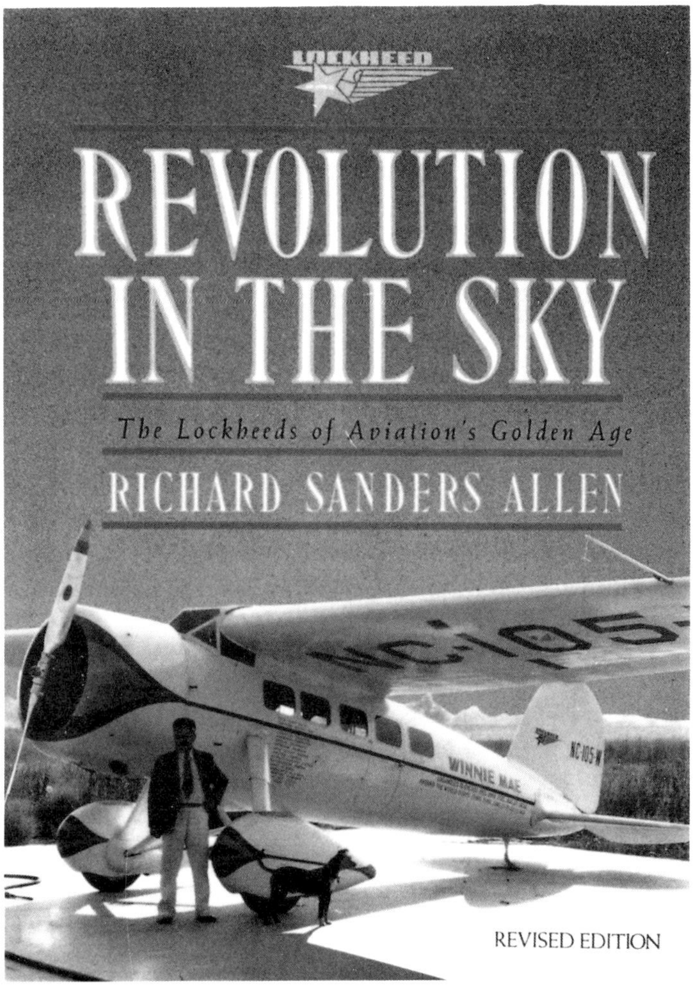

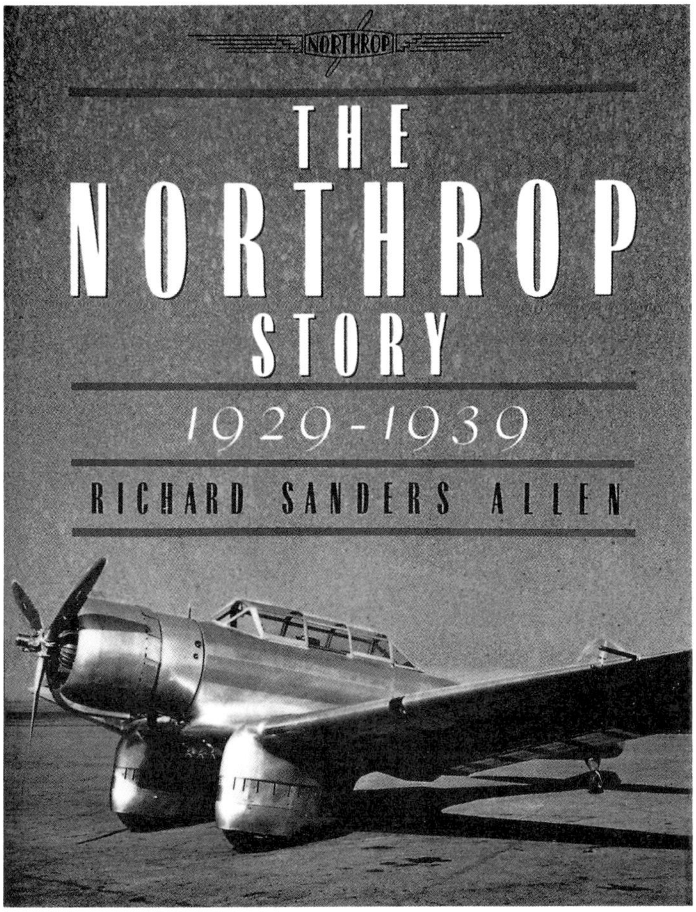

REVOLUTION IN THE SKY: THE LOCKHEEDS OF AVIATION'S GOLDEN AGE

Richard Sanders Allen

A reprint of the classic 1964 study. This is the fascinating story of the single-engine Lockheeds flown by Charles Lindbergh, Wiley Post and Will Rogers, Amelia Earhart, and Jimmy Doolittle.
Size: 8 1/2" x 11"
250 b/w photographs, 12 drawings, maps
256 pages, hard cover
ISBN: 0-88740-584-3 $37.50

THE NORTHROP STORY 1929-1939

Richard Sanders Allen

From flying wings to polar explorers, from air racers to air liners, here is the full story of the single-engine airplanes designed and constructed by Jack Northrop during aviation's golden age.
Size: 8 1/2" x 11"
150 b/w photographs
178 pages, hard cover
ISBN: 0-88740-585-1 $29.95